A Walk with Jennifer

{Based on a True Story}

Debi – I hope you enjoy Jennifer's story.

Mary Richardson

Mary Richardson

Endorsements

What people are saying about . . .
A Walk with Jennifer

"The story of Jennifer Hayse is both compelling and emotionally gripping. I found myself not wanting to put the book down, as page after page, the details of her tremendous faith in God and her courageous battle with breast cancer unfold in this dynamic true story. Richardson invites the reader to take <u>A Walk with Jennifer</u> and to participate in the Christian fellowship of the Jen Possible Team where everyone shares in witnessing the strength of a young mother's fight to survive. This book inspires, and brings great hope and peace to the reader. What appears to be a tragedy turns out to be a beautiful testimony – all for the Glory of God!"

Pastor Terese Rea, *Director*
Precious Jewels Women's Ministry
Community Christian Church
www.cccsterling.org

"I quickly became a member of the Jen Possible Team as this beautifully written story of hope unraveled. Richardson stated it was 'her honor' to be entrusted with writing the testimony of Jennifer Hayse, and now it is my privilege to endorse her book. As we walk with Jennifer, we discover that enduring hardship, with Grace, is a personal choice in life. And above all else, Jennifer reminds us that we never walk alone when we choose to walk with God!"

Robin Sullivan, *Christian Radio Host*
WMUZ 103.5 Praise Company Revival
www.robinsullivan.com

Dedication

*In loving memory of
Jennifer Ann Hayse
1971 ~ 2006*

*This book is dedicated to
her three children
Nicholas, Natalie, and Angelina*

Acknowledgments

〽

God is first in my life therefore my first acknowledgment is to Him, for without Him, I am empty and lost. It is because of my personal relationship with Jesus Christ that my life is no longer a stagnant pool of murky water. He restores me each day with Living Water and I shall never again live a water-resistant life. I humbly give all praise and acknowledgment to the risen King.

As with life, writing this book was a matter of choice which led to many other decisions in the process. One of the hardest choices was deciding what to include and what to leave out of the story. Therefore in so doing, I realize some people will be let down by their exclusion. I hope they will understand how difficult this decision was as I wrote, and rewrote, Jennifer's story countless times.

I wish to thank my dearest friend, Sue (Hotton) Blocker, who planted the seed of thought for this book as we walked with Jennifer along the shore of Lake Michigan. I believe you experienced more sleepless nights than I over the fruits of this publication. I might still be on page one had it not been for your faithful expectations, your Christ-like motivation and of course, your editing skills. I am blessed and honored to be your friend.

I wish to thank my very good friend, Candice Meyer, whose talent and love for reading helped to bring this book to a final close. The seasons within this book reflect the hard work and love you pour into the beauty of God's living garden. I am grateful our friendship continues to blossom and grow.

I wish to thank the outstanding members of the Jen Possible Team for their prayers and encouragement. I know as you read these pages you will be filled with precious memories of our dear friend, co-worker, and sister-in-Christ. I feel ashamed to see my name only as the author of Jennifer's story because countless hours of your time were also dedicated to this endeavor. However, it was God who orchestrated the events that are so colorfully painted on these pages, and I am truly indebted to all of you for every inspirational stroke of the brush.

I wish to thank Debbie Norris and the women in my Tuesday evening Bible study for your prayers over the last three years. As well as, a personal note of thanks to Lori Reiber for your time and prayerful review of the manuscript.

I lack the ability to fully thank the members and pastoral staff where I joyfully worship at Community Christian Church in Sterling Heights, Michigan. I fall short in expressing my thanks to Pastors Tony and Terese Rea for the dedication and love you continually show to others while serving our Lord and Savior. You have taught me to be still while listening carefully for the spiritual sound of abundant rain.

Mentioned last, but always first in my heart are my beautiful children; Christopher Cody and Jessica Marie. Forgive me for not telling you more often how thankful I am that God blessed my life completely with being your mother. Thank you for loving me while I was so deeply immersed in writing this book. Your maturity in Christ and wisdom in understanding God's plan demonstrates your firm belief in Him. How blessed we are to have Jesus as the head of our household!

I pray that everyone who reads these pages is filled with the knowledge that God is in control of his or her life, and He alone charts the path that we as Christians must follow. It is during our time here on earth, that we make the choice to be obedient to His call and to walk through storms as Jennifer did, with great faith and trust in our Savior.

Author's Note

A *Walk with Jennifer* is based on a true story, recounted with as much accuracy as possible by myself and others who inwardly knew Jennifer Ann Hayse. However, given the sensitive nature of what unfolded, the names of certain physicians and the identity of certain hospitals have been changed. Any resemblance between these fictional names and hospitals, and the names of real persons and places, is strictly coincidental. None of the people or events within this book were invented, and while some conversational details are beyond the scope of human recollection, a portion of the dialogue was recreated through interviews and other supporting documents. I cannot vouch for its precise accuracy in all instances, but I can vouch for its truthfulness.

A Valentine's Day Wedding

~ *Introduction* ~

❝**D**o you, Jennifer Ann Toby, take Keith Alan Hayse to
have and to hold, from this day forward, for better,
for worse, for richer, for poorer, in sickness or in health,
until death do you part?❞ The minister joined their hands,
and Jennifer whispered, "I do."

It was Valentine's Day, 1993. The morning clouds gave
way to a clear sky, and the day's temperature was unusually
mild for Michigan. The sun's reflection shone brightly over
the blanket of fresh snow making it sparkle like thousands
of tiny diamonds.

The wedding guests were enjoying the walk along
Oakwood Boulevard through the historically picturesque
town of Dearborn. They soon arrived at the Inn, located in
close proximity to Greenfield Village and the Henry Ford
Museum.

The Inn's colonial structure and decor provided a perfectly romantic atmosphere for their wedding. Inside the
quaint, old-fashioned chapel was where Jennifer married
Keith, the first and only man she had ever loved.

*   *   *

Eleven years passed since the day she and Keith exchanged wedding vows and Jennifer remembered that day clearly, because it was a beautiful Sunday afternoon on Valentine's Day. Once more it was her favorite time of year, mid-February, 2004, but in contrast from her wedding day, the temperature today was cold and dreary. The sky was filled with clouds that were low, dark, and gray. Jennifer could feel them surrounding her in a shameless effort to suffocate her with their sadness. Without the sun, the vacated piles of snow reminded her of frozen dirt and the winter miracle from more than a decade ago was no longer sparkling like thousands of tiny diamonds.

Year after year, the routine breast self-examinations were engrained into Jennifer's lifestyle. At times the monthly practice seemed more of a nuisance than anything else, until one unsuspecting morning she felt a lump in her left breast. Her hand trembled as she felt the lump a second time. There was no mistaking it, she had discovered what every woman fears, and the timing was dreadful . . . *she was ten weeks pregnant.*

*   *   *

Jennifer was thirty-two years old and teetering on the brink of her life falling apart. She waited nervously in the doctor's private office. Inside the lining of her pocket she felt a missing round button. She had kept it ever since her daughter, Natalie, was born and somehow had never found the time to sew it back in place.

The door suddenly opened, and a quick formal exchange of greetings took place between her and the physician. On the desk sat a manila folder with her name in bold black letters. Dr. Zechariah Jordan opened the file, and a brief scan of the mammogram report gave him time to regain his composure. He removed his glasses and for the first time looked directly into her eyes . . . *and she knew.*

He explained the diagnosis in layman's terms, and her world slowly began to unravel. His rigid outline sat stiffly behind the desk in front of her, and Jennifer found it difficult to comprehend what he was saying.

This was Jennifer's worst nightmare. It was the unspeakable fear she had buried deep inside the locked hallways of her mind. She asked to see the medical report. She took her left hand from her coat pocket and the round smooth button fell. It was spinning wildly out of control and then gradually stopped. The button remained on the floor, no longer needed, its purpose forgotten.

The words in front of her were blurry as they faded in and out of clarity. Her mind was like the lens of a camera, trying desperately to focus and make sense of the medical terminology. However, there was no point in denying the truth, for she was holding the proof in her hands. The only words she understood were . . . *highly suspicious of malignancy.* Then without warning came the shattering diagnosis: *bi-lateral breast cancer.*

*   *   *

Jennifer Ann Hayse was a believer in Jesus Christ, and by faith, she endured stages of suffering most of us will never know – let alone ever experience. She was a young woman with remarkable courage, the sort of courage everyone prays for during the worst of life's turbulent storms.

She fought countless battles during her illness, and all the while she was influencing the lives of many people. All have since come to realize their individual faith in God was magnified by witnessing Jennifer's life. As a result, all become better equipped because of their participation in her life, to help others in knowing God and His perfect plan for all of us.

* * *

Take an inspirational journey beginning in Plymouth, Michigan, then travel six thousand miles across the Atlantic Ocean to the Holy City of Jerusalem, where God beckons Jennifer to come while she prays for a miracle.

A fresh pot of coffee is waiting for you, pour some into your best-loved cup and bring it to your favorite place of solitude. The light in the den is glowing, and the fireplace is inviting. Resting over the back of your grandmother's wicker chair is your pink Angora sweater. Place it lightly over your shoulders to keep the chill away, and curl your legs up comfortably on the cushioned footstool near the warmth of the glowing fire. With the turning of every page, mark your footsteps next to hers and come along as we journey with her and forever take . . . *A Walk with Jennifer.*

* * *

"Be joyful always; pray continually;
give thanks in all circumstances,
for this is God's will for you in Christ Jesus."
1 Thessalonians 5:16-18

Stellar Pink Dogwood
Summer of 2003

~ 1 ~

"Hello, my name is Jennifer Hayse." The young engineer smiled and extended her hand saying, "Welcome to Visteon Powertrain, you must be Mary Richardson."

"Hello, it's nice to meet you, Jennifer." Mary returned the smile.

Jennifer helped Mary with the single storage box in the chair next to her and asked, "Are the rest of your belongings in your car, Mary?"

"No, everything is right here," Mary said and patted the lid to the box. She picked up her briefcase and waved toward the lobby door indicating to Jennifer that she would follow.

Jennifer led the way through a maze of partitioned work spaces and said, "This is where I work." She placed Mary's belongings haphazardly on the file cabinet and speaking over her shoulder, she told Mary to place her briefcase anywhere. Jennifer then took three metal component parts from the desk and suggested, "First, let's go for coffee before we begin our day."

Mary scanned the cluttered area and noticed there wasn't an inch of unoccupied space, either on the desk, under the desk, or above the desk. Open boxes and piles of electronic parts were scattered everywhere, and countless screws were thrown about like discarded marbles.

On a chair, dozens of green wiring boards were piled high. They were stacked like a house of cards about to collapse. A yellow sticky note dangled from the pile, identifying the stack as *NAM-3XX*. A second note read, *Testing Complete . . . Cathy.*

Mary set her briefcase on the floor and followed Jennifer down a hall of identical workstations, all of which were heaped with gadgets and miscellaneous components designed to operate the automobile. A few desks away, Jennifer dropped off the parts she was carrying and left a return note saying, *ESU-1XX . . . Jen.*

"This is where Cathy Britton works, Mary. She is my job-share partner for imported vehicles and you will meet her tomorrow." Jennifer then continued down the main corridor toward the employee lunchroom. She was blindly following the irresistible aroma of freshly brewed coffee.

As they walked along, Mary mentally charted her new surroundings and realized that starting over again, after working twenty-five years in a manufacturing environment was not going to be an easy thing to do.

"I'm glad you're a coffee drinker, Mary." Jennifer said while waving good morning to the men in the lunchroom. Weaving a path through her co-workers, Jennifer went directly for the pot of coffee. She handed Mary the first cup and then introduced her to everyone.

"This is Mary Richardson, and today is her first day with us in Powertrain, so everyone, please try to be extra nice!" At once a chorus of fake groans filled the room. Jennifer smiled and apologized to Mary, "They're only teasing."

"Hello, my name is Bill Hardy," he nodded at Mary.

"And I'm Duane Lanyon," he shook her hand enthusiastically.

"Mary has been transferred to our Engineering Section." Jennifer said, while pouring a generous amount of vanilla hazelnut flavoring into her coffee along with a packet of sugar. She explained to Mary, "Years ago, Duane and I worked briefly together at the Visteon Technical Center and now he is moving back into our engineering section." Jennifer nodded at the older of the two men and said, "Bill and I have been working together for almost two years."

Duane then asked Mary the reason behind her unusual transfer to their engineering section. She explained that the manufacturing plant where she worked had been closed and as a result, she was given this new assignment working in the Powertrain division.

"Starting over again is great, huh?" Duane grinned because he had been transferred several times in the past and understood Mary's circumstances.

"Such is life," she returned his grin.

While listening, Jennifer added more cream to her coffee mug. Mary watched her and wondered if there would be any trace of coffee left by the time she was through. Duane tossed his tea bag into the trash can and said, "We're happy to have you on board, Mary."

"Thank you," she sipped her black coffee.

Bill reminded Duane they had a meeting in five minutes. They said good-bye, and walked down the hall toward the conference room.

*   *   *

Jennifer added a touch more coffee to her cup before taking Mary back to her cluttered workstation. Once there, Mary looked for a place to set her coffee down but couldn't find a spot. Instead she finished drinking it while Jennifer answered the telephone.

While waiting, Mary glanced around Jennifer's work place and noticed a Disney poster tacked on the wall along with several crayon drawings on brightly colored paper. Next to the childlike art, and hanging lopsided, was a framed diploma from the University of Michigan – Dearborn: College of Engineering.

After ending her telephone call, Jennifer jotted down a note and asked, "Are you ready to learn about Powertrain control modules?"

"Is that what this is?" Mary held up a circuit board.

"No, that is what we call a printed wiring board." Jennifer began explaining the process in small increments. After awhile she concluded by saying, "These parts are used to operate the vehicle, and each module has a separate PWB that is circuited for special design features."

"The PWBs are components of the module?" Mary asked.

"Exactly, and when they are complete, we ship them to the customer via your expertise!" Jennifer smiled.

"When is your next shipment?" Mary looked around at the clutter.

"In two days," Jennifer said nonchalantly.

Mary chuckled and asked, "Will you be ready in two days?"

"Well, I could use your help, Mary." Jennifer placed her finger to her lips, hiding a smile.

"No problem I'll help you, and once the modules are shipped your workstation will be cleaned up."

"Not really," Jennifer confessed. "It looks like this all the time."

*   *   *

Cathy Britton was at home preparing dinner for her family when the telephone rang and the caller ID told her who it was. "Hi, Jennifer," she answered.

"Hi, Cathy, are you busy?" Jennifer was still at work shutting down her laptop.

"No, I've got a minute," Cathy said.

"I just want you to know the ESU modules are ready to be shipped."

"Excellent." Cathy preheated the oven and said, "I'll ship them tomorrow."

"Good, this will give you a chance to meet Mary."

"Oh, I forgot we have a new co-worker. What is she like?" Cathy asked.

"Mary is very organized and she has an incredible attention span!"

They both laughed, knowing their own limited ability to stay focused at times.

"I've got a great idea," Jennifer said jumping to another subject.

"What?" Cathy said as she peeled an onion.

Jennifer lost her train of thought and asked aloud, "Where did I put my car keys?"

"Try your purse," Cathy suggested while reading the recipe in front of her.

Jennifer felt inside her coat pocket and said, "Never mind, I found them." She then began searching for her grocery list.

"What was your great idea, Jen?" Cathy read from the cookbook using the tip of the cutting knife as a reading guide.

"Oh, I can't remember my idea." Jennifer started to button her coat and said, "I need to stop at the store before getting Nicholas and Natalie from daycare." Her busy fingers stopped when they reached the place where there was a missing button.

"What are your plans for the weekend?" Cathy asked.

"Keith and I promised the children we would fly kites, ride bikes, and plant flowers."

"Wonder Woman strikes again!" Cathy sliced a green pepper.

"I suppose, but I'm disappointed because I just talked with Keith and he has to work." Jennifer kept looking for the grocery list and said, "So the family celebration will take place without him."

"You celebrate everything, Jennifer."

"I do not," she said in mock defense.

"Oh yes you do," Cathy teased.

"We should celebrate everything." Jennifer smiled thinking of when she celebrated her last wedding anniversary, and thinking of romance, she said, "This weekend Bill drives to Louisiana where he will meet Rima and her family for the first time."

"Already?"

"Yes." Jennifer saw the pink heart drawn on her desk calendar.

"Wow, May 24 is this weekend?" Cathy wondered where the time had gone.

"Mmm-hmm, spring is here, and love is in the air," Jennifer sang.

"Now, Jen, please don't be disappointed if your attempt at playing Cupid fails."

"My attempt won't fail because this is a match made in heaven!"

"Okeydokey," Cathy said, hoping Jennifer was right.

Jennifer stopped looking for the grocery list because it was late, and she needed to leave. Like all working mothers, she was anxious to see her children. As she prepared to leave the office, she disconnected herself from the role as a working engineer and reconnected with her true identity . . . *motherhood.*

*   *   *

Cathy hung up the telephone and after reading the entire recipe, she asked aloud, "Why am I slicing a green pepper?"

"There's one in the refrigerator." Her husband, Jim, called to her while walking into the kitchen.

"What?" Cathy looked at him, confused.

"A green pepper – there's one in the refrigerator." Jim took off his jacket and hung it over the kitchen chair.

"Why are you home?" she asked her husband.

"Where else should I be at five o'clock?" He wondered what she was fixing for dinner.

"Beef stroganoff," she said, reading his mind.

"With green peppers?" he asked.

Cathy sweetly replied, "Yes, Jimbo, beef stroganoff with green peppers."

Eating one of the green slices, he asked, "What did you do today?"

"If you only knew," she murmured, thinking about her busy day.

"Where are the children?" He tugged her blonde ponytail.

"Emily is napping because she is tired and has a cold." Cathy took the ground beef out of the refrigerator, but she couldn't find the sour cream. "Did you see Rebecca and Ryan outside playing when you drove up the driveway?"

"No." He reopened the refrigerator to pour himself a glass of juice.

"Find the sour cream, please," she said while the onions started to brown.

Jim found the dairy product, placed it on the counter and left to change out of his work clothes. Cathy emptied the scraps from the cutting board into the garbage disposal. Looking out the window, she regretted spending the entire day inside cleaning the house. She watched the vegetables swirl and disappear down the drain.

She lowered the flame under the frying pan, placed the rolls in the oven, and then went upstairs to wake Emily from her nap. The little girl reached her arms toward her mother and Cathy kissed her forehead, grateful there was no trace of a fever.

"Let's go, Kiddo." Cathy patted her youngest child on the legs and lifted the blanket. She helped the two-year-old out of bed, and they walked down the stairs.

As she came into the kitchen, Jim asked, "Are the rolls in the oven?"

"Yes, they're almost ready." A few minutes later, once everyone was served Cathy sat at the table and asked, "Who has homework?"

"I do!" Ryan loved learning and doing his schoolwork.

"And what about you, Rebecca, do you have any homework?"

In response, her black silky hair swayed back and forth, indicating no.

"No homework, are you sure?" Jim asked.

The wave of black silk changed directions; it was now moving up and down. Rebecca drank her milk and smiled at her adoptive parents.

Cathy looked at her husband and said, "Jim, why don't we do something fun this weekend?" She thought of Jennifer's plans with her children, and suddenly, she was eager to be outside enjoying the warmer weather.

"Like what for instance?" Jim was a school teacher and he loved to organize fun activities.

"Let's fly a kite, plant some flowers, and simply celebrate spring!"

*　　*　　*

Ten minutes later, dinner was through and one by one the kitchen chairs emptied. Cathy started to protest but stopped herself when Jim told the children, "Only one hour of play-time and then you have to come back inside."

He stepped into the family room and reached for the tele-vision remote. He then sat in the recliner, raised his feet, and prepared himself for a relaxing evening.

"I have Bible study tonight," she reminded him.

"What time?" He was flipping through the local news stations.

"Six-thirty." Cathy cleared the table and shook her head. She had been leaving at the same time every Wednesday evening for five years. She glanced at the television screen and said, "Ryan will do his own homework, but go through Rebecca's backpack to check for math assignments. Emily might need some Tylenol before going to bed, but check her temperature first, okay?" When Cathy didn't hear a response, she turned off the faucet and listened to the familiar sound of snoring. "Okeydokey," she whispered and decided he could nap until it was time for her to leave.

She dried her hands and left the kitchen to look over her Bible study homework for that evening. The class discus-sion from last week was on Christian friendship and unex-plainable suffering of the righteous. The women at church were studying the Book of Job and the endurance of the Old Testament character. Job was a man who lost everything, yet in spite of his loss, he remained devoted to God. Cathy walked outside, reflecting on how quickly the good inten-tions of Job's friends turned from comfort to judgment.

She went around the garage to the back patio wondering if the bulbs she planted last year were going to blossom. She inspected the leaf-covered ground, but could not find any signs of plant life. She looked up and waved to the neighbors adjacent to her backyard. The Herders would soon be leaving for Texas, and a new family would move into the neighborhood. Cathy's son, Ryan, was sad because his school friend was moving away, but Cathy prayed with him, asking God to bring a loving family to their neighborhood.

Before leaving for Bible study she gave one last glance toward the Herders' backyard and with anticipation of meeting new people, she prayed for the opportunity to plant seeds of faith in the hearts of strangers.

~ 2 ~

Bill was enjoying the drive in his 2001 Quicksilver Corvette Z06. America's love affair with the automobile manifested itself in Bill Hardy, and working in the auto industry provided him with a passionate career as a core electrical engineer. His heart raced in unison with the 385HP engine under his grip. He shifted into sixth gear and relaxed into the driver's seat.

A remarkable turn of events had taken place during the past five months and now he was on his way to Louisiana to meet Rima Holland. It all began with Jennifer during the second week of the New Year. His thoughts wandered back to that early morning coffee break.

"Good morning!" Jennifer greeted him as she walked into the lunchroom.

"I know the sound of that whimsical voice," he said, laughing. "What are you brewing this morning besides coffee?"

Jennifer walked toward him, and Bill knew by her delightful smile that she was bursting to share good news. "Bill, what are your plans this morning?" she asked.

"Why, Jennifer, what are you plotting?"

"Your future," she beamed at him.

"Oh?" He was thinking about a donut for breakfast, but instead, he closed the bakery box.

"Stop by my desk, and we'll talk."

He reconsidered the donut, knowing the sugar would help him keep pace with Jennifer.

She waited, while down the hallway, he balanced his donut, a coffee cup, and his morning paper. At her desk, she started her computer and explained to him, "Over the holidays Keith and I drove to Louisiana to spend New Year's Eve with my grandmother."

Bill listened as he settled into the extra chair.

"You see, my Grandmother Catherine celebrated her ninetieth birthday on December 31 and we wanted to surprise her, but it didn't go as planned."

"Oh, why not?" he asked.

"Honestly, Bill, our trip turned out to be more about you than Grandmother."

"What does your grandmother's birthday have to do with me?" He regretted eating the donut and tossed the sugary napkin into the wastebasket.

Jennifer took a deep breath and smiled before saying, "What I'm about to tell you is going to change your life, Mr. Hardy!"

"I'm listening." He was intrigued.

"I'll start at the beginning. While visiting Grandmother, she was complaining of chest pains so we took her to the emergency room."

"Will she be all right?"

"I'm hoping she will recover, but she has other medical complications. Right now she is home recovering, but there is a silver lining to every cloud." Jennifer's eyes sparkled.

"I'm listening." He could not hide his smile.

"While waiting at the hospital, Bill, I met Rima Holland, who is Grandmother's caregiver. Over the past year, Rima and I have talked on the telephone several times, and she is taking excellent care of Grandmother."

Finishing his coffee, he said, "Keep going."

"It took several hours before Grandmother was admitted to the hospital, and during that time, Rima and I became better acquainted. We had a very long, woman-to-woman talk about important matters of the heart."

"What does that have to do with me?"

Jennifer rolled her chair closer and in a hushed voice, she said, "Bill, Rima is a grown woman, she's a mature Christian, and she's not married."

He jerked his head in surprise. "Are you playing matchmaker?"

"Yes."

Bill didn't know what to say.

"I can't explain it, but my heart tells me there was another reason for me to make the trip to Louisiana other than to celebrate Grandmother's birthday."

Paying closer attention, he asked, "What do you mean?"

"Well, I think you should become acquainted with Rima over the telephone to determine whether or not there is a romantic connection." Jennifer wheeled her chair back, waiting for her words to sink into his heart.

That was five months ago, and today Bill was an hour away from meeting Rima and her family in DeRidder, Louisiana. To Bill, having someone special in his life was spectacular, and soon enough their nightly conversations had brought them to this point.

He smiled, remembering the southern edge to Rima's voice when she made plans for them to meet around seven o'clock at the Stage Coach Inn. He was experiencing great peace regarding his future and his heart told him this evening would mark a turning point in his life.

The sunset glowed across Beauregard Parish and brought together two hearts from completely separate and unique lifestyles. Even though Bill and Rima lived hundreds of miles apart the threads of Christianity would soon tie . . . *their futures together.*

*   *   *

Duane and Janis loved working outside, and this was their first spring living in Milford. Last year, the move from Redford was not easy; however, the timing was right, and they were pleased with the rustic design of their new home. It was the sound of a creek hidden among the trees in the backyard that motivated them to make the purchase and the property was large enough for their sons, Jacob and Justin, to unleash their roughhousing outdoors.

Their weekend chores came to an end as the pine tree shadows fell across the property line. Nature's sundial was ending another day of rewarding work. Duane had waited all weekend and now that it was Sunday night, it was time to talk with Janis. While contemplating his words, he turned on the side faucet to the hose.

Tomorrow he would officially start working at his new office, and like most men, he separated work from his personal life. He balanced the two aspects more accurately when they were compartmentalized. Work was work, and home was home. Duane pulled the hose around to the front yard, deciding now was as good a time as any.

A layer of dust hung in the air as Janis swept away the last of the topsoil. "You were right, Duane, we only needed a few yards of dirt." She was slapping her work gloves over the grass.

He began to hose down the porch and wanting to make her laugh, he inched the stream of cold water toward her tennis shoes. He grinned as she jumped to avoid a trail of cold mud. He redirected the stream, and the ripple of mud inched toward her toes. She stepped over it, trying to get out of its way, but it followed her like a shadow. If she stepped to the right, it was there, then back to the left, and it was beside her.

"Stop clowning around," she warned.

But he couldn't resist trying for her left shoe.

"You are so annoying." Halfway through his redirect, Janis saw it coming and walked away.

"Whoa, wait a minute!" Duane called out to her.

Ignoring him, she took the rake and walked toward the shed. Duane fought with the nozzle, trying to turn off the green snake. He finally caught up with her, and taking the rake from her hand, he asked, "Did you get wet?"

"You're such a kid." She tapped him on the shoulder with her dirty gloves and walked away.

"Wait, Janis, we need to talk before the boys get home."

"Talk about what?" she stopped to ask.

"We need to talk about my job."

Dread invaded her thoughts because she was all too familiar with the financial roller coaster ride when working in the automotive industry.

"I've been transferred to the V.E.M.A. building in Dearborn," he blurted.

"When did this happen?" Janis crossed her arms.

"About two weeks ago." Duane squinted into the setting sun.

"What does this mean?" She tapped her right foot.

"It means," he said, trying to ignore the squishing sound of her wet shoe, "that starting tomorrow, I work at V.E.M.A., and nothing else changes."

"You're wrong, Duane, because starting tomorrow things change around here."

He smiled and tried to unfold her clenched arms.

"From now on, each evening I want you to take one minute to tell me something about your workday."

"What?" he protested.

"I mean it – starting tomorrow," she said, emphasizing her point.

Seeing the boys come up the driveway, he quickly apologized and agreed.

Janis walked ahead of him into the garage. "Come on, boys, it's time to eat," she called to her sons while slipping out of her damp shoes.

"Yeah, your mom is tired, so don't give her a hard time." Duane smiled at Janis.

Jacob and Justin pushed their way into the house. Duane untied his muddy boots and placed them next to her damp shoes. He rearranged the boy's bikes so she could get into the car in the morning. He then turned on the outdoor lights and closed the garage door.

Washing his hands in the laundry tub, he thought about his promise. Take one minute to talk about work? Not bad at all, he thought as he dried his hands on a paper towel, knowing . . . *a promise is a promise.*

*   *   *

The next morning, Duane could not miss the note taped to his computer asking for help. The smiley face drawn on the bottom of the paper told him it was from Jennifer. He put his lunch on the file cabinet and started his computer, and then taking a note pad with him, he walked toward the test lab.

Turning the corner, he bumped into the department manager. "Oops. Sorry Al," Duane apologized to his boss and then asked, "Welcome back, and how was your vacation?"

"Our vacation was great." Al regained his balance and said, "Sheila enjoyed camping in the RV and visiting with our grandkids."

"It sounds as if you enjoyed it, too."

"Yes, it made me think more about retirement." Al opened his day planner before asking, "Did anything important happen while I was gone?"

"Not that I'm aware." Duane wanted to ask his boss about the mystery behind his work transfer, but he didn't. "I'm going to the test lab right now because Cathy and Jennifer will be shipping modules today."

Al marked it on his calendar and said, "Good, this will be Mary's first shipment for our department. Did you get a chance to meet her?"

"Only briefly because I was busy unpacking." Duane grinned, recalling Mary had unpacked in less than ten minutes.

"We have a section meeting in an hour, so I will introduce you and Mary to everyone at that time." Looking at his watch, Al left and headed toward another meeting.

Duane continued walking down the hall and through the double doors to the test lab where the engineers wanted to spend their entire day. Jennifer had spent several months preparing the bill of materials and schematics for today's shipment. She was waiting patiently for the stamp of approval from the lab technician when Duane joined the crowd near the workbench.

"Good morning, Duane!" Jennifer handed him a plate of brownies.

"No, thanks," he waved away the temptation.

"Umm, Jen makes the best brownies." Cathy nudged him while licking her fingers.

Jennifer continued to offer the dessert until Duane caved in. He looked for the smallest piece, and Cathy was right; they were delicious.

"Go ahead and ship the modules." The technician announced as he unfastened the wiring harness from the test equipment. Jennifer clapped her hands in delight since the launch was a success and the modules could be shipped without any issues.

"So, what can I do to help?" Duane asked.

"Not a thing," Jennifer said while handing him a pink napkin. "I only wanted you to come and celebrate our successful test launch."

"I was tricked?" he asked.

"Yep, you were tricked," Cathy said, laughing.

"You don't need my help?" Duane mildly complained.

"No."

They all laughed at how quickly their past work camaraderie resurfaced.

"Okay, I'll see you two at the section meeting," Duane said, walking away.

"What section meeting?" Cathy jumped off the stool.

Duane smiled over his shoulder, and said, "The boss is back in town!"

*　　*　　*

Mary saw her manager walking down the aisle toward one of the many conference rooms. Al was tall and lanky, making it easy to follow him and since she was not sure where the meeting was, she kept him in sight. She maneuvered through the maze of hallways and after following him closely, she stepped into the conference room and took the first available seat.

"Good morning!" Jennifer sang the words as she walked in and passed the plate of brownies to Al first.

"Thank you." He closed the door behind Cathy and turned to his staff. "Before we get started, has everyone met Mary?" Al pointed in her direction, explained her job responsibilities, and then he nodded toward Duane and said, "You all remember Duane, correct?"

The room filled with lighthearted moaning.

"Such grumbling, considering Duane and Mary are here to help." Al turned to his new employees and said, "They really are great people; they just like to complain."

Mary smiled.

"You'll get used to it." Duane whispered to her.

*   *   *

Thirty minutes later, the meeting ended and the majority of engineers left. Cathy took the last brownie while Jennifer brushed the crumbs off the table and into the wastebasket.

"So, Jennifer, have you heard from Bill yet?" Cathy asked.

"Yes!" she sang the word.

Duane forgot about Bill's trip to Louisiana, but Al heard the question and was intrigued. He was standing in the doorway, needing to leave yet wanting to stay. Mary remained seated because she wanted to become better acquainted with the tight-knit group.

"Bill drove to Louisiana?" Al sat back down.

"Yes, and he enjoyed meeting Rima and her family."

"Wow!" Cathy said.

"Bill Hardy has a girlfriend?" Al asked Jennifer.

"Yes, they started talking the first of the year."

Mary silently counted the span of time – January until May was only five months.

"He will be back on Wednesday." Jennifer wouldn't say anything more.

Everyone understood they would have to wait until then for more news. Al stood and moved his chair back in place and everyone else did the same. Cathy and Jennifer headed to their desks and made plans to go for a walk during lunch. Mary made her way back to the shipping dock, knowing the truck driver would be waiting for his freight.

Duane hurried to his desk, and thinking of his promise last night to Janis, he dialed his home phone number. With no answer, he listened to his own voice on the recorder and left a short message. "Hey, remind me to tell you about Bill when I get home tonight."

He smiled at how easy it would be keeping his promise now that he was working with Cathy and Jennifer. Duane even thought that maybe it would be nice someday to have Janis meet them because they were all close in age and lived similar lifestyles. He remembered Cathy being very open about her Christianity, and since Jennifer was her friend, he was certain she was also a believer. He thought the situation was perfect and last night's promise will be easy to keep.

Little did Duane realize at the time, what dramatic changes were about to take place in his life, and how his tranquil family would soon be intertwined with the families of his entire work section. God's plan would soon demonstrate to him what a wonderful woman of faith . . . *he had married.*

*   *   *

The following week, Cathy and Jennifer sat waiting at Senate Coney Island restaurant for Bill to join them. Sitting in their booth, Jennifer faced the door while Cathy stirred her coffee. She was waiting for Jennifer to start their conversation and after a few moments, she casually asked, "Do you have a headache, Jen?"

"Hmm?" Jennifer drew her eyes away from the front door.

"Are you okay?" Cathy was concerned.

Jennifer nodded and sipped her flavored coffee.

"You seem out of touch lately are you sure everything is all right?"

"I think so – "

"What do you mean, you think so?" Cathy inquired.

Without answering, Jennifer waved to Bill. "I hope he has good news!" She turned around in the booth and said, "I'm excited about their romance, Cathy, and I've been praying for this moment!"

"Jen, please don't get your hopes up," Cathy advised.

Bill sat next to Jennifer, and before the conversation began, the waitress took their lunch orders.

Jennifer turned sideways and said, "Bill, you look happy."

"I am happy, thanks to you." He lifted his glass of pop and nodded.

Jennifer knew it was a good sign and encouraged him to speak openly.

"Should I start at the beginning?" he asked.

"Yes." Jennifer was ready to learn about his feelings.

"Okay, on the way to Louisiana, I stopped at the National Corvette Museum – what a great place," he teased.

"We don't need you to start at the *very* beginning!" Jennifer sighed.

Cathy and Jennifer were on the edge of their seats. Bill laughed and started again with sincerity. "I knew from talking with Rima that we had a lot in common and it would be hard to imagine we wouldn't get along, but I was still a little nervous about meeting her and her family."

Cathy exchanged a quick glance with Jennifer, and during their lunch, Bill told them everything. He spent three days with Rima and her family, camping at Hodges Garden, a state park in Florien and while camping, everyone had the chance to become better acquainted.

In the mornings, they stayed by the lake, and in the afternoons, he and Rima found time for privacy and walked the trails around the park. In the evenings, they enjoyed the campfire and talked long after her family said good night.

After he finished, Cathy exchanged another astonished glance with Jennifer.

"When are you going back?" Jennifer asked.

"We made plans for the Fourth of July," he said.

In delight, Jennifer clapped her hands and Cathy fell back into the booth, speechless.

*   *   *

After lunch, they walked outside and stood next to Jennifer's vehicle. With both hands in his pockets, and rocking from heel to toe, Bill was sincere when he declared, "You know, Rima is someone I could easily fall in love with."

Jennifer and Cathy were not certain whether it was his tone or his actual words that made them stare at him.

"What?" he grinned.

"I'm a little surprised," Cathy said, stammering.

"I'm not." Jennifer hugged Bill and abruptly said to Cathy, "I won't be going back to the office with you this afternoon."

"Jennifer, wait a minute; this day has been confusing!" Cathy rubbed her temples and asked, "Why not?"

"I have plans this afternoon." Jennifer quickly climbed into her vehicle and waved to them as she drove off.

"Bill, that's awfully strange," Cathy commented.

He unlocked the doors to his Corvette and asked, "What do you mean?"

"Jennifer was supposed to help me with the Aston Martin schematics this afternoon." Cathy climbed into the sports car, and remembering Jennifer's uncharacteristic mood from earlier, she said, "Jennifer was very quiet before you came into the restaurant."

Bill waited for an opening in traffic and made a quick turn onto Rotunda Drive.

"And that's not like her," Cathy finished her thought.

"You're right," Bill agreed.

"I hope everything is okay." Cathy turned in the passenger seat and caught a glimpse of Jennifer's vehicle through the budding tree branches of a . . . *Stellar Pink dogwood.*

Pearly Gates
Autumn of 2003

~ 3 ~

As soon as Jennifer got home she called her obstetrician. The voice message at the office said they were closed for lunch and to call back, after one o'clock, which would be in fifteen minutes. While waiting, she leaned against the counter and studied the clutter of art decorating the refrigerator door.

Held by a daisy magnet was a fairy princess she helped Natalie with last weekend. The colors were a variety of soft pink, yellow, and blue with a glossy jade green. On the other drawing, Nicholas used his favorite colors of brown, gray, black, and navy to color a space rocket. She taped his to the door because he asked her not to use a flower magnet for his picture. The two separate drawings clearly demonstrated the difference between her children.

She glanced at the kitchen clock and noticed enough time had passed, so she redialed the telephone.

"Ridgeway Medical Center for Women, how may I direct your call?"

"Dr. Barbara Harris, please." Jennifer said.

"Are you calling for an appointment or for test results?"

"An appointment, this is Jennifer Hayse." She paced the kitchen floor.

"When was your last visit?"

"It was a few months ago, sometime back in March." She remembered her last appointment, vividly.

"And what is the reason for your appointment?"

Jennifer held her breath and said, "I found a small lump in my left breast."

A few moments later, her appointment was scheduled for Monday morning, June 2, at nine-thirty; she wrote down the date and time before hanging up.

She looked outside and noticed the weather was mild, so she decided to go for a long prayer walk. She found her spring jacket in the downstairs closet and slipped into a pair of walking shoes. She grabbed a water bottle from the refrigerator and stepped outside, as usual, the neighborhood was quiet for this time of day.

Jennifer unscrewed the cap and took a sip, as her thoughts began to wander, she prayed the lump was hormone-related, perhaps even a side effect from her recent miscarriage. She took another sip of water, and turning the corner, she increased her pace to speed walking.

Several thoughts flooded her mind as she pumped her arms in unison with her legs. Repeatedly, she told herself she was too young for breast cancer, besides statistically she was not in the right age group for serious risk factors. She maintained a rapid pace for the next five blocks.

Slowing, she turned onto Pond View Drive, gradually her mind cleared and was in harmony with her heartbeat. She reached the end of her driveway and opened the mailbox, hugging the letters to her chest, Jennifer closed her eyes and erased all negative thoughts as she prayed . . . *Dear Lord, help me to be still and know that You are God. (Psalm 46:10)*

*   *   *

It was dark outside before Keith came home, and Jennifer was asleep on the couch. She woke at the sound of his voice and gave him a drowsy welcome.

"Sorry for waking you, I thought you would be upstairs in bed." He kissed the tip of her nose and sat down, exhausted.

"No, I wanted to wait for you to come home, Keith."

"Don't you have to work tomorrow?" he asked.

"Yes, at six o'clock in the morning." She tried to stop yawning.

"You better get some sleep then." He walked into the kitchen and asked, "Are there any leftovers?"

"Yes, there is some lasagna in the refrigerator." She finger-combed her auburn waves back into the hair clip that slipped out during her nap.

Keith opened the containers of food while Jennifer reached for a saucepan.

"We need a microwave," he said.

"I don't like microwaves." Jennifer poured herself some apple juice and told him there was time if he wanted to change out of his work clothes. She adjusted the flame on the burner and washed her hands before fixing him a salad. By the time he came downstairs, his meal was ready. "You see, Keith, that was just as easy as using a microwave."

He sat down at the table and said, "Once the children get older, our lives are going to be busier, and you will want a microwave."

Jennifer did not comment as she sat next to him and finished her apple juice.

"How were the kids today?"

"Natalie misses you terribly and Nicholas wanted to play a computer game, but I couldn't locate the file." She covered another yawn. "He wanted to call you at work so you could tell his mommy how to use the computer," she smiled.

"Tomorrow night I'll link an icon to the desktop for him." He finished his dinner and got up.

"Keith," she said, reaching out, "I have to talk with you about something important."

"I'm listening." He stood by the counter, sorting the mail.

She watched him go through two days of envelopes shuffling the occupant mail from the rest.

"Where is the credit card statement?" he asked.

"I paid it yesterday along with the electric bill."

"Good." He kept sorting the mail.

"Keith, we need to talk." Jennifer's tone of voice got his attention.

He said the first thing that came into his mind. "Why, are you pregnant?"

"No." And with that her tears started to fall.

He followed her to the couch and asked, "What's wrong Jennifer?"

"This afternoon I made an appointment to see Dr. Harris on Monday." She wiped her tears and said, "Keith, I found a lump in my left breast four days ago."

Caught off-guard and not prepared for the news, he tried his best to console her. "That's not unusual, Jennifer, because you have found lumps before that come and go with your monthly cycle, right?"

"Yes, but I'm not on my period right now." She blew her nose.

"Sweetheart, we've been through this before, and it's probably nothing." He placed his arm around her shoulder.

"I hope you're right."

"What time is your appointment?"

"It's at nine-thirty." She sat cross-legged on the couch.

"Do you want me to go with you?"

She shook her head.

"Listen Jennifer, by ten-thirty on Monday, you'll be out of the doctor's office and smiling."

"I hope you're right, Keith." She rose from the couch and kissed him good night.

"I'll be up in a minute." The eleven o'clock news came on and Keith wanted to watch it before going to sleep.

Jennifer walked past the kitchen table, ignoring the dirty dishes and the empty glass of milk that needed to be cleaned up. She locked the front door, turned on the porch light, and with a quick flash the bulb burnt out and darkened her footsteps. She turned and carefully climbed the stairs to their bedroom and set her alarm clock for five-fifteen.

Tomorrow, she and Cathy would prepare documentation for the quality review meeting and she needed to get some rest. She pulled back the covers, sat on the bed, crossed her legs and folded her hands in prayer . . . *Dear God, thank You for my children's quiet and peaceful sleep, protect them through the night; keep their dreams soft and light. Thank You for bringing Rima and Bill together, I pray they will honor You by bringing joy and happiness to each other. Dear God, I pray Monday morning will come and go quickly without any cause for concern.* She finished the prayer the way her grandmother had taught her as a child . . . *I love You, Jesus, because You first loved me. Amen.*

Loving memories of her grandmother gave Jennifer a reason to smile. She laid down trying to end her day with peaceful thoughts. She turned on her side and started to fall asleep, but the gentle weight of her right breast caused pressure on her left side where she discovered the lump. The discomfort mounted to a low-level degree of pain, and she moved to lie flat on her back. A single tear fell onto her pillow as she tried to find rest.

*   *   *

45

It was Saturday morning when Mary heard the telephone ring above the sound of the washing machine. She stepped over the pile of towels and closed the laundry room door, catching the telephone on its last ring.

"Hello?" she answered.

"Hi, Mary."

"Sue, I was just about to call you." Mary walked into the living room and sat in her favorite chair. She elevated her feet knowing the next hour would be spent visiting. She had known Sue for twenty-seven years and during that time they had formed an unbreakable bond. Although for the last fifteen years, careers and family circumstances cast them in different directions, they still treasured and preserved their friendship.

"How is your new job?" Sue asked.

"You know, Sue, I actually like my new job." Mary grinned.

"Really?" Laughter filled the telephone line from Chicago.

"You're surprised, aren't you?"

Sue continued to laugh because, yes, she was surprised.

"I think my new job will be much different from what I've been accustomed to in the past." Mary stated.

"Oh, why is that?"

"Well, for one thing, the people are nice, and I'm not working in manufacturing." This was Mary at her best: straightforward and honest.

Between bouts of laughter, Sue asked for an explanation.

"Well, I've been working in manufacturing where everything must be done just-in-time, but in prototype you have oodles of time to complete your work, and the atmosphere is not so demanding."

"That makes a huge difference." Sue agreed.

"Also, my co-workers are different, Sue, maybe it's because they're engineers." Mary anticipated the next comment.

"Now Mary, my daughter is going to be an engineer, remember?"

"Can't you talk Nicole out of it?" she teased.

"No!"

"You're not trying hard enough," Mary said with mock discipline. "Time will tell at work, but for now, everyone is on their best behavior. The engineering group is a large mix of all ages, from young adults with babies to grandparents with years of experience and guess what?" Mary wiped away the dust from the end table while she talked.

"What?"

"I had a one-person welcoming committee for my first week on the job."

"You had what?" Sue could not keep from laughing.

"Seriously, my manager was on vacation during my first week, and I suppose he didn't want me wandering the halls without any direction or purpose, so he assigned a young engineer to keep me company," Mary explained.

"Oh boy, your manager sure doesn't know you, does he?" Sue laughed.

"Not yet, but I enjoyed all the attention, and Sue, you would have been proud of me because I was actually pretty nice during my first week."

"Mary, you are terrible." Sue watered the plants on her window sill and asked, "Who was the engineer assigned to welcome you aboard?"

"Her name is Jennifer Hayse and she graduated from the University of Michigan. Her degree is in electrical engineering, and she is bright, cheerful, and full of energy!"

"She must be young," Sue sighed.

"Yes, she is, and I'm old enough to be her mother," Mary sighed.

"We are getting older, aren't we?" Sue laughed again. "I'm glad you think it's funny." Mary loved hearing the sound of Chicago laughter.

"Jennifer sounds very nice."

"She is, and so is everyone else."

"God has blessed you again, Mary."

"Yes, He has." On her way into the laundry room, Mary poured herself another cup of coffee.

"Well, I'm excited because your new job will give us something extra to talk about." Sue began to make herself oatmeal for breakfast. "And that's what I love about our friendship, Mary. We can talk for hours about anything."

*   *   *

After ending her telephone call, Mary rubbed the numbness from her left ear. She was transferring clothes from the washer to the dryer when she jumped at the sound of her son's deep voice. The high school football player laughed and said, "You know Mom, one of these days, you're going to hurt yourself."

"Christopher, you scared me." Mary scolded.

The teenager lowered his six-foot-two frame to give his mother a kiss on the cheek. "Were you talking with Sue?" he asked.

"Yes, did our laughter wake you from your beauty sleep?"

"Yes, it did, can you keep it down next time?" He yawned and stretched to the ceiling. "What's for breakfast?"

After starting the washing machine Mary followed him into the kitchen, and said, "Have some cereal with a banana." She pointed to the fruit bowl and reached for the dry cereal box.

"Mom, how bad does fruit have to get before you'll throw it out?" He held the discolored banana in the air.

Mary's daughter, Jessica, joined them in the kitchen. She grinned at her older brother's comment and pointed at the wastebasket. Christopher tossed the banana into the garbage.

"What time do you both start work this morning?" Mary asked.

"In an hour," Jessica said while making toast.

"Well, you'd better hurry then because it's a twenty minute drive to Stony Creek." Mary watched her daughter casually take a bunch of grapes and stroll over to the kitchen table.

Christopher walked into the family room, clicked the remote, and the sound of morning television filled the house.

"Don't worry Mom, we have plenty of time." Jessica poured a glass of milk and asked, "Would you grab my toast and the peanut butter?" She flashed a radiant smile at her mother as she twisted her long black hair into a ponytail.

Mary went to the table and handed Jessica the peanut butter and toast. The morning sun was shining directly across her daughter's lovely profile which outlined her beautiful silhouette. Mary smiled and asked, "What time will you and Christopher get off work today, sweetheart?"

"The golf course will be busy." Jessica glanced out the bay window and said, "We probably won't be home until after dark."

Thirty minutes later, Mary stood on the front porch watering the petunias and waving good-bye to her children, who drove off to work in her son's pickup truck. The sound of the noisy muffler filled the streets of the quiet neighborhood as they left the subdivision.

Back inside her home, Mary silenced the sound of the television with one click of the remote. She went to the kitchen, added bananas to the grocery list, and then brought her coffee and daily devotional with her outside to the patio table.

There was peace in her household, and in her life; it was a genuine peace from the presence of the Holy Spirit. Mary acknowledged the countless blessings God had bestowed upon her family as her thoughts instantly turned to prayer . . . *Dear God, thank You for my wonderful children, their summer jobs, and the love they have for each other. Thank You for my career and help me to adjust to the changes You have brought my way. Give me maturity in my faith and wisdom to use this opportunity to show others Your kindness and love. Amen.*

*   *   *

It was eleven o'clock Monday morning before Keith telephoned Jennifer, he stepped outside his office and hit the speed dial number for her cell phone, and she answered on the first ring.

"How did things go?" he asked.

"Dr. Harris says I'm fine, but I'm not sure I agree."

"Why not?" His question was abrupt.

"It just doesn't seem right, Keith."

"Why not?" he asked a second time.

"Because this lump is different from others in the past – it hurts."

"Did you tell her that?" He was looking down at his shoes.

"Yes, but she said there was no difference."

"Well, she is the doctor." He watched the traffic on the busy street.

Jennifer wished she felt more confident.

"Besides, if the pain continues you can always go back for another examination," he said.

"I suppose you're right," she sighed.

"I have to get back to work, but we'll talk about this later tonight." He said good-bye and went back into the building. Jennifer stood in the hallway at Ridgeway Medical Center for Women browsing the list of health issues posted on the information board. She chose two pamphlets from the selection, both on the subject of breast cancer and then placed them inside her backpack while waiting for the elevator.

She stepped inside with another woman and quietly rode down to the main floor where she opened the lobby door and walked out into the parking lot. She calmed herself down with inner words of encouragement and told herself she would read the pamphlets to learn more about the warning signs of breast cancer. Soon she was feeling better and taking the doctor's medical advice, she let the worry drift from her mind; like butterflies floating on the breeze, her concerns were carried away.

*   *   *

Mary parked next to the garage entrance outside the V.E.M.A. office building. It was mid-July, and the early morning temperature was already above eighty degrees. She left the windows halfway down in her vehicle and walked toward the entrance.

"You better roll your windows up," Duane called out to her.

"Why?" she yelled back at him.

He smiled at how easily she became frustrated and said, "Because it's supposed to rain this morning."

"No, it's not." Mary jingled her keys at him and walked through the door he held open.

"Yes, it is." Duane continued to hold open the door giving her time to reconsider, but his grin was misleading.

"Are you joking, Duane?" she asked.

"No, he's serious this time, Mary," Cathy said, walking in behind her.

Mary studied Duane for a moment and then went outside to roll up her car windows. He held the door while Cathy stood inside the entrance, smiling and listening to the sound of distant thunder. Mary was back inside just before the rain began to fall.

"You cry wolf a lot," she smiled at him.

"I agree with her, Duane." Cathy shook her finger at him.

"I was just trying to help." He lifted both hands in self-defense.

It was then, the thunder crashed, and the rain started to pour. They watched as the drops splashed onto the dry pavement.

Mary stared off in the distance and said, "The farmers need the rain."

Duane thought it was a strange remark, but he left without commenting.

"How are things going, Mary?" Cathy soon asked.

"Well, I'm making progress with cleaning my portion of this huge storage room." Mary punctuated the remark with a nod while unlocking the door.

Cathy looked into the room and said, "Don't kill yourself trying to keep it clean."

"Don't worry, I'll only straighten out my area and leave the rest alone."

"Good for you," Cathy jabbed Mary's shoulder. "Although, Jennifer mentioned you were going to help organize her workstation."

"We tried," Mary said, laughing, "and we failed."

"You know, I'm not sure Jen could find things if her work area was organized and besides, she manages things perfectly."

"You both do, Cathy, and believe me; I know how difficult it is being a working mother."

"It is hard, isn't it?" Cathy stared down the hallway and then said, "Jennifer and I have been meaning to ask you out for lunch, Mary. Would today be a good day?"

"Yes, today would be great, thanks."

"Okeydokey." Cathy smiled.

~ *4* ~

Cathy and Jennifer sat across from Mary in the restaurant booth. The waitress took their orders and left them a carafe of hot coffee. While Cathy and Jennifer mixed their blended brews, Mary drank her first cup. She was pouring her second one when Jennifer asked, "Are you comfortable with your new job?"

"Yes, thank you for asking." Mary admired Jennifer's sincerity and added, "I enjoy the work and the people."

"We are nice people," Cathy joked.

Jennifer smiled and waved across the dining room at two women who were walking toward her table. "Hello, Kathy and Susan," she said. After an exchange of greetings Jennifer made a quick introduction, "Mary, this is Kathy Walsh and Susan Abraham."

"Hello, Mary." Kathy said, "We've passed each other in the hallway, but have yet to meet." They shook hands.

"It's nice to meet you," Mary said.

"I don't believe we've met either, Mary, I am Susan."

"Hello, Susan."

"Jennifer, what's new with Bill?" asked Kathy.

"Ditto," Cathy asked, "What's the scoop?"

Susan and Mary smiled at each other.

"It's not my place to say anything yet," Jennifer stated.

54

Kathy was noticeably pregnant and had to lean into the booth so the waitress could get through. Mary offered to slide over and make room for her to sit, but she explained they couldn't stay. Kathy then asked Jennifer, "Do you think Bill has an announcement to make?"

"We shouldn't speculate," Jennifer said and then sipped her coffee.

"You're right," Kathy said. "It was nice meeting you, Mary."

After they left, Cathy tried again, "Jennifer, tell me what's new with Bill."

Jennifer shrugged her shoulders and changed the subject by saying to Mary, "Kathy is one of our core engineers and she works with Bill."

"She is dynamite!" Cathy cut in.

"Is this her first child?" Mary asked.

"No, she has two children, Rose and Jacob," Jennifer said. "She is pregnant with their third child, and her husband's name is Bob."

"When is she expecting?"

"Any minute," Cathy answered.

"Does Susan work with Kathy and Bill?" Mary wondered.

"Yes, Susan was transferred to our engineering section the first of the year, but I worked with her years ago when she was a design engineer," Jennifer explained. "Although we don't see each other as much as we used to and it's been a long time since we've talked. She's a lovely woman, and everyone respects Susan."

"Susan is a strong Christian." Cathy finished her lunch and said, "So am I, and so are Kathy, Jennifer, Duane, Bill, and Al." Cathy leaned forward with her elbows on the table and wondered, "How about you, Mary, are you a Christian?"

"Yes, I am but there have been times when I've strayed from my faith, and thankfully, God pursued me and carried me back into His fold."

"Praise God!" Cathy said, and then she explained, "My upbringing in God's Word was from my mother in a traditional environment, but now my family attends a Christian church, and we love it."

Mary added, "Like you Cathy, I grew up in an atmosphere surrounded by doctrine, but now I attend a Christian church where I am surrounded by the Word of God. My mother taught me from an early age to believe in God and it was her example of faith that guided me into seeking a personal relationship with Jesus Christ." She then turned to Jennifer and asked, "What about you, Jennifer, how did you come to know the Lord?"

"It was my grandmother who taught me about God when I was young and with each story she told, I couldn't wait to hear another one." Jennifer's eyes sparkled with memories. "Grandmother would rock me in her wicker chair while telling me all kinds of stories from the Old and New Testaments."

Jennifer paused, and Mary waited for her to continue, but when she didn't Cathy broke the momentary silence.

"We are sisters-in-Christ, and watching our mothers and grandmothers raise their families in faith is a wonderful testimony." Cathy thought for a moment before saying, "Sometimes it takes witnessing another person's life and how they overcame a trial to bring us closer to God."

"You're right Cathy," Mary said. "My mother overcame tremendous personal heartache by virtue of her faith, which helped me to eventually place my trust in God."

"Your mother sounds like a strong woman," Jennifer remarked.

"She wasn't strong in stature, Jennifer, she was petite like you, but she was a tower of spiritual strength to her six children." Mary would never forget her mother's faith in God.

"Is your mother alive?" Jennifer asked.

"No, she passed away two years ago just before Christmas." Mary put on her reading glasses to divide their lunch bill.

"Oh, I'm sorry." Jennifer's compassion was genuine.

"Christmas is a sad time of year for a loved one to pass away." Cathy opened her wallet.

"Yes it is, and Christmas is much different now without Mom."

"You miss her, don't you?" Jennifer could tell.

Mary nodded.

"My children better miss me when I'm gone and not just at Christmastime." Cathy lightened the conversation.

"They'll miss you all the time, Cathy," Jennifer remarked.

"Hey, Jen, your two beauties would be lost without you." Cathy admired Jennifer's motherly nature.

"Yes, they would miss me." Jennifer inwardly sighed.

There was a silent connection forming among the three of them; it was an unseen gravity with a spiritual force that was braiding their lives together.

> "A cord of three strands is
> not quickly broken."
> Ecclesiastes 4:12

*   *   *

After lunch, Bill found Jennifer and Cathy working in the test lab. He quietly came up behind them and in his baritone voice, he announced, "I commend you both for your outstanding patience!"

"We've been waiting all day to talk with you," Jennifer replied, with her hands resting on her hips.

"I will no longer keep you in suspense." He dramatically bowed to them.

"Let's go for a walk!" Jennifer suggested because she loved the opportunity to walk with friends.

Leaving the building, they immediately noticed a significant change in the weather. The abundance of rain from earlier in the day had caused an increase in temperature along with a rise in the humidity.

"Don't you love Michigan?" Cathy commented while stretching her arms out through the invisible afternoon moisture.

"What a change in the weather," Jennifer said.

"Why, did it rain this morning?" Bill joked.

"Yes, it was thundering and lightning, Bill. Where have you been?" Cathy jabbed his arm.

"I've been lost in my thoughts," Bill smiled.

"Cathy and I are going to let you do all the talking, Bill." Jennifer started to walk underneath the shade of the overhanging branches.

He waited a moment before saying, "I called a realtor yesterday because I'm going to sell my house."

"Sell your house?" Cathy was surprised.

"Shush," Jennifer placed her finger against her lips.

"Yes, four years ago when my mother passed away, I moved in without giving it much thought. At that time it was the right thing to do, but now things have changed."

Jennifer smiled, and Cathy could not take another step. They waited for his explanation.

"I want to purchase a new home for my bride," Bill announced.

"No way!" Cathy shouted.

Bill rocked back and forth on his feet, enjoying the look of surprise on Cathy's face while Jennifer simply smiled because she had suspected the good news all along.

Across the parking lot at work, Kathy noticed the excitement from the group and called out, "What's going on?"

Jennifer waved to her, and Kathy walked over to join them. Bill was beaming as he told her, "Rima has accepted my proposal of marriage."

"Congratulations!" Kathy cheered.

*   *   *

For the second time that afternoon, Duane was in the parking lot with Mary, helping her empty boxes of trash from the storage room. "Are you sure all these files should be thrown away?" he asked.

"Yes, I'm sure," Mary answered.

"Okay, if you say so." He dumped the container and noticing the crowd of people underneath the trees, as he put down the trash he pointed to them and said, "Mary, this can wait because I think we're missing out on some news over there."

Mary glanced over at the huddled group of engineers.

"Come on Mary, let's join them." Duane didn't wait for a response. He dropped the trash bin and asked as he approached, "Hey, what's all the excitement about?"

"Rima and I are getting married!" Bill said.

"Attaboy!" Duane shook his hand.

"Bill, have you set a date yet?" Cathy interrupted.

"Yes, September 6," he answered.

"Oh, good, we have fourteen months to prepare," she told Jennifer.

"No, Cathy, I meant six weeks from now," Bill corrected her.

The group stirred with renewed commotion. Kathy squeezed in another word of congratulations before leaving. Duane laughed at the rapid exchange of wedding plans between Cathy and Jennifer, while Mary stood amazed. She turned to Bill and said, "I thought you just met Rima for the first time a couple of weeks ago."

"He did," Cathy and Jennifer answered simultaneously.

Mary glanced back at Bill and noticed the reserved man she met two months ago had indeed changed and it was obvious that he was in love.

"I never thought I would be blessed with love and marriage at this point in my life." Bill stopped walking and explained to Duane that on his first trip to Louisiana, he shared his feelings of love with Rima.

Jennifer then told everyone, "I've talked with Rima many times in the last few weeks, and I know for certain that she is deeply in love with Bill."

"God has a future plan for you and Rima." Cathy told him.

"Yes, I know He does, and I realize this may seem out of the ordinary because things came together rather quickly. However, I can assure you that Rima and I are in agreement with getting married. We are equally yoked in our faith and we believe that our marriage is the work of the Holy Spirit."

Jennifer was so happy that she clapped her hands, again.

"Are we invited?" Cathy abruptly asked.

"Of course, after all we can't get married without Jennifer because she introduced us."

"I'm sewing matching dresses for Natalie and me to wear at the wedding." She told everyone.

"Wonder Woman strikes again," Cathy elbowed Duane in the ribs.

The small group walked back into work. Jennifer talked with Cathy about wedding plans, celebrations, and parties. Bill was half-listening to their conversation since his thoughts began to wander about his future and his bride. Duane was smiling because there would certainly be something to tell his wife, Janis, tonight at dinner.

*   *   *

Two days later, Dr. Barbara Harris thumbed through the posted medical chart and was bewildered when she saw who was waiting inside the examination room. She opened the door and said, "Mrs. Hayse, I'm surprised to see you again so soon."

"Hello, Dr. Harris, and yes, I was just here a few weeks ago."

"What is the reason for your return visit?" Dr. Harris sat down.

"Yesterday I found another lump, but this time the lump is in my right breast." Jennifer's voice cracked when she explained, "Also, the first lump in my left breast has increased in size and I'm concerned that my condition is more than just fibrocystic changes."

"When was your last period?" Dr. Harris asked.

"July 1."

"Is there any chance you could be pregnant?" Dr. Harris reached under Jennifer's knees to extend the examination table.

"No, I'm not pregnant." Jennifer lay flat on the paper-covered vinyl.

"How old are you, Jennifer?"

"I'm thirty-one."

"You are still very young," Dr. Harris said. "How have you been since your miscarriage last March?"

"Do you mean emotionally or physically?" Jennifer tried to relax.

"Both." Dr. Harris continued to examine the soft tissue area on the left breast.

"Ouch!" Jennifer winced.

"I'm sorry, you can sit up now." Dr. Harris covered her with the paper gown and asked, "How old are your children?"

"Nicholas is four, and Natalie is two and a half."

The physician wrote the information down in the medical chart before closing the file and said, "Although statistically, you are not within the age parameters for any major concerns, I think you should have a mammogram."

Jennifer was relieved and nodded in agreement.

Dr. Harris said, "Until we have the lab results there is no reason for concern. I believe the lumps are fibrocystic masses that developed after your miscarriage, which was only five months ago." Dr. Harris turned to wash her hands. "This was your third miscarriage, correct?"

"Yes." Jennifer felt sadness every time she was reminded of the past.

"I can assure you, Mrs. Hayse, having a mammogram will put your mind to rest."

"I certainly hope so," Jennifer said.

"On your way out today, make an appointment for a mammogram, then I will see you in a couple of weeks with the test results." Dr. Harris was finished.

Jennifer discarded the uncomfortable gown and left the examining room. She took the first available opening for a mammogram on Wednesday, July 30. The receptionist gave her an overview of the test procedure. Jennifer placed the information sheet in her backpack and left Ridgeway Medical Center for Women.

*　　　*　　　*

Once inside her car, Jennifer telephoned Keith. "Are you busy?"

"No, why?" he asked.

"I just left the doctor's office," she said.

He hesitated before asking, "What's wrong?"

"Keith, I found a second lump in my right breast last week, and Dr. Harris was able to see me this morning."

"Jennifer, why didn't you tell me sooner?" he asked.

"Because, I didn't want you to worry."

"Well, I'm worried now, what did the doctor say?" Keith rubbed his forehead.

While walking to the parking lot, Jennifer explained what happened in the doctor's office and said, "I'm scheduled for a mammogram, Keith."

"Does Dr. Harris feel there is something wrong?"

"No, this is just a precaution." Jennifer started her SUV and turned on the air conditioning. "Keith, I know my body and these lumps are not the same, which gives me reason to believe something is not right." She pulled out into traffic and waited at the first stop light.

"I'm certain the test results will put your mind at ease, otherwise are you feeling all right?" He couldn't tell by talking with her over the telephone.

"Yes, I'm going back to work, and I'll be home around six o'clock."

"Okay, but don't wait on me to eat dinner."

"You're going to be late again?" It was the third night this week.

"Yes."

Seeing the entrance ramp to the expressway, Jennifer said good-bye and placed both hands on the wheel, merging carefully onto I-275 North. In thirty minutes, she would be in Dearborn and back to work. This would give her enough time to update the module changes and send them out before the end of the day. She turned up the volume to her favorite radio station, WMUZ, and her thoughts were filled with Christian music.

*   *   *

It was late in the afternoon, and Jennifer was satisfied with the updates Al needed. Her wandering thoughts were interrupted when he asked from the doorway if she had completed the task.

"Yes, I just e-mailed the file to you and the launch team."

"Very good, thanks." Al asked when she would be shipping the modules to the United Kingdom.

"The shipment will go out the beginning of next week." Jennifer turned off her computer and asked, "Is there anything else you need?"

"No, have a good night." Al turned to leave.

Jennifer was glad the workday was through, she got her backpack, turned off the overhead light, and left her workstation. As she walked down the hall, her path was blocked by the janitor's cleaning cart. She moved it out of her way and into the copy room where Susan was standing.

"Hello, Susan," she greeted her friend.

Susan was reading a magazine and she didn't hear Jennifer.

"Hi, Susan," Jennifer stood next to her at the copy machine.

Startled, Susan closed the magazine and quickly folded it upside down in the tray. "Jennifer, you frightened me," she placed her hand over her heart.

"I'm sorry." Jennifer noticed an edge of sharpness in her voice, which was out of character for Susan.

"No, I'm sorry, Jennifer, I thought everyone had gone home because it's almost six o'clock."

"It is late and I was just leaving."

Susan looked away and didn't respond.

"Is everything all right?" Jennifer stepped closer.

Ignoring the question and wanting to change the subject, Susan said, "Kathy told me about Bill, and I know you're happy for him." She stacked the copied material in front of her. "It is exciting when someone declares their love and shows commitment, such as Bill."

"Yes, it is exciting and their wedding date is set for September 6."

Susan leaned against the copy machine and held tightly to her documents.

"Bill and Rima are in love and see no reason to wait," Jennifer said.

"I agree, there is no reason to wait because life is too short and we shouldn't put off sharing happiness and love with one another." Susan added.

Jennifer waited before asking, "How are your husband, Abe, and children, Michelle and Matthew?"

"Abe is doing well, he is a wonderful husband, and the children have – " Susan accidentally dropped the magazine she was holding.

"Here, let me help you," Jennifer offered.

"No, please don't – "

Jennifer picked up the Monthly Medical Journal for Women with the leading cover article, "*What you need to know about Breast Cancer.*" It was the same article Jennifer had planned to read. Slowly she handed Susan the magazine.

"Thank you." Susan lowered her eyes and turned away.

For a moment, they stood in a room filled with silence. The janitor interrupted them by rolling out his cleaning cart. The elderly man tipped the brim of his frayed working cap, and without saying a word, left the room.

"We'll talk later, Jennifer." She tried to leave but Jennifer reached out to stop her.

"No wait, Susan, please tell me what's going on."

Susan held her breath and said, "I have just been diagnosed with breast cancer." She took a long time before exhaling. "It doesn't seem possible, Jennifer, and I have not had a lot of time to grasp this news."

"Oh, Susan, forgive me for not knowing something was wrong because you have been so quiet lately." Jennifer's eyes brimmed with tears.

"I am always quiet when I am in prayerful meditation with our Lord." No longer trying to conceal the copied documents, Susan busied herself with restacking them.

Instantly, Jennifer wanted to help, "What can I do to help you Susan?"

"Simply pray for me." As the tears fell down Susan's face, she said, "My medical leave begins the end of this week and God alone knows how long I will be gone, but I know He loves me and His will for my life is perfect."

"Yes, His will is perfect and we all love you, Susan." Jennifer hugged her.

After saying a long good-bye, Susan gathered her things and left the building. She drove through the back parking lot to the front entrance. Jennifer also left and pulled directly behind Susan's vehicle, they waved to each other through windows and mirrors. Susan turned north toward Canton while Jennifer turned south toward New Boston. They were traveling the same road in life, but for now, they were heading in opposite directions.

"For my thoughts are not your thoughts,
neither are your ways my ways . . ."
Isaiah 55:8

~ 5 ~

Jennifer was troubled over the second diagnosis of fibro-cystic disease because she was certain her condition was more serious, and after talking with Dr. Harris, Jennifer asked to be referred to a surgeon for a second opinion. Today was her scheduled appointment and she had just signed the patient register at Ridgeway Medical Center for Women to be seen by Dr. Zechariah Jordan.

While waiting to see the surgeon, Jennifer's eyes were drawn to the photographs displayed on the lobby walls in art gallery fashion. The waiting room was filled with soothing music and soft lighting. Without question, it was all designed to relax those who were waiting.

Jennifer recognized the artwork from Israel because they were well known pictures of the ancient structures and mountain landscapes of Jerusalem. An inner peace transpired as she viewed the black and white photographs of *The Western Wall* and the *Tower of David*. There was a beautifully framed coastal sunset over a resort area called *The Nahariya* and she wondered if the hotel was near the Sea of Galilee.

One of the photographs was titled *Mineral Rich Water – World Famous Medicinal Qualities*. She thought of Jesus healing the sick near the waters of the Dead Sea and soon Jennifer was mesmerized with Dr. Jordan's artwork.

The last photograph caught her attention: *The Beit She'an – A House of Rest and Quiet*, located in the Jordan Valley. She thought how wonderful it would be to enjoy rest and quiet . . . *Dear Lord, guide me through this appointment and help me to trust Your will for my life.*

*   *   *

Jennifer was prepared for bad news as she followed the medical assistant past the examining rooms directly into the doctor's office. The woman placed her medical chart on the surgeon's desk and said, "Dr. Jordan will be right with you, Mrs. Hayse."

"I don't need to be examined?" Jennifer questioned.

"No, I was told to bring you into the office." The woman said and then left.

Jennifer looked around the finely decorated masculine office. The colors were a mixture of soft gray and burgundy, and directly behind the doctor's leather chair were several framed documents. The center diploma was proudly displayed and read: *Grossmann Medical University of the Negev, Israel* with the name, Zechariah Jordan, M.D., in bold print.

"Mrs. Hayse, it is my pleasure to meet you, I am Dr. Jordan." He walked in and sat perched on the edge of the desk, and his mannerism was filled with confidence. Jennifer guessed his age was close to her own.

"Barbara tells me you're anxious about your mammogram, so let me get right to the point." He crossed his arms and leaning slightly forward he said, "You do not have breast cancer."

Jennifer felt the room sway, as if the earth had stopped revolving, and it was several seconds before she blinked and asked, "You're certain?"

"Yes, I am certain because what you have are fibrocystic tumors, this is very common in women who have experienced multiple miscarriages, and your mammogram indicates no reason for concern." He walked over to his desk and sat in his chair. "This is good news, yes?" he asked.

"But what about the pain . . . ?"

He interrupted her and said, "Mrs. Hayse, your demographic profile doesn't match any of the current statistical research for breast cancer." He began searching through his top desk drawer. "Simply put – you're too young, and you have no family history . . . "

She interrupted him and said, "Yes, I do have a family history on my mother's side." Jennifer repositioned herself closer to his desk, trying to capture his attention.

A trace of annoyance was evident as he closed the desk drawer. He put on his glasses and opened her file. He scanned the medical records and impatiently said, "Yes, yes, I can see your family history." Dr. Jordan tossed his glasses on the desk and sat back in his chair. "However, your family history does not change the mammogram results." He pressed his fingertips together, making a pyramid, and waited.

"You're telling me, I don't have breast cancer?" Jennifer was not convinced.

"You do *not* have breast cancer."

"I am fine then?"

"If the pain persists, come back in six months, and we'll determine if there has been a significant increase in the fibrocystic tissue."

"You don't feel a biopsy is necessary?" Jennifer wanted reassurance.

"No, a biopsy is not necessary, is there anything else?" he asked.

Jennifer looked at her folded hands and tried to understand why she was not one hundred percent satisfied, then she asked, "My husband and I would like to have another baby, is there any reason why we should wait?"

"Dr. Harris is your obstetrician and she should answer that question." Dr. Jordan looked at his expensive watch. "As I said, the fibrocystic cell tissue accumulation is not uncommon after a miscarriage, please believe me." He walked to the door and understanding his body language, Jennifer stood. She thanked him, and then left.

As she rode down the elevator, her stomach growled, whether it was from nerves or hunger she was not sure. She stopped at the store in the front lobby for coffee and a granola bar. The intake of calories helped to curb the sudden onset of weakness, and the tension between her shoulders began to disappear.

"Mrs. Hayse?" someone called.

Jennifer turned and said, "Hello, Dr. Harris, I just came from Dr. Jordan's office."

"Well then, you should be smiling," Dr. Harris said.

Jennifer shifted her backpack to the other shoulder, and feeling a bit uneasy, she asked if Dr. Jordan should have performed a biopsy.

"I can't answer that question because he is your surgeon." Dr. Harris turned to catch the open elevator doors when Jennifer stopped her.

"Doctor, what about the pain and the increased swelling?"

"If the pain continues Dr. Jordan may have to surgically remove the cysts."

Jennifer looked around and since the lobby was not busy, she lowered her voice and asked, "Keith and I would like to have another child, Dr. Harris. Do you see any reason why we should wait?"

"I see no reason why you should wait." Dr. Harris wished her well and pressed the elevator button for the third floor.

As Jennifer watched the metal doors close, she tossed her empty coffee cup into the trash can and left. Once outside the building, she dialed Keith's cell phone, and in her soft lyrical voice, she left a message. "I can't wait to meet you for our dinner date tonight: seven o'clock at our favorite restaurant!"

She shielded her eyes against the bright sun, and looked both ways before crossing to the next row of parked cars when a shred of doubt invaded her thoughts . . . *am I really okay?*

She concentrated on the reassuring words of her physicians while envisioning the peaceful artwork of Israel that graced the walls of Dr. Jordan's lobby and soon, all doubt vanished and she was bathed with inner peace. The tiny butterflies in her stomach calmed their beating wings as she made the Biblical connection to the doctors' names . . . *Zechariah – the prophet, and Jordan – the river and valley.*

*　　*　　*

"Happy ten-and-a-half anniversary!" Jennifer raised her wine glass across the white linen tablecloth to her husband, Keith.

"Happy anniversary." He smiled and tasted the wine. "You look nice tonight, Jennifer. Do you like the shawl?" he asked.

"Yes, it's a lovely anniversary gift." She admired the soft fabric.

"I was hoping you would wear it tonight." Keith glanced at the menu and asked, "What would you like for dinner?"

"Whatever you order is fine with me." Jennifer took a small sip of wine while Keith ordered their meals and after the waiter left, she said, "We have a lot to discuss this evening."

71

"Yes we do, but first I want to know the results of your mammogram."

"It's all good news, Keith," she smiled.

"Whew!" He raised his wine glass.

"I'm sorry for all the concern during the last couple of months."

"None of it was your fault, Jennifer, I'm just glad it's over."

"I am, too." Her soft laughter filled the refined dining room.

"Shush," he whispered. Keith was opposite in personality from Jennifer and he was uncomfortable with showing any emotion, especially in public.

"Keith, we can try for another baby," she whispered to him.

"Now *that* makes me happy." He teased her and finished his wine.

"Since we are blessed with a son and a daughter, the gender of our next baby will not matter." Automatically, thinking of motherhood, Jennifer slid her glass of wine across the table for him to finish.

"I love your rationale." He drank from her glass.

"Whether we have a little boy or a little girl, just having another baby will make everything perfect." She adjusted the shawl over her shoulders.

The waiter brought their appetizers, and Keith placed two stuffed mushrooms on Jennifer's plate and asked, "What other news do you have?"

"Let's talk about your work," she invited him.

"There is nothing new at work." He buttered a slice of bread and asked, "What other news do you have to tell me?"

Jennifer waited a moment before saying, "We need to make plans to drive to Louisiana because Bill and Rima are getting married . . ."

"Whoa, wait a minute, Jennifer." Keith leaned into the table and said, "We drove to Louisiana the first of the year and we don't need to do it again anytime soon."

"Keith, we must go to their wedding because not going would be rude."

"Who else is going?" he sighed.

"Cathy is going." Jennifer knew what he was going to say.

"Good, I'm sure you and Cathy will have a wonderful time." He sliced his filet mignon.

"Fine, I'll go with Cathy." She sliced her filet mignon and told him, "You can stay at home with the children."

"Jennifer!" He almost choked.

"Now Keith, would it be easier to drive to Louisiana, or to stay home with Nicholas and Natalie?" She knew the answer, and so did he.

"Jennifer?" he pleaded.

"Yes?" she smiled.

"The next time you play matchmaker, be sure the couple lives within five miles of our house." He tried to hide his grin.

"Sweetheart, I'm glad you want to go as a family."

After a pause, he asked, "Have Bill and Rima set a date yet?"

Jennifer mumbled, "September 6."

"Now, Jennifer that changes everything." Keith wiped his mouth and finished the last of her wine. "I don't know if I can get the time off work with such little notice."

"I hope it won't be a problem." She placed her napkin on the table and took his hand. "Keith, I need to visit with Grandmother Catherine one last time."

The waiter quietly cleared their table.

"It's a long trip, Jennifer, but let me talk with my boss tomorrow about scheduling the time off. What else is new?"

Keith knew she wanted to visit with her grandmother and he understood the reason.

Jennifer suddenly felt a cold shiver. She lifted the shawl higher around her shoulders and could not stop the tears from blurring her vision. "Keith, I am very grateful for my mammogram results today. God has been good to us, and I want us to enjoy our time together."

"We enjoy our time together, Jennifer." A tinge of guilt hit his stomach.

"I mean time together as a family with our children, not just the two of us."

"I can't help that my work schedule is unpredictable." He placed his napkin on the table and reached for the glass of wine, but it was empty. "Jennifer, I know it's hard when I'm not around to help."

"I'm not referring to the times when you're not around, Keith, I'm referring to the times when you are there." She softly said, "I understand you must work odd hours without notice and I don't have any issues with those arrangements. What I am asking though, is when you are home to please spend some time with me and the children instead of spending time alone playing games on the computer."

He knew she was making a valid point, so he didn't comment.

"Let's do things more often as a family," Jennifer said.

"Okay, I'll teach the kids how to play computer games with me," he teased.

"You always make me smile." She blushed and asked the waiter for more coffee. "Now, let's talk about your job."

He moaned and rubbed his forehead.

"Keith, the other day at work, I spoke with Duane . . ."

"Who is Duane?"

"You know who Duane is," she stated, seeing through his personality, "and he was on the telephone talking with Janis . . ."

"Who is Janis?" he grinned.

"Janis is Duane's wife and he was telling her about Bill's wedding."

Keith continued to smile.

"The point is, Mr. Hayse, Duane was talking to his wife about his job, and from now on, I want you to be more open and talk to me about your job."

"You want me to change? I thought you loved me just the way I am," he winked.

"Hmm." She frowned and despite herself, her lips curved in response.

"Is there anything else we need to discuss?" He looked at his cell phone.

"Yes, do you remember Susan?"

"Jennifer, you have too many friends at work, and I can't remember all of them."

"Susan Abraham is a close friend who is now on medical leave."

"Oh, what happened?"

"Susan has been diagnosed with breast cancer."

Keith was struck by the close proximity of Susan's diagnosis and Jennifer's recent experience. He thought for a moment and said, "Yes, I remember her."

Jennifer told him about the conversation she had last week with Susan. "Her diagnosis and my appointment with a surgeon today – the timing is so close; do you realize it could have been us instead?"

Keith was grateful when the waiter interrupted them with their check. After signing the receipt, he stood and helped Jennifer with her chair, saying, "Sweetheart, don't worry. I'm sure everything will work out for Susan."

*   *   *

Early the next morning, Cathy walked toward Duane's desk with two questions on her mind. She found him rummaging through stacks of paperwork and placing documents into storage boxes.

"What are you doing?" she asked.

"I'm placing some old documents into storage." Duane didn't stop what he was doing to visit.

"When did you become a neat freak?" Cathy sat in his chair.

"Just recently." He placed a sealed box under his desk.

"Duane, it looks like you're hiding things," she observed.

He was embarrassed and said, "I am hiding things."

"And who are you hiding things from?" she wondered.

He shifted his stance and said, "I'm hiding things from Mary because she's a neat freak and it makes me nervous."

"Oh, Duane that's ridiculous!" Cathy laughed.

"Shush," he placed his finger to his lips. "Haven't you noticed she's throwing everything out?" He sealed another storage box. "I'm afraid she's going to clean her way down the hall, and when she comes to my workstation, I don't want anything out of place." He was frustrated and mumbled, "I'll bet there isn't one thing in her house that she doesn't use every single day."

"Duane, you're too funny. Mary is only interested in her own workstation. Although, I heard she tried to help Jennifer organize things, but it didn't work." Cathy knew her remark would refuel his thoughts.

Duane quickened his pace and changing the subject he asked, "Cathy, what is it you came to talk about?"

"Oops, I almost forgot," she tapped her forehead. "Did you hear Kathy had her baby over the weekend?"

He continued to pack and said no.

"She and her husband, Bob, named their baby girl Lydia." Cathy helped by handing him a pile of documents from the table next to her and said, "Jennifer has a card at her desk for the family, be sure to sign it and, did you get Bill and Rima's wedding invitation?"

"Yes," he stopped working, "but Janis and I won't be able to go."

"Boo! Why not?"

"Our boys, Jacob and Justin, will be finishing base-ball and starting soccer at that time. Will you and Jim be going?"

"No, Jim's going to stay home with the children, but I purchased my airline ticket yesterday and my plans are to be gone three days."

"Will Jennifer be flying with you?" Duane sealed the last box.

"No, she and Keith are driving down with Nicholas and Natalie."

"That's a long trip to make with two little kids," he mumbled.

"You know Jen, she is Wonder Woman!" Cathy handed Duane a black marker to fill out the label for the storage boxes. "Besides, she wants to stay a few extra days and visit with her grandmother."

"Bill said the other day that Jennifer's grandmother wasn't feeling well." He looked around his office and for the time being, he was satisfied.

Mary stepped around the corner and asked, "What brings you both into work this early?" She then noticed the storage boxes and instantly rolled her sleeves up, wanting to help.

"Oh, I don't need any help, Mary. I'm only storing some documents. I'm not throwing anything away." Duane quickly turned to Cathy and suggested, "Why don't you and Mary go for coffee?"

"Great idea!" Cathy jumped out of the chair and came to his aide.

"Duane, you of all people know how quickly I can clean out an office and I don't mind helping." Mary smiled, knowing she was making him a little nervous.

Cathy laughed and took Mary by the arm and directed her toward the lunchroom. As they walked away, he heard Cathy say, "I think you make Duane nervous, Mary."

"I can't imagine why," she laughed.

~ 6 ~

This was Cathy's first visit to Louisiana, and she was enjoying the unique scenery, especially the Spanish moss. The self-sustaining air plant rested lazily over the full branches of the sycamore trees. She walked up to Cabin Five at Hodges Garden and knocked on the screen door.

"Is anybody home?" From inside the rustic cottage, Cathy heard a small protest coming from one of the Hayse children.

Jennifer called out and told her to come inside. Nicholas was playing on the rug by the charred fireplace, and Keith was reading a computer magazine. Little Natalie sat on the kitchen counter with pink foam rollers in her hair. Cathy wasn't sure whether Jennifer was putting them in her daughter's hair or taking them out.

"Do you have any coffee?" Cathy asked.

Jennifer nodded toward the stove and, helping herself, Cathy asked, "Where's your cup?"

"I haven't had any yet." Jennifer finished and thanked Natalie for being patient.

Cathy handed her a cup and poured her own. "Did you bring any flavor packets with you?"

"Yes," Jennifer grumbled, "but I can't remember which bag I packed them in."

Cathy then noticed the luggage piled high on the floor. "Are you staying longer than five days?" she asked.

Jennifer said no, and winced at the bitter taste of black coffee.

Cathy grinned and asked, "Have you walked down by the lake yet?"

Jennifer looked out the window and saw patches of blue water through the tall pines. "I didn't realize we were this close to the water." She turned to Keith and asked, "Would you keep an eye on the children while I go for a walk?"

He told her yes.

Jennifer turned off the coffee pot and slipped into her tennis shoes then followed Cathy outside and down the narrow path toward the beach.

Cathy said over her shoulder, "Well, Jen, you deserve a round of applause for bringing Bill and Rima together."

"Cathy, it was God's plan – not mine."

"Yes, of course, but you responded to the divine call when God placed it on your heart." Cathy took off her sandals to get her feet wet. "Besides, not many people go out of their way now-a-days to make others happy, but you did Jennifer. You saw the possibility for romance and look what has taken place in such a short time."

"It is wonderful." Despite her happiness, she felt melancholy.

"You don't sound very excited, Jennifer." Cathy followed her up a sandy incline and asked, "You love weddings, so why aren't you happy?"

They sat in the grass with their feet resting in the sand. Jennifer scooped up a handful of it and watched as the grains slowly slipped through her fingers. She squinted into the sun and answered, "I've been thinking a lot about my grandmother lately."

"I know you do, Jen, but why does thinking about her make you sad?"

"Because after today Rima will leave for Michigan, which means my grandmother will have a new caregiver, Mrs. Perez, and I am concerned the change will confuse her."

A gust of wind brushed sand from Cathy's feet onto Jennifer's lap, "Oops, sorry!"

"That's all right." Jennifer stood and said, "Let's walk along the water's edge while we talk."

Cathy slipped back into her sandals and caught up with Jennifer on the shoreline. "How long will you be staying after the wedding?" she wondered.

"A few days because I want to meet Mrs. Perez and make sure she knows to contact us, either by telephone or e-mail, in case of an emergency."

They walked along quietly, enjoying the chirping of birds perched in the wooded acres before Jennifer said, "Let's talk about the wedding."

"Okay, since you're the wedding coordinator, I'm sure you've seen the bridal gown. Will you describe it to me?"

"No Cathy," Jennifer gently chided. "You can patiently wait another couple of hours before seeing Rima's very own creation when she walks into the rose garden."

"Rima designed her own wedding gown?" Cathy stopped in disbelief.

"Yes, she was her own seamstress, too."

"How was that possible? Rima only had six weeks to design and sew her own wedding gown!"

Jennifer tossed a pebble into the water and told Cathy that soon after Rima met Bill, she went to a dressmaker's shop to purchase the fabric for her wedding gown.

"Wait a minute, Bill proposed over the Fourth of July weekend, but Rima bought the fabric back in May?"

"Yes, Rima was in love, and she knew in her heart, Bill was in love, too."

"Ah, gotcha!" Cathy understood.

"I feel there is something very special about this wedding." Jennifer gazed out at the sky.
"What do you mean?" Cathy kicked at the water's edge. "I'm not sure how to explain it, other than to say I have a sense of peace knowing Bill and Rima are getting married."
"I think it's because you don't want them to spend their lives alone, Jen." Cathy looked out over the lake and said, "It would be lonesome not having someone special to love."
They talked a little while longer before walking back to Cabin Five. Cathy offered to help with getting the children ready for the ceremony, but Jennifer declined. Cathy then said good-bye and walked along the pine needle path to her own cabin.

*   *   *

The bushes within the rose garden were holding onto their last petals and because of the time of year, they displayed only a glimpse of color among their aging branches. A strong fragrance of past buds still lingered in the air, floating across the afternoon breeze. The wedding guests were seated, and were listening quietly to an Eastern Kingbird and a Yellow Breasted Dickcissel sing in harmony. The soothing splash of lake water against the quarry rocks added to the natural homespun music for the outdoor ceremony.

Bill stood in the gazebo waiting for his bride to join him in the rose garden. Soon enough the bridal party was in place followed by the little flower girl, Natalie, who walked down the stairs and from her wicker basket, dropped rose petals that covered the wooden steps. Jennifer encouraged her daughter forward with a smile and before long, she stood next to her mother in her matching beige, yellow, and green sunflower dress. The minister raised his hand toward the top of the stairs, and everyone stood for the bride.

Rima placed her hand on her father's arm, and they walked down into the garden. Her bridal gown was a mirror image from the days of long ago. Reflecting the era of the late 1800s, her design was modest and dignified. It spoke of the long-established and time-honored history of Beauregard Parish in southern Louisiana.

The guests stood as the minister gave a prayer of blessing over the couple. The traditional wedding captured the hearts of everyone as Bill and Rima exchanged their vows. The groom then kissed the bride, and as husband and wife, Mr. and Mrs. William Hardy turned to greet their guests.

*   *   *

After their meal, Cathy and Jennifer enjoyed wedding cake and coffee outside, sitting in the cool shade of the trees. Keith offered to take the restless children to the play area by the lake and Jennifer watched as her family walked toward the playground.

"You did it." Cathy tapped her coffee cup with Jennifer's and said, "Bill and Rima are a perfect match."

"I agree, Rima has a beautiful heart and she loves Bill."

"So, who is next on your list?"

Jennifer smiled, "I'm sure someone I know is waiting for me to play matchmaker!"

"You go girl." Cathy placed her coffee back on the table and glanced around. "Hey, wait a minute; it looks like everyone is leaving."

They walked into the dining room to look for the newlyweds.

"They're gone?" Jennifer asked.

"It looks that way," Cathy answered and then linked her arm with Jennifer's as they walked downstairs toward the play area. "I have a feeling our friendship with Bill as we once knew it will be changing now that he's a married man," she said.

"I think so, too." Jennifer admitted.

Keith and the children were at the playground. As Cathy and Jennifer joined them on the swing set, they leisurely sat, gliding back and forth in the evening breeze. Natalie was gathering yellow dandelions among the fluttering of tiny white butterflies and Nicholas played by the water close to his dad. Jennifer noticed her son's clip-on tie was missing and wondered if she would find it before leaving tomorrow.

*   *   *

The next day, Jennifer stood on the front landing of the Louisiana country home that she had come to love so much. Mrs. Perez held open the screen door and inquired, "Mr. and Mrs. Hayse?"

"Yes, I'm Jennifer, and this is my husband, Keith."

They stepped inside the old farmhouse and stood in the tiny living room. When Jennifer did not see her grandmother, she asked if she was outside sitting in the shade.

"No, your grandmother, Mrs. Toby, is not feeling well today."

"She's not feeling well?" Jennifer asked.

Mrs. Perez explained to Jennifer that while she and Keith were driving to DeRidder from Michigan, her grandmother's health took a sharp decline.

Jennifer looked at the small country kitchen and asked, "She's not awake?"

"No, your grandmother is in her bedroom."

Mrs. Perez told Keith there was fresh lemonade on the picnic table and suggested, "Why don't you go outside with the children and let them play on the tire swing?"

Keith knew it would be best for Nicholas and Natalie to be occupied. He took them by the hand, through the kitchen and out the pantry door.

"How is Grandmother doing?" Jennifer asked Mrs. Perez.

"Dr. Nelson came by two days ago to increase her pain medication. I'm sorry, Mrs. Hayse, but I believe your grandmother's time is near."

Slowly, Jennifer sat in the worn green vinyl chair by the lamp stand and began to cry. Memories of past love and comfort she had known all her life were running through her mind.

Mrs. Perez reached for a box of tissues and handed them to her. "Your grandmother is not in any pain. She rests comfortably during the day and hardly wakes up at night."

Jennifer sank further into the chair as fresh tears surfaced.

"My Dear, I know this is difficult," Mrs. Perez said.

Jennifer blew her nose before asking, "Dr. Nelson, did he say when – "

Mrs. Perez held out her hand to Jennifer and said, "It won't be long."

Jennifer stood in the humid living room and glanced over at the window, wondering if it were closed and then noticed the curtains barely moving. She had forgotten how humid it gets in the Bayou, even in September. She raised her hands and gathered her long curls into a higher ponytail, hoping it would take the weight off her neck and allow for a small amount of cool breeze. She patted the moisture on her forehead with the back of her hand as she stepped into the hallway.

*   *   *

The first door on the left was Catherine's room and once she got closer, Jennifer could see the outline under the coverlet of the tiny frail woman. All her life, Catherine Toby, was held in high esteem by others; partly because of her staunch morals and integrity, but mostly because of her faith in God. The congregation at Mountain Hope Baptist Church knew her personal testimony and through the years, many of them had accepted Jesus into their lives after learning of God's love through Catherine's story.

The tiny bedroom was uncluttered just as it always was in the past and next to her bed was a beautiful wicker rocking chair. It was Catherine's handmade wedding present from her charming husband. Jennifer traced her fingers over the worn braids of natural reed that now barely supported the back of the old rocker.

In her younger days, it was in this chair that Catherine would nurse sick babies back to health, and then years later she would sit by candlelight reading the Bible, waiting for rebellious teenagers to come home safely. Then sweetly, a generation afterwards Catherine would comfortably rock in the chair with her grandchildren securely on her lap. It was in this chair where she sang to them and taught them of God's blessings and His love.

Jennifer quietly maneuvered between the dresser and the bedside because she did not want to startle her grandmother from a sound sleep. On the nightstand leaning against the tarnished brass lamp was an unframed photograph of her, Keith, and the children from their visit last year at Christmastime.

There was a water glass with a straw dangling over the side, and next to it were various prescription bottles. A tube of pink lipstick rolled and fell against an open jar of hand lotion, and a faded dry washcloth hung over the knob of the nightstand. Jennifer felt faint as shadows circled across the four walls from the slow-moving ceiling fan. The motion was making the room feel smaller and more humid than when she first stepped in.

Keith quietly asked from the doorway, "Are you okay?"

She didn't answer him because she didn't know if she was all right or not. Instead she asked, "Where are the children?"

"They're on the tire swing, but Mrs. Perez is watching over them."

"Oh, Keith, that old swing is dangerous," she said, peering out the window.

"Don't worry, it will hold their weight." Keith was standing by the window on the opposite side of the bed. He pulled back the sheer linen curtain and watched Natalie playing in the yard and from across the room he said, "Catherine seems smaller, doesn't she?"

Jennifer sat in the wicker chair and smoothed away a white curl that had fallen onto her grandmother's creased forehead. She was surprised at how soft the touch of Catherine's face was against the back of her hand and she wondered if her own skin would feel that soft at the beautiful age of ninety.

"I know this isn't how you expected things to be when we left the hotel this afternoon." Keith walked over and placed his hand on Jennifer's shoulder.

"No, I didn't expect to find her slipping away." She placed her hand over his and cried, "It looks like I won't have an opportunity to say good-bye."

It was sad to see his wife's grandmother so frail, because Keith had known Mrs. Toby for years and she had always been active. He didn't know of anyone who could tell a story with such energy and flair as Catherine did, and it was hard to comprehend how quickly her health had deteriorated.

It was obvious the heart attack Catherine had endured at the beginning of the year was more damaging than first expected and now he was glad they made the drive to see her one last time. The humidity in the room was stifling and he wanted Jennifer to get some fresh air. He held out his hand and suggested, "Let's go outside and decide what our plans should be for this evening."

* * *

Under the apple tree, Mrs. Perez was slicing fresh fruit for Nicholas and Natalie. They just finished eating the sandwiches she had given them earlier. She saw their parents across the yard and called out, "Come and sit in the shade." She pointed to the other side of the picnic table. "Can I make you something for lunch?"

"Yes, thank you, Mrs. Perez, whatever my grandmother has in her kitchen will be fine."

"I'll make tuna salad sandwiches." She replaced the lid on the peanut butter jar and stacked the plates to carry them back into the kitchen.

"What should we do, Keith?" Jennifer asked.

"I'm not sure, but you look awfully tired. Do you feel all right?"

Without answering him, she shaded her eyes from the bright sun. Keith was right, she wasn't feeling well.

"I think we should go to the hotel and take a family nap," he said, trying to coax her into a smile. "Maybe it's the humidity, Jennifer, but you look worn out. I think all the preparing for the wedding, on top of the long drive from home, may have been too much for you." He knew Jennifer's natural coloring was near porcelain, but today she was very pale.

"I am tired," she said.

"You need to rest, and tonight we can relax by the hotel pool, have a late dinner, and in the morning we'll decide what to do."

They turned at the sound of the creaking screen door and watched Mrs. Perez bring out their lunch and a jug of cool lemonade. She placed the tray on the picnic table and said, "These are sweet baby pickles that Catherine jarred last year and I thought you might enjoy some with your lunch."

Keith poured Jennifer lemonade while she helped herself to a sandwich because she had forgotten to eat breakfast and was very hungry.

"I checked on your grandmother, and she's still resting." Mrs. Perez asked, "If you would like, I can take the children for a walk in the garden while you have lunch."

Jennifer replied with a nod and wiped the corners of her mouth with a paper towel from the tray.

"Come, children, let me show you what is left of your great-grandmother Catherine's summer garden." Nicholas and Natalie jumped from opposite sides of the tire swing and followed Mrs. Perez to the garden gate.

After eating, Jennifer made the final decision. She told Keith, "Give me half an hour to visit, and then we'll leave."

"Do you want me to go in with you?" he asked.

"No," she replied.

*   *   *

Walking into the farmhouse through the pantry door, Jennifer noticed the canned vegetables and fruits her grandmother had been preparing for as long as she could remember. She ran her hand across the old wooden storage shelf. She recognized the piece of wood and knew it had never been replaced since the day Catherine moved from the city to this small piece of property. The same warp and bend to the wood had been there since she was a little girl.

She washed her hands at the kitchen sink and through the window she could see the children picking beans in the garden. She dried her hands and placed the towel over the wooden peg that served as a holder and then she leaned gingerly against the old hammered tin sink. She was filled with a sadness she could no longer contain. She felt the surge of hot tears rush down her cheeks and she welcomed the emotional relief.

"Oh, Grandma!" she sobbed.

Jennifer waited until the tears subsided before she left the kitchen. She walked down the hall and into the bedroom. She wanted to talk with her grandmother, even if she was no longer capable of responding. Maybe, Catherine would understand that she had driven far to see her – one last time.

She sat perched on the edge of the wicker chair and leaning in closely she whispered, "Grandma, it's me, Jenny, and I've come to visit you." She moved closer and the tears continued to run down her face. There was no sign of understanding or movement from Mrs. Toby; she did not recognize the familiar lyrical voice of her favorite granddaughter.

"Grandma." She took Catherine's hand and caressed it against her tear-stained cheek. She closed her eyes and allowed countless memories to rush through her mind of days long ago that were now gone forever, and of a time that was now . . . *passing away.*

With her eyes closed, Jennifer whispered a prayer, one that she knew if the woman resting before her could hear, would bring back the sparkle that once shone brightly in her eyes . . . *Dear Heavenly Father, thank You for giving me this wonderful woman during my life and for keeping her until this day so we could visit one last time. I know You are waiting to take her and I am filled with joy because soon she will be filled with the presence of Your glory. I know Grandma will be with You in heaven, and I know she'll be there waiting for me on the day my journey ends.*

For the last time, Jennifer brushed back the stubborn white curl that always fell out of place and it was then Jennifer remembered one of her Grandma's favorite scriptures.

"Gray hair is a crown of splendor;
it is attained by a righteous life."
Proverbs 16:31

Jennifer smiled for Catherine, and without saying good-bye she left the room while the old wicker chair softly rocked on its own. She knew in her heart this was the last time she would visit Louisiana.

*   *   *

It was mid-October, when Keith and Jennifer were at home celebrating Natalie's belated birthday. Their lives were busy and full, just like many other couples with young children. Jennifer was saying good-bye at the front door to the last of their party guests. Keith was in the kitchen searching for an antacid tablet to help neutralize his stomachache. He just finished explaining to Bill and Rima that he would like them to take the children for a walk because this would give him the time he needed to talk privately with Jennifer. She then came into the kitchen just as Rima was walking out the patio door with Bill and the children.

"Good idea, Rima, let's all go for a nice walk." Jennifer was happy, and it had been a wonderful day filled with celebration.

Keith balanced an armful of presents and said, "No, Jennifer, we should stay inside and clean up this mess."

"You want to clean the house?!" She teased him and took the presents from his hand.

Keith helplessly glanced over at Bill and quick to respond, Bill told Jennifer that they would like to spend time alone with the children. Natalie threw her little arms around Uncle Bill's neck and gave him a kiss on the cheek while Rima waited outside with Nicholas.

"Okay." Jennifer watched them leave and then started picking up pieces of wrapping paper and torn gift boxes.

"We'll get this later, Jennifer; right now I want you to come into the kitchen with me." He took her hand and guided her steps over piles of discarded birthday paper.

"Natalie had a wonderful time today, didn't she?"

Keith didn't respond.

She filled the sink with soapy water and said, "Keith, I'm thankful we're able to create happy memories for our children's birthdays."

She looked through the window at the pond across the large fenced-in yard. She saw Bill and Rima securely holding her children's hands pointing to something that was splashing in the water.

"You know, Keith, it was Grandmother Catherine who always made my birthdays memorable. She would bake a white almond cake with her special butter cream frosting and then she added a drop of red coloring to create the perfect shade of pink, just to make it special for me."

She continued with telling him that if it were not for her grandmother's dedication and guidance in her life, she would have only vague and disconnected memories of her childhood.

The knot in Keith's stomach tightened because he dreaded spoiling the day.

Jennifer finished the dishes and started the garbage disposal and over the churning of the motor he said, "Sweetheart, I have something important to tell you." He stood beside her at the sink and as the warm water ran over her hands, Jennifer noticed the sadness in his brown eyes, and her heart began to pound.

Late last night, after everyone went to bed, Keith had opened his e-mail and received the news that Catherine had passed away peacefully in her sleep. She was now in heaven standing at . . . *The Pearly Gates.*

~ 7 ~

A utumn had arrived, and today was a perfect scene from the canvas of Norman Rockwell. Now that most of the leaves had fallen, the sun was finally able to shine over the secluded home on Dorn Court. It was Candice's favorite time of year, and raking the yard was a chore she enjoyed. The pine needles hid among the fallen leaves and with every sweep of the rake it stirred an earthy bouquet.

"Walt, I need your help with this bag of leaves." Candice called to her husband.

He climbed the steep grade from the gravel driveway and found his wife almost lost amongst the brilliant colors of nature. She wore an orange corduroy jacket with brown slacks, and around her neck she tied a colorful light wool scarf, matching the time of year.

"Hold still," he said and plucked the fallen leaves that were tangled in her short blonde hair. "You look nice today, Candy, are we expecting company?"

"Yes, Mary is coming over for lunch."

"What time will she be here?" He picked up the rake and began walking toward the tool shed.

"She plans on coming over at one o'clock." Candice carried a broken clay pot from the porch steps and followed him to the side driveway.

"I hope you don't mind, but I was thinking about going to the hardware store this afternoon." Walt latched the old wooden doors closed.

"No, I don't mind because then you can stop at the market for a few things on your way home." Candice tossed the broken pieces of clay into the dumpster.

"Sure, write me out a grocery list." The sound of his voice faded as the long strides of his tall frame quickly carried him into the house.

Once inside the kitchen, Candice stirred the chicken soup, and then lit a few candles to place on the counter. When Walt asked for the grocery list, she handed him the notepaper.

"Milk, bread, and eggs?" He tucked the paper into his shirt pocket before saying, "Candice, I can remember three things."

After thirty years of marriage she still couldn't anticipate his demeanor.

"I was thinking about stopping by Pastor Helm's place on the way back from town," he told her.

"Take your time," she said jokingly.

"Well, how long will Mary be here?"

"I don't know Walt, four, maybe even five hours." She laughed, and followed him into the garage.

"What on earth do you women talk about?" He climbed into his Lexus.

"Honey, we talk about you!" Candice yelled over the noise.

She went back into the house and followed the aroma of freshly baked bread from the oven. She placed the warm pan on a cooling rack next to the mixed green salad. Then, she brought two glasses down from the china cabinet and set them next to the cheese platter. She stirred the soup one more time, making sure the noodles were tender.

*　　　*　　　*

Mary slowed down as she approached the road sign warning drivers the pavement was about to end. The washboard gravel road was passable this time of year, but she knew a visit to the Meyers' home during winter was near impossible because of the snow. For years, her last social call with Candice took place late in October and Mary missed visiting once it snowed. She enjoyed the way Candice always decorated her home so beautifully for Thanksgiving and Christmas.

On the road ahead of her, a cloud of dust was forming, indicating another driver was coming from the opposite direction. Over the top of the hill she saw the Lexus and knew it was Walt. She slowed down to say hello.

They stopped, and once the dust settled, they opened their car windows. Mary had not seen Walt for some time and she was glad to talk with him because she knew he was excited about retiring the first of the year.

"Where are you going?" he laughed.

"I'm going to your house," she smiled. "Where are you going?"

"Candy has me running errands," he mumbled.

"You're going to the hardware store, aren't you?" Mary knew him well.

He laughed at her foresight and asked, "What did you bring for dessert?"

"I brought pumpkin pie with walnuts and a dark caramel glaze topping."

"Did you bring whipped cream?" he asked.

"No," Mary sighed.

"Well, let me get my grocery list out and write it down," he teased.

Another cloud of dust formed across the plowed cornfield meaning a vehicle was approaching. "Are you joining us for lunch?" Mary quickly asked.

"Nope, I don't want to interfere with you girls." Walt laughed.

They rolled their windows up, waved good-bye, and drove off.

*   *   *

There was no road sign for Dorn Court, although Candice said there used to be a wooden arrow pointing in their direction. At one time it was nailed to an old apple tree and Mary recalled seeing it once, but that was years ago. She turned left onto the narrow lane that would bring her to their front door. As she drove under the shaded covering of the trees, the sun blinked through the branches, shedding light on the dusty road ahead. The colors were brilliant and it was a magnificent change of season.

She parked on the side driveway, close to the tool shed and noticed the surrounding trees grew bigger every year. She could barely open her car door without hitting the lower branches and she had to crouch down while getting out of the vehicle.

The prize-winning show dogs, Hawk and Moose, started barking at the sound of company. Even though the dogs were confined to the backyard, they always gave a startling jump to any visitor. She walked up the lawn pathway carrying the dessert with her to the front door.

"Mary, it's good to see you!" Candice greeted.

Mary did enjoy visiting Dorn Court and embraced her longtime friend.

Candice stepped away from the front door and wanting to stay outside, she asked, "Isn't this a gorgeous day?" They stood under the ivy-covered oak trees and watched the chipmunks eat at the dried Indian corn, pinecones, and pumpkins that were heaped on the front doorsteps for decorations.

"Oh, darn those little chipmunks, Mary; they keep tipping over my arrangement!" Candice fixed the display, and laughing, she said, "Come on inside." They walked under the stone archway and through the leaded glass doors.

Mary placed her sweater on the old wooden church bench in the foyer and asked, "Is that chicken soup I smell?"

"Mmm-hmm, it's the only kind I know how to make." Candice adjusted the flame under the soup kettle and turned the warm bread out of the baking pan. She poured two glasses of hot cider and carried the cheese platter with her saying, "Let's visit on the patio first."

Mary picked her sweater up on the way outside and since the backyard was heavily shaded, she knew the temperature would be much cooler. Candice swept the leaves off the padded chairs and placed the snacks on the table. She walked over to the railing, next to Mary, and admired the beauty of the season.

"God is a colorful artist," Mary acknowledged.

"Yes, He is, and every year He paints a masterpiece for our enjoyment. Just look over there at the Silver Beech trees." Candice pointed to the trees nearest to the railing. "And those Tulip trees there on the left, with the gray trunks, are my favorite. Let's turn the patio chairs around so we can enjoy the colorful view."

"Candice, you know all the names of the trees in the forest and the flowers in the fields, you're just like my friend, Sue."

"When you retire, Mary, I'll teach you everything I know." Candice laughed.

"All I want to do is relax when I retire," she commented.

"Relaxing will be the last thing you'll do, Mary." Candice passed the cheese and crackers. "I'm so involved with our church in Dryden, by serving on the committees and helping out, there is no time left to relax." She looked at the acres of trees behind her home and said, "God has blessed me through the years and now during my retirement, it's time for me to seek the Lord more diligently in order to learn His purpose for me during this season of my life."

Mary listened while Candice told her about the plans for creating a meditation garden on the grounds at Holy Redeemer Lutheran Church. "I'm a member of the Garden Angels Club, which aligns perfectly with my talented green thumb." Candice smiled and said, "You know, Mary, a lot of creativity is used in landscaping and I pray one day we'll have a spectacular meditation garden at the church so others can enjoy it." Candice said.

Mary asked, "Whereabouts will the garden be?"

"It will be next to the gathering room by the front entrance."

"Are you referring to that steep incline?" Mary was surprised.

"Yes, although it will be difficult, it is the perfect spot." Candice took a slice of provolone and quoted Matthew 19:26: "With man this is impossible, but with God all things are possible."

*   *   *

An hour later, they finished lunch and Candice carried a tray with sliced pie and warm coffee to the living room. They talked about their families and mutual friends when Candice then asked about Mary's new position at work.

"Something is on the horizon with my new job," Mary said. "I have the feeling that God's hand is moving rapidly in my life, and in the lives of those around me. It's almost like the feeling you have just before it rains when you can't see the storm clouds or hear the thunder, but you know the abundance of rain is coming."

"I know that feeling and it is hard to explain." Candice held her china cup and saucer.

"You're right and I don't know where to begin." Mary sipped the excellent blend of roasted coffee beans.

"Well, start off by telling me about the people you're working with," Candice suggested.

"That's easy enough; the group I'm working with is mostly young engineers – except for me, of course."

Candice laughed.

"Seriously, their children are in toilet training while mine are in driver's training which makes us generations apart in age." Mary continued explaining, "For instance, I had lunch the other day with one of my co-workers, Jennifer Hayse, and during our conversation I discovered she was born the year *before* I graduated from high school."

"Oh, please stop." Being a few years older than Mary, Candice enjoyed the friendly ribbing.

"And, Jennifer has children, which means I could be a grandmother."

"Look at it this way, Mary, on the positive side being around younger people helps to keep us young." Candice poured more coffee from the silver decanter and said, "Tell me more about Jennifer; what is she like and how old are her children?"

They talked until the sun slipped behind the neighbor's barn and soon the shadows blanketed the empty cornfields as the deer slowly ventured out for their evening meal.

*　　*　　*

It was the third night this week that Jennifer had not slept well and now she was downstairs in the early morning light, watching the kitchen clock automatically change from six-fourteen to six-fifteen. Five months passed since she discovered the first lump in her left breast. It was then she began charting weekly breast self-examinations to document any change in size or location of the two lumps.

Daily concerns over the onset of the second lump consumed her thoughts, and several times she wanted to call Dr. Jordan, but felt foolish in doing so because he clearly explained that she had fibrocystic disease and not to worry. Yet, she could not keep from wondering why the changes in her breast tissue were occurring.

The telephone rang and before answering it, she checked to see who would be calling this early in the morning. It was Susan Abraham.

"Hello Susan, are you all right?" Jennifer asked.

"Yes, I'm fine, and I know it's early. Have I disturbed your household?" Susan laid her hand on the worn cover of her Bible. "I was sharing my thoughts with the Lord when the need to talk with you was placed on my heart."

"I'm glad you called Susan, how are you feeling?" Jennifer asked because Susan had begun her chemotherapy treatment.

"I'm doing well, however I have bursts of energy and then no energy at all." She refolded the medical pamphlet in front of her from the surgeon's office.

"Are you getting rest?" Jennifer wondered why she was awake so early in the morning.

"No, I get very little rest because having breast cancer keeps me busy." A trace of melancholy was in her voice.

"I'm sorry, Susan, is there anything I can do?" She walked into the foyer and leaned against the stair railing.

"No, there is nothing that needs to be done because we have the support of many friends and both our families, who are there to help us." Susan tapped the pen in front of her and said, "We just need everyone's prayers."

Jennifer sat on the bottom step of her staircase and placed her hand over her mouth because she didn't want Susan to hear her sobbing. The lack of sleep plus her own health concerns were beginning to place a toll on her emotions.

"Jennifer, please don't cry," Susan's words were barely audible. "One of the most difficult things about having cancer is when you realize that your disease is hurting those you love."

"I understand," she sniffled.

"I'm sorry for not returning your recent telephone calls, but it takes time adjusting to the changes that cancer brings into your life." Susan set the pen aside and said, "It's hard to imagine one day everything is fine and your life seems to be in order, then suddenly you're in the midst of a horrific storm. All of this without any warning – there were no clouds, not even a change in temperature, but down came the rain, the thunder, and the lightning."

"There were no warning signs, Susan, or any other indications of breast cancer?" Jennifer asked.

"Before I discovered the first lump?" she asked.

"Mmm-hmm." Jennifer walked back into the kitchen.

"No, there were no warning signs. I was not sick and there was neither inflammation of the breast tissue, nor any swelling or tenderness, it all happened very quickly." Susan snapped her fingers and began tapping the pen again. "However, I have learned one important thing."

"What is it, what have you learned?" Jennifer eagerly asked.

"I have read that breast cancer is not like any other cancer because it is a heterogeneous disease, which means it is different for all ages and all types of women."

"I didn't know that, Susan, tell me what else have you read?"

"I have read that in women over the age of forty-five, the types of cell formations are different than the cell formations in younger women."

"Is that good or bad?" Jennifer pulled back the kitchen curtain to glimpse at the morning sun.

"It all depends on your age," she laughed mildly.

"May I ask how old you are, Susan?"

"I'm forty-two, which statistically places me on the border line of the safe side of breast cancer."

"What do you mean by the safe side of breast cancer?" Jennifer was now picking up toys in the family room.

"I'm learning if a woman is diagnosed under the age of forty, her cancer can be more aggressive and more difficult to detect. Medical research shows that breast cancer appears to be less aggressive in women over the age of forty-five."

Jennifer stood still with an armful of stuffed animals and realized this was not good news for her because she was well under the age of forty-five. "Susan, are you sure?" she questioned.

"I believe so, yes." Susan noticed Jennifer's voice took on a worrisome tone and she sensed Jennifer was seeking information, not just carrying on polite conversation.

"Breast cancer is more aggressive in younger women?" Jennifer asked.

"This is what the statistics are indicating." After a slight pause she asked, "Jennifer, why are you asking such meaningful questions? Is everything all right?"

"I'm not sure." The stuffed animals dropped from her arms.

"What do you mean?" Susan sat up straight and rested her hand on the Bible.

"A few months ago, Susan, I found a lump in my left breast." Jennifer felt relief in telling another woman.

"Have you seen your doctor?" Susan placed the chiffon wrap her mother sent from India across her lap for added warmth because suddenly she felt a cold shiver.

"Yes, I saw my doctor right away." Jennifer then told Susan what had transpired so far, including the medical diagnosis and her growing sense of apprehension.

*   *   *

Moments later, after hearing the soft whimpering of her children, Jennifer ended her telephone conversation with Susan. The morning sound of the radio alarm grew louder as she climbed the stairs and with each step she was determined not to concern herself with the ongoing discomfort she was feeling. At the top of the stairs, Keith gave her a kiss and tugged on the sleeve of her robe while mumbling, "Good morning."

Jennifer smiled at him and then went to wake her son, Nicholas first. She found the four-year-old laying crossways on his rumbled sheets. His head was pressed against the wall, causing a tuft of soft brown hair to stand on its own and his left sock dangled from his big toe.

"Nicholas, it's time for school." Jennifer placed her hand on his belly and gently rocked him back and forth. "Nicholas Hayse, this is your mommy singing to you!"

Keith stood at the doorway, listening to her sing and then asked, "What time did you get up this morning, Jennifer?"

"I was up very early." She stood and picked up a pair of jeans and a t-shirt off the floor from yesterday. She tossed them over her arm and opened the closet door to get clean school clothes. She handed them to Keith and whispered, "Make sure he uses the bathroom before you get him dressed." She left and went down the hall to wake her daughter, Natalie. Along the way, she dropped her son's clothes into the over stuffed hamper.

"Good morning, Natalie, how is mommy's baby this morning?" Jennifer gave a woeful sigh as the toddler jumped out of bed and ran toward her open arms. "You're growing up too fast!"

Natalie squeezed Jennifer's neck, planting kisses in her mother's long hair.

"What would you like to wear this morning?" Jennifer opened the bottom dresser drawer to let her daughter choose an outfit and Natalie picked out a white blouse with tiny pink butterflies. "Butterflies are my favorite, too." Jennifer looked for a pair of pants to match the embroidery on the blouse and not finding a pair in the dresser, she turned to look in the closet.

"We're going downstairs," Keith hollered from the hallway.

"Okay, start breakfast, please." Jennifer was on her knees going through a storage box of baby clothes and it was not long before she found what she needed. She was putting things back when she noticed a yellow infant sleeper with an embroidered teddy bear holding colorful balloons. She leaned back on her heels and traced her hand over a stubborn baby formula stain.

She thought how quickly time was passing as she caressed a baby blanket with Disney characters. How many times had she used the blanket after her children's bath or to rock them back to sleep during the middle of the night? Newborn babies were extra special to Jennifer because an infant was God's gift, and she prayed one more of His wonderful gifts would be given to her.

"Jennifer, what do you want the kids to have for breakfast?" Keith called out from the kitchen.

"They can have cereal or yogurt," she answered. A smile filled her heart as she placed the baby items back in the box, hoping she would be placing them into the dresser drawers soon. The loving thoughts of a newborn baby lifted her spirits, and as she walked down the stairs she shook off the dark feeling that was preventing her from being happy.

Christmas Holly
Winter of 2003

~ 8 ~

Rima Hardy was captivated by the crystal formation of the cascading snow as she realized that none of the frozen molecules of vapor were the same. She compared the snowflakes to God's children, who are also uniquely formed by His hand, for every child of God is different and no two are alike. She watched the winter miracle through the frosted windows, and knew back home in DeRidder, the temperature was still warm. "Bill, how long do y'all think it will snow?"

"Oh, it will probably snow until next spring, Rima." He grinned and laid the newspaper on the kitchen table.

"What I meant, Mr. Hardy, is how long will it snow today?" She enjoyed his dry sense of humor.

"The weather report says it will stop early this afternoon with less than three inches of accumulation, but the weather report is probably wrong."

"Well, let's hope they're right about the snow. Do you have a busy day planned at work?" She stood next to the table by the window.

"Yes, I have a lot to do before the Christmas holiday break."

"How much time do y'all get off from work?" she wondered.

Bill looked at the calendar on the kitchen wall and squinted through his glasses. "Let me think for a minute, I have a few days of vacation time left, plus the holidays which gives me a total of sixteen days off this year."

"That's a lot of time." She stared at the calendar and gave out a low whistle.

"Is there somewhere special you would like to go for Christmas?" he asked.

"No." Rima placed her hand against the window and felt the cold air seep into her palm, leaving the image of her handprint behind.

"Rima, come sit down, please." Bill pulled out the chair next to him. "I need to talk with you about something important regarding work."

"I don't reckon I'd be of any help to y'all about engineering."

"This is about Cathy and Jennifer." Bill spun the butter knife in circles while he talked. "In the past, we have always planned a Christmas lunch just for the three of us, but this year it seems – "

"But this year it seems what?" she asked.

"Well, this year is different because you are my wife, and I don't want to offend you by going to lunch with female co-workers." The knife stopped spinning.

Rima was deeply touched and said, "Jennifer and Cathy are your friends and I reckon it would hurt their feelings if y'all didn't go out together for a special Christmas lunch."

"I'm glad you understand, Rima, but it feels awkward now that we're married."

"Mr. Hardy, how could I not love your honesty?" She kissed him tenderly and said, "I want you to go as planned this year, but next year I expect y'all to invite me!"

"Absolutely, next year it will be the four of us." Bill glanced out the window at the weather and said, "I'd better leave for work." He walked to the front door and put on his jacket. "Don't plan an early dinner this evening because traffic is much slower when it's snowing."

Rima handed him gloves and a scarf. She kissed him good-bye and waited as he drove away before she closed the door. She rubbed her hands together and walked back into the kitchen . . . *Dear Lord, protect my husband this morning, and thank Y'all for our marriage. May we always show respect and love for one another as we did on this glorious winter morning!*

*　　*　　*

Ignoring the pain in her neck, Cathy cradled the ringing telephone on her shoulder. She balanced milk and strawberry jam in one hand while opening the refrigerator with the other. "Hi, Jennifer," she answered.

"Hi Cathy, how is the weather in Plymouth?" Jennifer rolled her chair closer to the computer and scanned through her e-mail while talking.

"It's getting worse and Jim just found out the schools are closed today." Cathy watched the snow rest outdoors on the swing set. "You're not planning on driving into the office this morning, are you?"

"No, there is nothing urgent that needs to be done today and luckily we made our last module shipment for the year a few days ago." Glancing through her messages, Jennifer saw an e-mail from Bill.

Cathy kept busy while talking and refilled the dog's water bowl.

"We have an e-mail from Bill about our Christmas lunch," Jennifer told her.

"That's funny because we were just talking about it the other day." She placed the bowl on the floor by the patio door for her dog, Bailey.

Jennifer said, "Bill wrote one sentence only, '*Where are we going for our Christmas lunch*?'"

"He is a man of few words, but nevertheless where are we going this year?"

It was Jennifer's turn to choose the restaurant because Cathy picked last year and Bill the year before.

"I will decide today and make lunch reservations for December 17, but I want to keep where we are going a secret until then."

"First, let me check my calendar." With her finger Cathy found the day open. "It's a winner!" She jotted down the lunch date.

"Keep your pen ready," Jennifer said while opening another e-mail. "Al sent out an invitation for our section Christmas party which will be on Saturday, December 27."

"Oh, that might not work for us, Jen. What time will Al and Sheila be having their party?"

"Two o'clock in the afternoon." Jennifer hoped Cathy and her family would be there.

"We have breakfast that morning with Jim's family." Cathy marked down the time and added, "But, we should be able to come as long as the weather cooperates."

"The snow is pretty, isn't it?" Jennifer looked out the window at the frozen pond.

"Yes, but winter reminds me of too many wet clothes and lost gloves," Cathy sighed.

"It is more work when you have children, isn't it?"

"You betcha." The family dog lapped at the fresh water and Cathy bent to wipe up the spill.

"Cathy, can I ask you a question?"

"Sure, go ahead." She patted Bailey and whispered, "Good dog!"

"After your third child was born, did you notice any big changes in your marriage?"

"Like what, for instance?"

"Well, did you notice there was not enough quality time alone for you and Jim?"

"Not really, it just got noisier around the house, but why do you ask?"

"Keith and I are trying for another baby!" Jennifer told her.

"Good for you!" Although happy, Cathy was surprised.

"I was upstairs yesterday looking through the baby clothes I'd put away last March." Jennifer leaned against the cold window frame and said, "If it were not for the miscarriage last spring, our little boy would be five months old this Christmas."

"Yes, I know." Cathy asked, "Jen, do you think you're ready to try again?"

"Yes, I asked Dr. Harris and she said there is no reason to wait."

"Then everything will go according to God's plan," Cathy said.

Jennifer placed her hand over her abdomen and silently prayed.

*   *   *

Mary was at work in deep thought when she jumped at the sound of Duane's voice behind her and although he felt bad for scaring her, Duane couldn't keep from laughing.

"Duane, don't sneak up on me." Mary was getting used to his horseplay and ignored his laughing. "What do you want?"

"I don't want anything; I just came to see if you were in the office this morning."

Mary took off her reading glasses and asked, "Why wouldn't I be at work this morning, Duane?"

"Oh, I don't know, maybe it has something to do with the fact that you drive sixty-five miles one way and we're in the middle of a blizzard."

"It's winter, Duane, it's supposed to snow." She closed the file cabinet.

"Is he bothering you, Mary?" Al came alongside Duane.

Duane pointed to himself and innocently asked, "Who, me?"

"Yes, you." Al and Mary said together, teasing him.

Al then asked him about the shipments to Australia and after giving a quick update on the progress Duane left Mary's workstation and headed toward the test lab. Al took a minute to write down the information in his daily planner and then asked Mary, "Did you get the invitation to our Christmas party?"

"Yes, it is nice of you and your wife, Sheila, to have everyone over."

"We enjoy company and we hope you and your family will come."

"What can I bring to the party?"

"Jennifer said you make a terrific chocolate cake," Al suggested.

"All right, mark me down for bringing dessert." Thinking the conversation was over, she returned to the task at hand.

"By the way Mary, I agree with Duane and think you should leave work before the roads become dangerous."

"Oh?" She was surprised.

"Yes, the weather forecast is now calling for more snow than first predicted."

"I didn't know, thanks Al." Mary looked away and inwardly admonished herself for never listening to the news or weather forecast.

"You're welcome, and just so you know – "

"Yes?" Mary looked at him.

"I don't expect you to drive into the office when the weather is bad because it's dangerous, so on days like today just work from home."

"That sounds good to me, thank you." She smiled and watched him walk down the hall toward the test lab. Mary turned off her computer, locked her desk and, grabbed her coat and gloves. She walked out to the parking lot and could not believe the accumulation of snow in just two short hours.

She shielded her face with a gloved hand as she hiked out to her car. She began to scrape the snow from the windows, but the majority of it fell on top of her feet and slowly trickled down inside her shoes. She opened the car door and tapped each foot against the floorboard before climbing inside. The sound of the wiper blades scratching against the frozen windshield made her nervous. Mary threw her soaked gloves onto the passenger seat and placed her cell phone in the cup holder.

She put the car in reverse, backed out of the parking spot and before moving another inch, she prayed . . . *Dear God, the snow is beautiful and thank You for the change of seasons. Be with me and protect my ride so I may enjoy Your beauty and splendor from the warmth and comfort inside my home. Amen.*

Everything was blanketed in white and it was three exhausting hours later when Mary guessed the location of her driveway. She pressed the button for the garage door opener and the slow-moving vehicle crept inside. By this time, her hands felt as if they were glued to the steering wheel and her back was aching.

Mary's daughter, Jessica, was standing inside the garage dressed and ready to shovel the driveway. She asked, "Mom, why are you home so early?"

"I'm home early because I have a kind-hearted boss, who told me I could leave work." Mary reached over and tightened the scarf around her daughter and asked, "Are you dressed warm enough?"

Layered in warm clothes, Jessica could hardly nod her head in response. Christopher was next to her and handed the smaller of the two shovels to his sister. He bent to kiss his mom hello and told her he was glad she was home safely.

"Mom, will you make us hot chocolate?" Jessica asked.

"Yes, once the driveway is shoveled." Mary grinned.

~ 9 ~

A l and Sheila Partington lived on a hidden street off the main road in Clarkston. This winter, the inland lake off their yard was frozen and covered in layers of early snow. In the summertime, their home was shaded with coolness by the covering of old hickory trees that stood tall in their back-yard, but today their home took on the inside warmth and cheer of good friends. It was decorated with seasonal trim, bringing in the beauty of nature while leaving the winter chill on the front porch.

Inside, beautiful fresh Christmas Holly with red berries covered the mantel above the burning fireplace where adults stood talking with each other and little children raced about everywhere. It was time to celebrate the Christmas season.

A small group sat at the dining room table rehashing a recent political debate. Someone made an effort to change the subject, but the attempt failed. A second group was sitting in the breakfast nook, laughing and sharing food from each others' plates – everyone was asking who had brought the Polish sausage because it was excellent.

Competitive word games and trivia contests were being played downstairs in the recreation room because after all, how could talented engineers get together without exercising their minds? Even on their Christmas break, there was still playful rivalry amongst friends. The noisy game of charades did not distract the two young chess players. From a distance, anyone could see the boys were brothers because they resembled each other along with their parents, Duane and Janis.

*   *   *

Jennifer was the official photographer and she moved from room to room, taking many photographs. Without interrupting any conversations, she captured friendly smiles in her photo lens, and you were now forever etched in her memory, and saved on her flash drive.

She wore a simple contemporary black dress with low heels. Her make-up was natural and in her hair she placed a sprig of Christmas Holly she had borrowed from the fireplace mantel. She artistically wove the branch into her long auburn curls and her colorful jingle bell earrings chimed while she adjusted her Santa hat to one side.

The two little children running toward her also wore Santa hats that were tied securely under their chins. Once Nicholas and Natalie were reassured that their mother was still among the crowd of strangers, they ran off to play downstairs with the chalkboard and puzzle pieces.

Mary caught Jennifer trying to take a snapshot of her, but Mary blocked the lens with her hand. Jennifer lowered the camera and pouted which resulted in a joyful smile from Mary. Instantly, Jennifer raised the camera and snapped the picture she wanted, and then she sat next to her at the table to share the desserts.

Mary asked why Keith wasn't with her and the children. Jennifer hesitated for a moment and placed a small handful of chocolate M&M's in her mouth. She politely finished before explaining her husband wanted to watch the football game instead of coming to the office party. Mary took a butter cookie covered in red sprinkles from the tray and snapped it in two. She listened to Jennifer explain that Keith had to work extra hours during the holidays, and today was his only day off.

Cathy was in the kitchen slicing ham, buttering rolls, and fixing plates for her three children while her husband, Jim, asked them what they wanted to drink. Al's wife, Sheila, was helping others with their plates; she expertly directed half the crowd into the basement and the other half into the dining room.

The microwave was buzzing, letting Janis know the cheese dip was ready to be served. She rummaged through the drawers, hoping to find a hot pad holder when Cathy tapped her on the shoulder and pointed to the drawer next to the sink. Duane opened a bag of nacho chips then reached for a bowl from the cupboard above his wife's head. He could smell her homemade cheese dip and couldn't wait to be the first one to try it.

Al stopped two toddlers from running down the hallway and avoiding a near collision; the little boys paid no attention to the almost hit-and-run incident. Once stopped, they asked him if there was any ice cream for the chocolate cake.

A few hours later, while everyone else ate dessert, Cathy and Jennifer sat together in the corner of the library on a padded window seat. Jennifer faced Cathy and confidentially whispered news to her best friend, and immediately Cathy smiled. They hugged and clasped their hands together, continuing their private conversation.

Mary watched from the doorway and saw a friendship between the two young women that was special. She recognized the all-knowing look in their eyes as they talked and listened to one another. Mary knew and understood that sort of bond because she was blessed with over thirty years of endearing friendship with Sue.

In the foyer, Bill leaned on the stair railing and told Rima he wished Kathy was at the party because he wanted them to meet each other. However, Kathy called Al earlier and said her two-year-old, Rose, woke up that morning with a high fever. In the end, Kathy and her husband, Bob, decided it was best the whole family stay at home this year. They didn't want to bring their newborn, Lydia, out in the cold and besides, next year would be different, they would all be there and the group of toddlers would be a handful.

*   *   *

To someone on the outside looking in, they would see a group of people enjoying each other's company, and everything would appear to be cheerful. But to the discerning wisdom of each adult inside the home, there was a trace of sadness at this year's gathering.

Missing from the dessert table were the mouthwatering scoops of Kulfi, which is the traditional saffron and pistachio ice cream that Susan and her husband, Abe, always brought to the office Christmas party. Along with the ice cream, Susan always went out of her way to make fresh Gulab Jamun and over the heavy pastry, she would drizzle a light cinnamon frosting. Everyone enjoyed the Indian cuisine that the Abraham family would make for their American friends.

However, this year Susan needed to rest and her family would be staying close to home holding their traditional holiday customs to a minimum. During this time, Susan needed to rebuild her white blood cell count because she was finished with chemotherapy and was scheduled for radiation the first of January. As with all families it was difficult for the children, Matthew and Michelle; however, the teenagers were strong in their faith and understood their mother's illness was in God's hands.

*   *   *

As the sun set, the party came to a close. The children were overtired, the food was put away and it was the perfect ending to a prosperous year. Jennifer asked to take one more group photograph and as everyone smiled for her, they couldn't help but notice the look of concealed happiness from within her. At the moment, her life was ideal, the doctors told her she was healthy, her children were thriving, her marriage was secure and above all else, she was anchored firmly in her faith.

Cathy and Janis piled the dishes into the dishwasher while Duane emptied the trash. Al and Sheila did their best to stop the offers of help because they didn't want anyone to feel obligated. They knew the ride home would be long and the fading daylight slipped away quickly toward the end of December in Michigan.

Jim stood in the corner of the kitchen with his three children bundled in hats and gloves, waiting for Cathy. She motioned for him to take them out to the car and she would be right behind them. Duane took Jennifer's keys and offered to warm her vehicle before she put Nicholas and Natalie into their car seats.

He walked outside with Jim and first helped him get his family into the back of the car then the two men shook hands and wished each other a happy New Year. Al put on his winter coat and boots so he could direct the cars out of the driveway with a flashlight. Ditches flanked each side of the dirt road and there was no outdoor lighting to guide the way.

Jennifer was in the living room bundling Natalie in a blanket and Mary was struggling to place a mitten on Nicholas' limp hand. The little boy was falling asleep while standing in front of her and she was making every effort to keep him upright. She glanced away for a second looking for his lost mitten when he suddenly toppled over into her arms.

Janis told Sheila to keep the leftover cheese dip because she knew Al loved the snack, and besides, she had more at home. She called down the stairs one last time for her sons to end their intense game of chess when suddenly Justin ran up the stairs, beating Jacob by two steps, then with true brotherly love, the older one shoved the younger brother aside while getting into his jacket.

Al opened the garage door and motioned for Duane to back in Jennifer's car, getting it away from the falling snow. Duane came inside the house to get the Hayse children so he could place them in the warm vehicle. Jennifer handed a pink bundle to him and Mary gave a sleeping little boy to Al.

Sheila brought out the only two coats left in the spare bedroom. Jennifer put on hers and said good-bye, once again wishing everyone a happy New Year. As she headed toward the door Mary stopped her and told her to finish buttoning the front of her coat. Jennifer laughed and said she couldn't because the missing button had fallen off the year after Natalie was born and she had not found the time to sew it back in place.

Mary asked if she had the lost button, Jennifer smiled, reached into her pocket and confirmed the missing button was still there. Mary told Jennifer to wear the coat and bring the button into work after the first of the year, and Mary would sew it back in place while they visited during lunch. Jennifer smiled, shook Mary's hand and said she would hold Mary to her promise.

Duane called from inside the garage, asking Jennifer how much gas she had, implying the car was plenty warm and she should be leaving before she ran out of fuel. Al held the driver's door open for her, and once inside, Jennifer carefully backed down the driveway. Duane offered to walk Mary to her car, but he only got halfway before she insisted he turn around and go back to his truck. He inwardly chuckled at her resistance yet at the same time he admired her iron will, and before leaving he wished her a happy New Year.

Bill and Rima walked arm in arm, slowly shuffling along the sidewalk to their vehicle because Rima was not used to navigating through the slippery snow. As they passed the Lanyons' car Janis leaned over the front seat console and waved good-bye to them. Duane ran across the snowy driveway and almost slipped and fell in full view of his two sons. He opened the truck door, and everyone heard the boys laughing at their father's clumsiness.

Mary switched her headlights to low beam and waited for Jennifer to back completely out of the driveway before she turned them on high beam. She waved good-bye to Al, who was still standing watch with his flashlight, making sure everyone got safely out to the road.

Just ahead of her, Mary watched four vehicles flashing their right blinkers. She waited as one by one they turned onto the main highway heading in the direction of their homes. Mary's vehicle was the last one to leave, turning left and driving opposite of everyone else.

~ *10* ~

〜🝔〜

I t was the third week of January and Keith held Jennifer's
hand as they walked along the midway enjoying the last
evening of their vacation. It was after dusk, and the warm
Florida temperature was a welcome change from their
escaped northern climate. They strolled along the paved
yellow brick road that led them toward the amusement park's
closing fireworks event.

The last four days were filled with parades, cartoon characters, jungle rides, and fun activities for the children. But,
tonight while Nicholas and Natalie stayed with a babysitter,
Keith and Jennifer wanted to enjoy the attractions of Disney
World designed with grown-ups in mind. Jennifer was
excited because the magical setting was the perfect place to
tell Keith the good news. She matched her footsteps left to
right with his and then pointed to a park bench suggesting
they rest for a while.

Keith stretched out his legs, and crossing his ankles
he said, "We can't stop for long because I'm about to fall
asleep."

"Well, I'm sure my news will wake you up." She placed
her head on his shoulder.

"What news?" he asked over the top of her auburn
curls.

"The home pregnancy test I took before we left on our vacation was positive!"

"Jennifer, how accurate are those drugstore tests?" he grinned.

"They are very accurate, Mr. Hayse!" She gently slapped his leg.

Keith leaned forward with his elbows on his knees. He folded his hands and turned sideways toward her, watching her smile grow. He leaned back, kissed the tip of her nose and whispered, "Here we go again."

She wrapped her arms around his neck and held him closely. It was a special moment for them, yet the crowd paid no attention to the young couple. Everyone was in a hurry to reach the stadium for the fireworks. Jennifer and Keith stayed behind and watched the flares light up the night sky from underneath the canopy of trees. Keith placed his arm around her as she watched the sky sparkle with every color in the rainbow.

Jennifer couldn't have planned a better time to announce the arrival of their third child. The reflection of the fireworks danced in her eyes as they cuddled on the park bench. During the grand finale, Jennifer thanked God for the beauty of the moment because all her dreams . . . *were coming true.*

* * *

The next morning Jennifer was up early, she tiptoed into the bathroom and turned on the cold water. She moistened a towel to wipe the back of her neck and down both her arms. She didn't recall experiencing drastic changes in her body temperature during her other pregnancies and somehow felt this pregnancy was different. She turned her wrists upward under the cold water, and gradually her body's temperature returned to normal. She decided a relaxing shower might help to ease the tension in her shoulders and the rumbling in her stomach.

She closed her eyes and allowed her thoughts to momentarily drift when the sound of insistent knocking forced her attention back to the present. Stepping out of the shower enclosure, she wrapped herself in a towel, and through the moisture she reached for the sink. Leaning closer, she wiped the mist away from the mirror. The joy from last evening faded as she studied her reflection and noticed the concern etched on her face. Instinctively she knew something was wrong and she could no longer deny it. The discomfort and mild pain in both breasts was increasing, and she didn't need further testing to confirm the size of the lumps had grown in the last few weeks.

Tiny droplets of water fell from her damp hair onto the bathroom countertop. She took the towel off and wrapped it around her head as she studied her reflection in the mirror. Jennifer knew her body well, and she was knowledgeable of the changes a woman experiences while pregnant. It was because of this knowledge that once more she began to second-guess the accuracy of the mammogram and question the surgeon's diagnosis.

Keith knocked on the bathroom door again and asked, "Do you want some coffee?"

She wiped away her tears, grateful the steam would help hide her conflicting emotions. She eased the door open slightly and asked, "What time is it?"

"Almost seven o'clock." He handed her a cup of flavored coffee.

"Thanks, I'll be out in a minute." For now, there was nothing she could do until she got home and called Ridgeway Medical Center for Women. She didn't want to alarm Keith again with more unconfirmed suspicions.

*   *   *

122

Cathy was at work and noticed it was just about time for lunch. She hit the save button and closed the open file she was updating. Although more work needed to be done on the schematics, she knew that skipping lunch was a bad idea. She left her workstation and walked to the lunchroom where Kathy stood by the microwave waiting for her lunch to heat up.

"We missed you at the Christmas party," Cathy said as she opened her box lunch.

"And we missed going, but when one member of the family gets sick it seems like everyone does." Kathy joined her at the table and asked, "How is your family doing?"

"Fine, we are back into the routine of school and homework."

"I keep forgetting your husband, Jim, is a school teacher." Kathy stirred her hot soup and said, "I'll bet it was nice having everyone home during the holidays."

"You betcha, and it's just as nice having everyone back in school." Cathy smiled and asked how baby Lydia was doing.

"Lydia is perfect! The third child is the charm!" Kathy smiled.

A gust of frigid air blew into the lunchroom as two employees exited the building. The women shivered and waited for the door to close. The temperature suddenly dropped, and the room was noticeably cooler than before.

Cathy waited before asking, "I've been thinking about Susan and I was wondering how she's doing?"

"She started radiation last week and she's doing well, considering."

Cathy leaned back in her chair and said, "I can't imagine what she must be going through."

"I can't either," Kathy added.

Both young women were thinking the same thing – *How would I respond to the diagnosis of breast cancer?*

Moments later Cathy broke the silence. "Cancer is such a private matter for some people and it's hard to know what you should or should not do for those who have been diagnosed."

"Yes, some people are very outspoken while others withdraw and want total privacy." Kathy finished her soup and said, "I'm sure Susan's faith and her family are all she needs right now and if she needs anything else, she will ask."

"You're right, and I believe it's important to determine the level of support the person wants when they are seriously ill so you don't interfere with their privacy."

"I agree, plus everyone's situation is different and knowing the person helps to understand what they're going through."

"You also need to determine how much support they have from their families because many families are torn apart today, either emotionally or geographically," Cathy said.

They sat quietly, dwelling on their own families and personal set of circumstances.

"I'm sure Susan will tell us if she needs anything," Kathy remarked.

"I know one thing, above all else she would ask for prayers," Cathy said.

"Yes, Susan has asked for prayers and she is getting a lot of support from her church."

They finished lunch and were walking down the hallway when they passed Jennifer's empty workstation and Kathy asked, "I haven't seen Jennifer lately, do you know where she is?"

"Yes, she was on vacation in Florida. She came back two days ago and was not feeling well, but she'll be back in the office on Monday."

"Oh, sick while on vacation – that's never fun," Kathy said. "Where in Florida did they go?"

"Wonder Woman went to Disney World." Cathy smiled.

"Where does Jennifer get her energy?" Kathy laughed.

"She is full of energy and she does a lot for her children because she wants them to have wonderful memories of their childhood."

*   *   *

The house was quiet and Mary was enjoying the peaceful sound of nothing when the telephone rang. "Hello?" she answered.

"Hi Mary, what time is the choir performance tonight?" Candice asked.

"It starts at seven o'clock Candice, how are the roads out by your house?"

"The roads are clear by us," she pulled back the draperies and peered outside. "I'm looking forward to hearing your daughter, Jessica, sing tonight at the concert."

"Yes, so am I." Mary enjoyed keeping in touch with her friends and always had time to chat and after a few moments, she asked. "So what are you doing to keep busy now that the earth is frozen and you can't work in the church garden?"

Candice blended the whipping cream into her hot cocoa and said, "Actually, I am working on the garden by going over the layout design for the spring planting. Right now I am placing the landscape tags from the plants over the design drawing to give myself a visual."

"This meditation garden has been a huge project for you, Candice."

"Yes, it has been and this year more people have helped which makes it enjoyable." She then asked if Mary wanted to know the names of the plants because the individual plants were carefully selected by the Garden Angels.

Mary said yes and placed a warm afghan over her lap.

"We purchased a lovely Stellar Pink dogwood for the front entrance along with two dozen morning glories, also known as Pearly Gates. We will plant them under the dog-woods so they can be in the shade. We also found Christmas Holly on sale and we bargained for a reduced price on several potted Bleeding Hearts." Candice studied the artist drawing in front of her and said, "Then, alongside the rock wall is where we will plant several Blushing Knockout roses."

Mary rested her feet on the coffee table while she listened.

"Let me see, we have Sedum Angelina near the slate rock steps and Walt helped to plant a struggling October Glory which is a red maple tree. There are plenty of lush Noble Firs that encircle everything with year-round color. In the spring we will plant twelve Elijah Blue fescues and we designed a triangle shaped bed for the Star of Bethlehem flowers. They will be near the front entrance by the gathering room to the church." Candice finished with explaining, "Our plans will be complete once we find room for the several pots of Jacob's ladder which are also known as the – Stairway to Heaven."

"There are Biblical references in almost every plant or flower you have chosen."

Candice finished her hot cocoa and said, "Yes, we honor Jesus through our choices because He loved the stillness in the Garden of Gethsemane."

"The plants will give more of a spiritual meaning to your garden, Candice."

"That is what we thought and the members of the church want the garden to be a living praise to God for generations to come. The Garden Angels also want it to be a place where believers can meditate and grow in their personal relation-ship with God."

*   *   *

Later, after ending her conversation, Mary was able to read one more chapter in her book before her cell phone rang, "Hello?" she answered.

"Hi, Mary, what are you doing?"

"Hi, Sue, I was being lazy and relaxing." Once again she curled her feet up and adjusted the afghan because after all, this is what wintry Saturday afternoons were all about. "By any chance are you in Michigan?" Mary was hopeful.

"No, I won't be back for two months," she sighed.

"I was hoping you were down the street at your sister Pam's house."

"Why, is there something special going on?"

"Yes, Jessica is singing tonight at Dakota High School with the senior choir, and I thought maybe if you were in town, you could join us."

"Oh, I wish I could be there." Sue missed living in Michigan.

"That's okay; you can watch her on television someday!"

"Mary, I think it's terrific the way you encourage your children."

"I'm simply following your wonderful example!"

"We are good mothers, aren't we?" Sue laughed. "So, what are you doing with your time lately, Mary?" She stroked the chocolate Labrador at her feet.

"I'm catching up on my reading and enjoying the lazy stillness brought on by the season of snow."

"What are you reading?"

"I'm reading the books you bought me for Christmas and my birthday."

"Oh, how do you like them?" Sue asked.

"They're excellent and I've marked almost every single page with notes." One of the books was on Mary's lap and she thumbed through it while talking. "But what has made these books special is the handwritten inscription by you."

"And I meant every word I wrote!" Sue said with encouragement because the gift of motivating others was paramount to Sue's character.

Mary then read the note aloud, "*'Mary, deep in your soul there are many stories to tell – may these two books ignite the fire'!*" She placed the book down and asked, "Sue, how will I ever live up to your great expectations?"

"I'm not the One with great expectations." She remarked while stroking Ruby's shiny coat.

Mary understood the spiritual meaning and said, "Sue, I will write a book once I have something worthwhile to write about."

"Mary, you have a million stories to write about." Ruby started barking, and Sue coaxed her into going outdoors. "That's why I bought you books filled with advice on how to write a book. I know that one day I will read a book with your name on the front cover as the author."

"Sue, everyone knows I'm a great storyteller, but an author? Goodness gracious!" Mary smiled and asked, "Let's change the subject, how was your birthday?"

Sue's birthday on the 29th followed Mary's on the 27th – December, of course.

"It was very nice and thanks for your presents." Sue opened the door and hollered for Ruby to come back inside. The Labrador wagged her tail and ignored the command. "I've got to go, Mary, because Ruby is chasing a terrified rabbit."

Mary smiled as the telephone signal between them abruptly ended.

~ 11 ~

D r. Zechariah Jordan's office was crowded for a Saturday afternoon and when Jennifer walked in the receptionist was busy talking on the telephone. The woman motioned to Jennifer that she would be with her in a minute. Once again, Jennifer found her eyes spiritually drawn to the photographs of the Holy Land and while waiting, she took one of the surgeon's business cards and tapped it against her open palm.

"May I help you?" the receptionist asked.

"Yes, my name is Jennifer Hayse, I was here last July and I need to schedule a follow-up appointment."

"Just a moment, Mrs. Hayse, let me find your chart." The woman disappeared behind several rows of vertical files.

Jennifer placed the doctor's business card inside her pocket and felt the familiar touch of the missing button from her coat. Unaware of her action, her fingers nervously polished the surface of the smooth, plastic disk as she thought . . . *I want my life to be normal without this dark storm cloud following me around.*

"Dr. Jordan's note in your file indicates you should have a repeat mammogram in six months. Have you had a second mammogram yet?"

Jennifer shook her head.

The receptionist handed her a printed instruction sheet and said, "Call this number to make an appointment – " She stopped speaking when she noticed Jennifer was crying.

"I'm sorry, but I'm nervous about having a second mammogram." Jennifer explained.

"Would you like me to make the appointment for you?"

"Mmm-hmm."

The woman handed her a tissue through the open window and then quickly dialed the medical lab, she asked Jennifer, "Which days are you available for the test?"

"I would prefer either Monday or Tuesday, please." Jennifer dabbed her nose with the tissue.

*   *   *

Before leaving Ridgeway Medical Center for Women, Jennifer called Keith because she knew he would be wondering why it was taking so long for her to run a few errands.

"Hi Keith, I'm running late and things are taking longer than expected." She pulled out of the parking lot and onto the main road. "I'm on my way home. How are the children?"

"Nicholas is coloring one minute and then playing on the computer the next minute, and Natalie has changed into three different Cinderella costumes since breakfast. I had no idea she had so many outfits, Jennifer. When did you buy them for her?"

She turned left onto the snow covered pavement of Ann Arbor Trail Road. She avoided answering his question and said, "I might have to stop at the grocery store, but it all depends on what you want for dinner tonight."

Keith was watching the NFL Playoffs on the television. It was a previously recorded game between the New England Patriots and the Philadelphia Eagles . . . *The Quarterback landed pretty hard on his shoulder* – the game announcer was saying. "When are you coming home?" Keith asked.

Jennifer sighed, "I'll be home after grocery shopping."

"How are the roads?" Keith turned up the volume a notch *. . . Good news, the Quarterback is up and off the field* – the fans cheered.

"The roads are fine, Keith, what do you want for dinner?" She had to raise her voice.

He inched forward on the couch, listening and watching the television *. . . there is a change in Quarterbacks and this is critical timing, folks.* "Yeah sure, Jennifer, do the grocery shopping before coming home."

She patiently said, "Keith, please put the children down for a nap."

"Touchdown!" He jumped off the couch and raised both hands in the air, unaware that in reality *. . . he was not winning.*

*   *   *

Three days later, Jennifer stood very still as she waited for the x-ray technician to step behind the glass partition and snap the mammogram film. Tears filled her eyes because the table compression was more painful than expected. The technician switched the x-ray plates and moved Jennifer closer to the metal table. She adjusted the lead apron across her midriff and, although the weight was heavy on Jennifer's opposite shoulder, it was a necessary precaution.

"This will only take a minute." The technician manipulated the machinery for the correct alignment and said, "Take a deep breath and don't move."

Jennifer heard the double click and saw a flash of light, indicating a few more seconds and she would be through. The moment the pressure clamp was released Jennifer dropped the heavy lead apron to the floor.

"That was painful," Jennifer murmured and wiped away her moist bangs. She took her clothes to the changing room and leaned against the closed door while waiting for the wave of nausea to subside. She placed a peppermint candy in her mouth, thankful she remembered to carry them in her purse. The mint helped to counter her squeamish stomach, and after feeling better she was able to get dressed, but before leaving Jennifer made certain the x-ray lab had the correct address for Dr. Zechariah Jordan at Ridgeway Medical Center for Women. The lady behind the desk double checked and assured her the results would be available in the next few days.

* * *

Later that morning, Bill held open the door as Jennifer walked into the front lobby at work. "How are you doing?" he asked with a smile.

She smiled back, told him she was fine and she wondered if Rima had talked with him yet.

"I understand from Rima that you have good news." Bill closed the door.

Jennifer said yes and shook off the snow from her wool scarf.

He stepped aside, avoiding the wet flakes. "Congratulations and when are you due?"

"I'm expecting the third week in September." She then lowered her voice and said, "I haven't told anyone at work yet, except for you and Cathy, because I want to wait until I am safely beyond the first trimester."

"I understand." Bill nodded in agreement.

"My due date is close to your first wedding anniversary."

"Yes, Rima said the same thing." With his hands in his pockets, Bill rocked back and forth on his feet.

"We'll have two wonderful celebrations at the same time!" Jennifer was happy.

"What are you celebrating?" Duane overheard the very end of their conversation.

Jennifer looked at Bill for help and he came to her rescue by saying, "You know Jennifer; she's always celebrating something." He then walked Duane down the hallway into the conference room to attend the weekly launch meeting.

Jennifer waved good-bye to them and then walked to her desk knowing there was a pile of work waiting for her immediate attention. She welcomed the opportunity to sink her thoughts into electronics, schematics, and modules because she wanted something to take her mind off medical offices and x-ray technicians in white lab coats.

*   *   *

Later that same day, Duane returned to his desk just as the telephone started to ring. He unloaded the modules he was carrying and answered the telephone on the last ring, "Hello?"

"Hi, are you busy?" Janis asked.

"Not anymore, I just got back from a lunch-and-learn meeting. I don't like eating and writing at the same time." He tried rubbing out the mustard stain from his sleeve.

"Duane, you eat and write at home all the time," she laughed.

"If you say so, what's up?" He knew his wife was right.

"Have you looked outside lately?"

"No, I haven't, do we have a lot of snow?" He was hoping for another blizzard.

"You're going to love it." She watched the snow cover the deck in the backyard. "I want you to remember how much you loved the mile-long driveway in the spring when we bought this house."

"It's not a mile long." He began tapping his pen on the edge of his desk.

"It certainly will seem like it when you're done plowing it."

"Why don't you start the tractor and do a little plowing first, and then I'll finish up when I get home?"

"Very funny." She gathered her heavy sweater around herself.

"What's for dinner?"

"I want to celebrate your first snow plowing of the season, so I made your favorite – hearty beef stew."

He grinned and said, "Speaking of celebrating, I heard Jennifer has some sort of celebration in the making."

"Oh?" Janis appreciated her husband including her in his work life.

"Yes, it's supposed to take place sometime in September."

*   *   *

Jennifer was thirty-two years old and teetering on the brink of her life falling apart. She waited nervously in the doctor's private office. Inside the lining of her pocket she felt the missing round button from her coat, she had kept it ever since Natalie was born and somehow had never found the time to sew it back in place.

The door suddenly opened, and a quick formal exchange of greetings took place between her and the physician. On the desk sat a manila folder with her name in bold black letters. Dr. Zechariah Jordan opened the file, and a brief scan of the mammogram report gave him time to regain his composure. He removed his glasses and for the first time looked directly into her eyes . . . *and she knew.*

He explained the diagnosis in layman's terms, and her world slowly began to unravel. His rigid outline sat stiffly behind the desk in front of her and she found it difficult to comprehend what he was saying.

This was Jennifer's worst nightmare. It was the unspeakable fear she had buried deep inside the locked hallways of her mind. She asked to see the medical report. She took her left hand from her coat pocket and the round smooth button fell. It was spinning wildly out of control and then gradually it stopped. The button remained on the floor, no longer needed, its purpose forgotten.

The words in front of her were blurry as they faded in and out of clarity. Her mind was like the lens of a camera, trying desperately to focus and make sense of the medical terminology. However, there was no point in denying the truth, for she was holding the proof in her hands. The only words she understood were . . . *highly suspicious of malignancy.* Then without warning came the shattering diagnosis: *bi-lateral breast cancer.*

The medical report fell from her grip, and she stared at the surgeon in disbelief. She wanted to scream, to lash out at him, but she didn't, instead she listened to an inner voice telling her . . . *Have no fear for I am with you.*

Dr. Zechariah Jordan listened to his inner voice and selfish desire to gain control. He started by saying, "I know this is alarming – " But his throat tightened and he couldn't speak, he tried again. "We need to quickly move forward – "

The invisible pressure on his vocal chords was intense and painful there was a powerful grip constricting his windpipe. He tugged sharply at his Gucci necktie while Jennifer rose and stood before him. She never took her eyes off him. He could not look at the beautiful, pregnant woman standing before him. He diverted his eyes and fumbled through her medical records.

In a choked voice he said, "A biopsy is the first step – "

"Yes, a biopsy should have been the first step. Why didn't you perform one last summer?" Her voice pierced the air between them.

"Back in July, the lab reports did not indicate – "

"You never listened to me back in July when I told you about my family history!" She refused to hide the anger in her voice. Her intense words didn't spark any recollection, and Jennifer knew she was right – he didn't remember her. Dr. Jordan removed his glasses, closed her medical file and shut his eyes.

"You don't remember me, *do you?*" The revelation shattered Jennifer's heart. She waited, giving him a chance to defend himself, but he couldn't. She turned and walked out of his finely decorated office leaving him alone to deal with his shame.

* * *

For the last time, Jennifer left Ridgeway Medical Center for Women and while walking out to her parked car, she remembered that Valentine's Day was this coming Saturday and she and Keith would be married eleven years. She looked toward the sky and noticed the day was cold and dreary. The sun was not shining and the clouds were dark and low. Jennifer could feel the clouds surrounding her in a shameless effort to suffocate her with their sadness. The vacated piles of snow reminded her of frozen dirt and the winter miracle of white was no longer shining like thousands of tiny diamonds. Everything was different now in comparison to her wedding day from eleven years ago, and Jennifer knew for certain that nothing would ever be the same again.

She slid into the driver's seat, turned on the ignition and the air ventilation. Her shoulders slumped and tears streamed down her face as she cried out . . . *Dear God, please, this can't be true!*

She felt a sudden wave of nausea, but she forced the bitter taste of sickness back down her throat and wiped the moisture from her forehead. She tightened her grip on the steering wheel. The effort was turning her knuckles white and the tears continued to fall from her swollen eyes. She was exhausted. Her hands lost their grip and fell onto her lap. They rested against the growing roundness of her abdomen, and unaware of her actions she stopped crying. She closed her eyes, leaned back into the car seat and forced her breathing into a slow and calm rhythm.

Soft words filled the interior of the vehicle as music from her favorite Christian radio station, WMUZ, played a familiar song. Jennifer recalled hearing her Grandmother Catherine humming the same beautiful tune countless times. The sound of modern music filled her ears as the words from long ago penetrated her heart.

How sweet was the sound as "Amazing Grace" floated through the air . . . *that saved a wretch like me.* Soon enough, Jennifer's pulse rate returned to normal, and the throbbing in her temples ceased . . . *through many dangers, toils, and snares.* She turned up the volume to hear more clearly the words . . . *'tis grace has brought me safe thus far.* The music rested several measures while Jennifer waited for these inspiring words . . . *and 'tis grace that will lead me home.*

*   *   *

The following evening they went out to celebrate their wedding anniversary plus Valentine's Day. After the movie theater, they went inside their favorite restaurant, Jennifer sat across the table from Keith and asked, "Do you remember our wedding day?"

The waiter placed a loaf of hot bread on their table.

"Of course I do," Keith said while slicing a piece of bread.

"What do you remember most about our wedding, Keith?"

He lifted a frosted mug of beer and thoughtfully said, "I remember thinking I was the luckiest man in the world."

"Do you still feel that way?"

"Yes, of course, why do you ask?"

Jennifer glanced over at the couple seated nearby. She was sure they were grandparents, and they too were celebrating this evening. The waiter then brought out their meals to the table and Jennifer thanked him.

"Did you like the movie?" Keith wanted to steer their conversation in another direction because he was familiar with the emotional changes his wife experienced while pregnant, but when she didn't answer his question, he tried again. "Did you like the ending to the movie, Jennifer?"

"No, it should have been a happier ending." She nonchalantly segregated the water chestnuts from the rest of the vegetables on her plate then twirled angel hair pasta around her fork.

Keith took another sip of frosted beer, trying to put his finger on what was bothering her when he decided it was time to see her smile. He lovingly brought out a black velvet box from inside his coat pocket that was trimmed in a silver ribbon. He handed her the gift and quietly said, "Happy Valentine's Day."

"Oh, Keith, I thought we agreed – "

He gently squeezed her hand and said, "No, Jennifer, we agreed last year not to exchange anniversary gifts, but this is a Valentine gift."

"This is so romantic!" Jennifer's smile showed her love for him. Inside the box was a delicate gold heart. She held it to the candle light before releasing the clasp, and with one swift movement the tiny gold heart was next to her own.

"And that, Jennifer, is what I remember most about our wedding day: your smile."

She couldn't keep the tears from escaping because her heart was filled with conflicting emotions. *Now is not the time to bring up the doctor's appointment,* she kept telling herself. "Keith, do you think that eleven years later our marriage vows are more significant now?"

He wiped his mouth and nodded in agreement.

"For better, for worse, for richer, for poorer?" Jennifer gripped his hand and repeated to him, "In sickness or in health, until death do we part?" She began to cry.

He leaned across the table and whispered, "I think this baby is another girl." He suspected her emotions were a natural response to her pregnancy.

Jennifer wiped her tears, straightened her shoulders and said, "I am getting too emotional, but whether the baby is a boy or a girl, it really doesn't matter because I'm just grateful to be pregnant again."

After sharing dessert they left the restaurant and on the drive home Jennifer kept telling herself . . . *Don't say anything yet, wait until you're certain.*

*   *   *

Twenty minutes later, Keith yawned while waiting in their driveway for the babysitter to come outside. Jennifer reminded him which street she lived on and what the young girl's name was. From inside his vehicle, he watched Jennifer's silhouette through the front room curtains as she nudged the sleeping teenager from the couch. In a hypnotic state, the babysitter walked to the car and fortunately, she would be home and sound asleep in no time.

It was fifteen minutes later when Keith was back in the driveway and for the second time that evening, he watched Jennifer's profile through the sheer curtains. The glow from the computer screen cast a shadowy outline across her face. Keith could tell by the way she peered at the monitor that she was deep in thought. He wondered what was so important to her that she needed to be surfing the Internet so late at night, and then he remembered how energetic she became each time she was pregnant.

He was sure this baby would be their second daughter and then all three of his girls, his wife and two daughters, would all have September birthdays. He smiled, thinking that a small three stone Sapphire bracelet would be the perfect gift for Jennifer next year on their twelfth anniversary.

He opened the front door and Jennifer quickly closed the medical website on breast cancer that she was researching. She sat casually in the chair with one leg tucked under, while her other bare foot began a nervous tapping of its own. He stood behind her and tightened his grip on her shoulders and said, "I'm ready for bed."

"I won't be long." She looked up at him and smiled.

He then bent to give her a kiss good night.

*   *   *

It was two o'clock in the morning when the printer finished the last page of the medical report Jennifer had studied. She had researched numerous sights on breast cancer staging because she wanted to be prepared for her appointment on March 12, to see the radiologist at Brandon Memorial Hospital.

Once again, she studied the chart showing the stages of breast cancer so she would be familiar with the medical terminology. She reviewed the diagnostic procedures and the three key aspects of the TNM staging and realized at this point a biopsy would be needed.

The light from the monitor vanished as she turned off the computer. She found the family cat, Simba, sitting on the kitchen counter purring softly under the light from the stove. She carried the tomcat to the pantry cupboard thinking that

Simba was the only feline she knew that waited until after dark to eat.

Jennifer placed dry food into his bowl by the patio door and crouched down to stroke him. At once, she wondered what it would be like to be Simba, to have no worries or troubles, and to know someone would always be there to love and take care of you. Jennifer understood that Simba lived such a life; the cat knew of no hardships, and he had no comprehension of his destiny. Simba gave her a thankful nudge and then left a half-eaten bowl of food before swooping down the basement stairs.

Jennifer remained sitting on the cold ceramic tile. She crossed her legs in front of her, placed her elbows on her knees, folded her hands, and bowed her head in prayer. She knew God was omnipresent and how vast His universe was, yet she knew He was right there with her at this very moment.

There on her kitchen floor, at two o'clock in the morning, God knew of her needs even before she prayed . . . *Dear God, I don't know where to begin because everything is uncertain, I need You to show me where to go for medical help. Please lead me in the direction You want me to follow – my only desire is to do Your will. Amen.*

Bleeding Hearts
Spring of 2004

~ *12* ~

As promised, the following Tuesday morning, Cathy met Jennifer at the doctor's office, but neither of them had a moment to talk before the physician entered the examining room.

"Hello, I'm Dr. Alfred Linwood." He shook Jennifer's hand and nodded in Cathy's direction. He wasted no time before asking, "Mrs. Hayse, tell me what has happened the last few months."

"The last few months have been terrible." Jennifer released a nervous laugh before reciting the medical chain of events which she knew by heart. After she explained things, she let out a deep sigh, wondering what she had done wrong or at what point had she missed the warning signs.

Dr. Linwood extended the footrest to the examining table and asked Jennifer to lie down. "I will exam you first and then explain in detail what needs to be done *today.*"

Cathy caught the emphasis on the word 'today'. She sat in the chair and gave Jennifer and the doctor as much privacy as possible. She focused on Jennifer's pink slipper socks that were moving in unison, they reminded Cathy of windshield wipers in a rainstorm. It was obvious Jennifer was frightened and so was she.

Dr. Linwood gave them no indication as to what he was thinking. He observed the thickening of tissue on the left breast and the apparent discomfort Jennifer was experiencing during the exam. He then pressed lightly underneath each arm and felt the swollen lymph nodes on both sides. He pushed the leg support back in place and helped Jennifer into a sitting position.

He sat down and made notes in her medical chart before closing the file and said, "I've compared your mammogram films along with the lab reports, and what I see is worrisome." He paused to clear his throat.

Cathy glanced from the doctor to Jennifer, and then back again to the doctor.

"I have scheduled you for a repeat mammogram *today.*"

Jennifer also noticed the emphasis on the word and she began to cry. Immediately Cathy was by her side, comforting her and listening to the physician.

Dr. Linwood knew the situation was serious and explained, "After you are done, the lab results will be sent to Dr. Jeremy Nash."

"I don't want another mammogram." Jennifer whispered to Cathy that the last x-ray had been extremely painful.

"I'm sorry, Mrs. Hayse, but we need three views of both breasts." Dr. Linwood said, "Your initial film was of the left breast only and the second film is incomplete because it only provided two views." He handed her a tissue and said, "Linda is the most experienced x-ray technician available and she will avoid any unnecessary discomfort during the procedure."

"If I had been your patient, Dr. Linwood, how would you have treated me?"

He hesitated, but then stated the truth, "I would have pursued the palpable lump back in July and immediately ordered a biopsy."

"I was told I was too young," Jennifer cried.

"Because of your family history, that assumption was wrong." He handed Jennifer a slip of paper and told her, "Give this to Linda downstairs in the x-ray lab."

He then gave a second note to Cathy and told her Dr. Nash is located across the street in the Brandon Professional Building and that Jennifer's appointment was scheduled for one-thirty that afternoon.

"What type of physician is Dr. Nash?" Jennifer asked.

"He is a surgeon."

*　　*　　*

Downstairs Linda paced the floor, waiting for the patient to come through the swinging doors. She had known Dr. Linwood for nearly fifteen years and never before had he personally called her at home to come in on a scheduled day off so she could process a mammogram film. Linda felt instinctively that Mrs. Hayse was another unfortunate victim of breast cancer and worse yet, Dr. Linwood told her the patient was ten weeks pregnant.

"Can you please help us?" Cathy asked the only person in the room. "We just came from Dr. Linwood's office, and he told us to ask for Linda."

"Hello, I'm Linda, and which one of you is Jennifer?"

Cathy stepped aside.

Immediately, Linda recognized the look of distress on Jennifer's face, she took her by the arm and said, "I promise to complete the test and have you finished as quickly as possible."

Cathy rested against the doorframe wishing this was all a huge mistake. She wished Jennifer had confided in her sooner because for eight months now, Jennifer had been on a roller coaster ride of uncertainty.

Linda was true to her word, and in no time Jennifer was finished. She asked them to wait another fifteen minutes while she viewed the x-ray for accuracy because Linda did not want Jennifer to leave until she was certain of the film's quality.

"You're all set, Jennifer," Linda said as she walked back into the lobby, "Dr. Nash will see you at one-thirty. In the meantime, do you have any questions?"

Jennifer did not know what to ask, but Cathy stepped closer and said, "Talk to us Linda, and tell us what to expect from Dr. Nash."

The waiting room was empty. It was during lunch so everyone was gone and Linda cautiously said, "I can give you some pamphlets on breast cancer . . . "

"No thank you, I've read them all." Jennifer's reply was short and abrupt.

Cathy reached over, placed her hand on Jennifer's shoulder and asked Linda, "What is Dr. Nash like?"

"I can assure you, Jeremy is a shoot-from-the-hip physician and he won't sugar coat anything." Linda knew professionally to end the conversation because she was not at liberty to discuss the x-ray films. Although she had enough medical experience to know the films were very clear and the results were obvious.

*   *   *

Cathy looked at the clock and knew they had plenty of time before seeing the surgeon. She suggested they stop for something to eat and while stirring her coffee, she mulled over several opening lines for a conversation. However each one seemed insignificant given the dire circumstances Jennifer was facing. This was the first meal she and Jennifer had ever shared in silence and it was heartbreaking.

Several moments passed before Jennifer said, "This is the nicest thing anyone has ever done for me, Cathy, thank you for rearranging your entire day just to be with me."

"Jennifer, this is what friends are for." Cathy looked at the clock above the cash register and wondered if it was working because every minute seemed like an hour. Cathy pushed her plate off to the side and Jennifer did the same. She then placed her elbows on the table and rested her head in her hands for awhile.

After a few moments Cathy said, "We need to leave, Jen, would you like to take a cup of coffee with you?"

"No, thanks." Jennifer stood and went to the ladies room before leaving.

Cathy paid the bill and waited for her outside. The temperature was getting warmer and the small patches of snow were beginning to melt. Spring was always a renewing time of year, but she didn't feel renewed at all. Cathy watched the water drip, one drop at a time, from the roof to the sidewalk.

Jennifer stepped outside and said, "I'm ready Cathy, let's go."

*   *   *

Inside the waiting room, Cathy found two empty chairs while Jennifer stood at the front desk and filled out the necessary paperwork. Two hours later, the constant ringing of the busy office telephone lines had intensified Cathy's headache. She glanced over at Jennifer who was now fast asleep in the chair across from her and Cathy's stomach tightened with concern.

The lobby door opened and an older woman whose name was Connie, stepped into the waiting room. She whispered to Cathy, "When you are ready, come with me, please."

Cathy tapped Jennifer's knee gently to wake her up and together they followed Connie to the first patient room on the left. Jennifer stood by the examining table waiting for a gown. The room was small and all three women kept moving out of each other's way.

"This is sort of like musical chairs, isn't it?" Connie displayed a weak smile when she handed a threadbare cotton gown to Jennifer. She told her the doctor would be in shortly and then she left.

*   *   *

Down the hall, Dr. Jeremy Nash, sat amongst piles of medical books and stacks of manila folders. His right ankle rested on his left knee. His thoughts were focused entirely on the medical report in front of him with Jennifer's name printed in bold black letters. He was not looking forward to his next appointment. He reviewed the mammogram films twice, but nothing would change the obvious. He tapped an inexpensive ink pen mindlessly on the rubber sole of his worn shoe. His next patient was thirty-two years old and ten weeks pregnant. He raked his hands through his thinning hair and thought of how terrible the next few minutes were going to be for the patient.

"Doctor?" Connie peeked around the half-closed door. She told him Mrs. Hayse and her friend were waiting.

He stood and walked down the corridor to the last examining room on the right and tapped briefly on the door before entering. "Hello, I am Dr. Nash." He focused all his attention on the young woman sitting on the patient table. "I'm sure this has been a long day for you, Mrs. Hayse."

"Yes, it has been a long day." Jennifer knew the routine and laid back.

Within minutes, his years of experience confirmed the diagnostic report. He continued with the exam and asked, "Do you work full time?"

"No, I work part time," Jennifer replied.

"And where do you work?"

"I'm an electrical engineer and I work at Visteon Corporation."

He then asked her to turn her head to the right so he could feel the left side of her neck, then back to the left, he asked. It was then he noticed the gold cross resting at the base of her throat. "Does your husband work?"

"Yes, he works full time as a computer specialist." Jennifer was scared.

"Do you have family close by?"

Jennifer held her breath, and Cathy stiffened.

"Yes, well sort of, anyway." Jennifer squeezed her eyes closed.

Dr. Nash looked directly at Cathy while asking Jennifer, "Do you have the support of close friends?"

"Yes." Jennifer's voice cracked and a single tear rolled down the side of her face losing itself in her thick auburn curls.

"You can sit up." Without another word the doctor left the room.

Jennifer trembled as Cathy placed a coat over her shoulders to help keep her warm. Cathy stood at the far end of the table wondering what to do when abruptly, Dr. Nash, walked back into the tiny examination room.

He exclaimed, "Mrs. Hayse, I am ninety-nine percent certain you have breast cancer." He knew the unfortunate chain of events that had brought Jennifer into his office. His face deepened in color showing his sympathy; he truly regretted being the one to declare the diagnosis.

Connie opened the door and placed a tray of orange juice and crackers near the sink then left without disturbing anyone. Dr. Nash handed the open juice container to Jennifer and her left hand trembled as she reached for it. He gave her a packet of crackers and said, "Let me know when you are ready, and we'll discuss your options."

Cathy was sick to her stomach. At once her headache turned into a migraine and she leaned on the table for support. Jennifer didn't open the crackers, but she did finish drinking the juice before asking Dr. Nash to give his medical recommendations.

He started by saying, "First off, the July mammogram when analyzed with the one taken today is remarkable in comparison. You have palpable masses, cystic and solid, in both breasts." He turned to the second page of the lab report and said, "I'm sure you have noticed the change in appearance on the left breast?"

Jennifer nodded and held the juice in both hands to keep from shaking.

"There are multiple, enlarged lymph nodes, primarily on your left side." There was additional data, but Dr. Nash felt no need to continue because he knew Jennifer was absorbing the seriousness of her disease. He closed her medical file and held it against his chest. "We can offer you the best medical care here at Brandon Memorial Hospital, but I'm sorry to say it is unfortunate that you have little time to make your decision. You do understand, Mrs. Hayse, that you must act quickly?"

Jennifer nodded and made eye contact with him while she prayed . . . *Dear Lord, show me what to do, please give me a sign.*

Dr. Nash was saying, "In comparing the two mammograms, I suspect your cancer is very aggressive." Once again, his eyes centered on Jennifer's gold cross. "You have two children, correct?"

Jennifer nodded.

"Mrs. Hayse, you must undergo a vigorous regimen of treatment to combat this disease." He crossed his arms, inhaled and said, "I want to be your doctor and administer the best treatment possible; however, your pregnancy complicates matters." He then advised her to terminate her pregnancy – immediately.

Cathy felt dizzy and her vision blurred since she was not prepared for that sort of medical advice. Jennifer straightened her back and squared her shoulders; she was not surprised.

Dr. Nash observed Jennifer's body language and after several moments of waiting for her response, he simply said, "I am sorry." As a physician, he wanted to justify and explain his medical opinion, but at the same time, he respected her choice.

Jennifer's gaze never met his eyes.

Before leaving, Dr. Nash again told her he was sorry.

After he left, Jennifer let her shoulders relax a little; she then turned to Cathy and asked for her backpack. Cathy's knees seemed locked in place. She could hardly move, but she did manage to reach the chair where Jennifer's backpack rested. Jennifer asked her to take out the pink folder from inside. As Jennifer flipped through the printed charts, she explained to Cathy the medical research she had conducted over the Internet.

She needed Cathy to help her review the written lab report because Jennifer needed to know the size of the tumors in order to classify the level and stage of her cancer. Cathy read the measurements from the mammogram dated that same morning while Jennifer did the comparison of the charts. They stood together as a team once more, but they were now working with medical statistics and data.

Cathy used her finger to guide her eyes efficiently through the medical paragraphs. She quickly located the information and said, "Here it is – 34mm on the right plus 16mm enlarged lymph nodes." Cathy waited while Jennifer charted out the measurements.

"What about the left side?" Jennifer dared to ask.

"The left side is – 27mm with irregular masses, multiple enlarged lymph nodes and – " Cathy stopped reading, sensing it was a sufficient amount of data for charting.

Jennifer laid the information against another staging chart from a second website, and both charts agreed. Cathy stood closer and leaned over Jennifer's shoulder. She was trying to read the charts rather than ask questions when unexpectedly Jennifer's trembling hands covered the information.

"The breast cancer has advanced to Stage III, Level B . . . *Cathy, I'm in trouble.*"

~ 13 ~

An hour later, Jennifer sat down at Cathy's kitchen table with thoughts about her future spinning through her mind. She understood from the charted measurements that her cancer was serious. They had finished their second cups of coffee when Cathy knew it was time for her faith, along with her Bible study classes, to be put into practice.

"Which Psalm reads . . . *'Be still and know that I am God'?"* Jennifer asked.

"Psalm 46:10," Cathy knew it by heart.

This marked the day the roots of their friendship became firmly anchored. Together, they were pole vaulted into a deeper spiritual level and Cathy promised to be there for Jennifer.

Cathy treaded lightly and asked, "How is Keith?"

"He doesn't know yet, but I'm going to tell him tonight." The involuntary jumping of Jennifer's left knee started on its own.

"Have you told Keith anything more since last summer?" Now that Jennifer had updated Cathy on the history of her doctor's visits, Cathy wondered how much Keith knew about her condition.

"No, because it was such an anxious time after the first false alarm and I didn't want him to go through the stress again." Jennifer blew her nose and further explained there was no need to tell him anything because the doctors said everything was fine.

Cathy couldn't argue as she may have done the same thing under the circumstances. They talked and prayed until the bottom of the coffee pot sizzled on the burner and after their time in prayer, Jennifer felt uplifted and renewed.

"Jennifer, how much have you learned about breast cancer in the last couple of weeks?" Cathy turned off the pot and rinsed out their empty mugs.

"Well, I've learned enough to know this isn't going to be easy, and I'm going to need all the help I can get." Jennifer simply smiled.

Cathy assured her, "I will schedule your appointments and coordinate the transportation to and from the doctor's office, plus I'll do the meal planning."

"Wait a minute Cathy, that's too much responsibility."

"No it's not because we're a team, remember?" Cathy felt like crying.

"Not anymore," she gently whispered.

"I don't understand, what do you mean?"

Jennifer stood next to her at the kitchen window and said, "I won't be going back to work, Cathy."

The reality of her diagnosis and the seriousness of the situation began to sink into Cathy's heart and mind. "This is horrible, and I don't know anything else to do for you right now other than to pray."

"I need your prayers more than anything, Cathy."

"Jennifer, I'm happy to hear you ask for prayers because I was worried you would be angry at God, you know, let down in some way."

"Oh, I have been let down, Cathy, but it wasn't God who let me down."

Cathy wiped her tears.

"For me to lose sight of God right now would be unthinkable." Jennifer looked through the kitchen window and explained, "My faith needs to grow like the trees, like the grass will grow in the spring, and the flowers will bloom in the summer." She turned to Cathy and told her, "My faith must grow like the mustard seed."

"Matthew, chapter 17," Cathy recalled.

"Matthew, chapter 17," Jennifer repeated.

Cathy finished rinsing their dishes and was wiping her hands off when Jennifer asked, "Do you remember how we used to dream about living next door to one another and starting our own business someday?"

"Yes, we were going to open a tea shop." Cathy remembered.

"Well, maybe we won't open a tea shop anytime soon, but we could be neighbors."

"What do you mean?" Cathy asked.

Jennifer was looking out the window and nodded in the direction of the home adjacent to Cathy's backyard and said, "You see that home over there with the big trees and the swing set?"

Cathy peered out her patio door and asked, "Do you mean the Herders' home?"

Jennifer pulled back the kitchen curtain and pointed. "Yes, that house right there, Cathy, wouldn't it be nice if Keith and I lived there? Our children would be the best of friends, and they could run back and forth across the yards, and we could sit and visit without having to drive so far."

"Jennifer!" Without realizing it, Cathy was shouting.

"Cathy, what is it?" Jennifer ran to her side.

"The Herders live in that home!" she said in disbelief.

"I'm sorry, Cathy, that was selfish of me to want to move into your friends' house."

Cathy turned and gripped Jennifer's shoulders and said, "Didn't I tell you, the Herders are moving to Texas and their house is for sale!"

Disbelief then traded places, and Jennifer saw a ray of sunlight shining brightly through the dark clouds.

"And we know that in all things God works
for the good of those who love him, who have
been called to his purpose."
Romans 8:28

*   *   *

It was Monday morning and traffic was light for the Motor City as Keith took the Woodward exit from I-94 to John R. Street. He followed the signs to Karmanos Cancer Institute which was straight ahead. He parked the car and helped Jennifer from the passenger side. He walked beside her, still dazed from all she had told him over the weekend. He could not say the words, let alone imagine his wife had breast cancer. He opened the lobby door, and they stepped inside the Institute.

Keith studied the directory and asked Jennifer, "Dr. Bouwman?"

"Yes, Dr. David Lee Bouwman."

"He is the Professor of Surgery and Director of the Alexander J. Walt Center." Keith tapped on the glass over the physician's title.

"Yes, that's him and Shari Franko is going to meet us here today."

Keith held the elevator door open for his wife and asked, "Again, how does my cousin know Shari Franko?" He wasn't sure about anything this morning.

"Shari owns Variations Salon in Dearborn, where your cousin gets her hair styled and it was she who introduced me to Shari over the telephone."

The elevator stopped, and they stepped into the hallway.

"You see, Shari was a patient of Dr. Bouwman's nine years ago." Jennifer kept her voice low and explained, "She is actively involved in the Susan G. Komen Detroit Race for the Cure each year and Shari was able to arrange my appointment this morning at Karmanos – see how God has blessed us?"

Keith stopped and stared as Jennifer walked past him. He was thinking . . . *God has blessed us?* He caught up with her and asked, "Shari is a total stranger, right?"

"No, I talked with her on the telephone last night," she smiled.

"Jennifer, you talked with Shari *one* time," he emphasized.

"What difference does it make how many times you talk with someone, I consider Shari my friend – an instant friend." She didn't understand his point.

"And she dropped everything to meet you here today, at Karmanos?"

Jennifer nodded and said, "Shari knows that being diagnosed can be frightening, and she wants to offer her support. You don't mind, do you?"

"No, but it does seem odd." He shrugged his shoulders and opened the door to Dr. Bouwman's medical office.

*   *   *

Shari was distressed after learning about Jennifer's unfortunate misdiagnosis. As she walked through the corridors to Dr. Bouwman's office, her mind paged through an album of memories; Shari was now a nine-year survivor.

Jennifer and Keith had been taken to the first treatment room and were waiting to be seen by the doctor. Shari waited outside the doorway and took a deep breath before tapping on the closed door. She was thinking of her first visit with Dr. Bouwman.

"Come in," Jennifer answered.

"Hello, I'm Shari Franko." She held the door ajar as the nurse recorded Jennifer's blood pressure and vital signs.

"Shari, how nice of you to be here for us." Jennifer sang the words.

After the nurse left, Shari handed Jennifer a gift in pink tissue paper and said, "I know you will have a ton of questions, so I brought you a copy of *Dr. Susan Love's Breast Book.*"

A second knock was heard, and the door swung open.

"Good morning, Mrs. Hayse." Dr. Bouwman's presence filled the room. He stood over six feet tall with wavy, charcoal gray hair and a full beard. His baritone voice spoke of authority and instantly, Jennifer felt safe.

*   *   *

It was two o'clock in the afternoon before Keith started to drive back to work. The morning was still hazy, but he understood the reality; there was no doubt, his wife had breast cancer. The results of the biopsy taken that morning would tell them the extent of her disease.

While at Karmanos they met Dr. Michael Simon, the Director of the Cancer Genetic Counseling Services and before leaving, the nurse had scheduled Jennifer to start chemotherapy the following week. They left Karmanos with a large packet of information and inside the envelope were signed medical leave documents for Jennifer's employer.

As Keith drove along, the sound of an impatient horn moved him across the intersection. His stomach involuntarily tightened, his palms were moist, and the steering wheel was suddenly very sticky. He powered down the window for a blast of cold air. Before leaving Karmanos, he called his supervisor and asked to meet with him later that afternoon. He pulled into his office parking lot and forgot to roll the window back up. He was moving in slow motion through a fog of events that were hard to believe. Keith knew his life was about to change significantly.

*   *   *

Shari retraced her footsteps outside Karmanos and into the parking garage. The sound of her cell phone's ring broke into her thoughts and the caller ID number made her smile; her husband's timing was always perfect.

"Hi, Sweetheart." She leaned against the cement column of the parking structure.

"How did things go this morning?" Jeff was across town, working.

"Keith and Jennifer have a long road ahead of them." Shari kicked at the loose gravel on the pavement and said, "Dr. Bouwman's concern for Jennifer was evident and when he explained things, I realized Jennifer's visit today was more urgent than mine was several years ago."

"Jennifer's case is very serious then," he surmised.

"Yes, I believe so and she begins treatment next week." Shari lifted her face toward the sky and said, "Jennifer is so young."

Jeff knew Shari was crying, and even though he was at a construction site, he offered to meet her at home if she wanted him to.

"No, I'll be fine."

"What are your plans now?" He waved to the crew of workmen driving through the front entrance gate at the construction site.

"I plan on doing the grocery shopping and running a few errands." Shari said.

"Do you want me to bring home dinner tonight?" He knew at times how difficult it was for his wife to mentor breast cancer patients, and it was obvious that because of her unique circumstances, Jennifer was going to be very special to Shari. "No, I'll fix dinner." She walked up the ramp to her vehicle and asked, "How long will you be at the investigation site?" "Not much longer." He handed the city inspector a yellow hard hat.

*   *   *

After Jennifer's appointment at Karmanos, she called Cathy to ask if she would tell their co-workers at Visteon about her diagnosis. The next morning, Cathy met with Al and he told her that Jennifer had called him the night before and he was still shaken over the news. He sat with Cathy and helped her compose her thoughts in preparation for the meeting with the rest of the group. Jennifer would not be returning to work, and she wanted Cathy to explain the reason for her leave of absence.

Jennifer's first chemotherapy treatment was March 25.

~ *14* ~

It was St. Patrick's Day, March 17, and since Mary was Irish, she enjoyed celebrating the special day. She wondered what sort of plans Jennifer had in mind for the day because true to her nature, Jennifer always celebrated everything. Mary walked down the row of workstations hoping that Jennifer would be at her desk, but Mary found her office space dark and empty. The computer screen was blank, and Jennifer's coat wasn't hanging over her chair. Thinking that she was late getting into the office, Mary wrote a note and placed it on Jennifer's still keyboard . . . *Coffee any time ~ M.*

Mary was walking toward the lunchroom when Duane stopped her and explained that Al had just called an impromptu meeting for the engineering department.

"Are you joking with me, Duane?" Mary never could tell.

"No, not this time Mary, there must be something wrong." He nodded in the direction of the conference room where others were milling in.

The conference room was full, but strangely quiet. No one was murmuring or guessing why the meeting had been called. Mary knew that in itself was unusual. Cathy was the last one to enter the room, and she closed the door behind her.

Al started by saying, "I'm sorry everyone, but Cathy and I have unfortunate news to tell you this morning."

The overcrowded room grew very still.

"I need everyone to be patient and to give Cathy their full attention." He nodded in her direction.

Cathy sat at the end of the long table with a yellow legal pad in front of her. She rolled the right, bottom edge of the top sheet tightly around her ink pen and focused on her notes. Without looking directly at anyone she cleared her throat and said, "What I am about to say won't be easy for any of you to hear because we all love her very much."

Everyone's eyes darted around the table. No one was prepared for what Cathy was about to say. Mary's stomach instantly tightened. She remembered Jennifer's empty workstation, and quickly glancing around the room, she didn't see her young co-worker in the crowd.

Cathy held her breath and said, "Jennifer Hayse has been diagnosed with breast cancer."

The group was in shock. They all spoke at the same time, their questions falling on top of one another as the room filled with tension. Al raised his hands and asked everyone to please let Cathy finish.

She nervously continued to curl the edge of the paper. She could feel everyone's personal agony on top of her own pain. "Jennifer's diagnosis was confirmed yesterday morning and today I feel that Jennifer can be compared to a modern day version of Job from the Old Testament." Cathy looked at those seated around her and explained, "The reason why I say this is because Jen has a very aggressive and uncommon form of breast cancer and the disease has already progressed to Stage III, Level B." Cathy stopped to clear her throat before explaining, "There are four stages to cancer and Jen is midway through the third stage."

The room exploded with questions and Al had to reach out to the engineers seated closest to him saying, "Everyone hush, please let Cathy finish."

". . . this is horrible." The trail of a sentence was heard.

"Yes, this is horrible, and unfortunately there is more news about Jennifer." Cathy did her best to contain her composure. She waited until she found the courage to say, "Jennifer is ten weeks pregnant."

Mary's hand covered her mouth to silence her words . . . *Dear God in heaven.*

Duane's heart sank he was thinking . . . *How can this be?*

Bill dropped his gaze to his folded hands . . . *How will Jennifer manage?*

Kathy closed her tear-filled eyes . . . *We're the same age.*

Cathy's voice was parched when she said, "I spoke with Jennifer last night and she wants to be very open about her illness. She doesn't want to hide things from anyone and finally, she wants all of you to know that she loves you very much." A tissue was handed to Cathy, while silent tears and soft murmurs could be heard from all four corners of the conference room. "Jennifer told me that she wants to continue with having parties and celebrating. She doesn't want cancer to stop her from enjoying life." Cathy blew her nose.

Al cleared his throat and said, "Sometime today we will post a sign-up sheet for meals and other suggestions on how to help the Hayse family. In the meantime, Cathy has prepared an e-mail to send to the other departments." He looked around the room and said, "Because as you can see not everyone is here; this way everyone will be notified."

"What does she want us to do first?" someone asked.

"Pray," Cathy quickly responded. "Jennifer wants us to pray and spread the word at your church so that her name will be placed on prayer chains everywhere."

"Cathy, is there anything else?" Al had two daughters close to Jennifer's age and his sorrow was evident.

She scanned the last page of her notes and added, "Yes, Jennifer wants all of you to tell your wives, daughters, mothers, grandmothers, sisters, aunts, and nieces; tell them to have an annual mammogram. Also, if the younger women feel something is wrong, tell them to trust their instincts and get another opinion. Jennifer wants them to know – they are never too young for breast cancer."

*   *   *

After everyone left, Cathy walked outside the building for privacy. She promised to call Jennifer after the meeting was over. She stretched her neck from side to side and the painful stiffness was obvious. It appeared the muscle tension in her neck was here to stay. She dialed Jennifer's telephone number.

Cathy relayed the meeting's outcome and the outpouring of help that was offered and Jennifer thanked her, because she realized the hardest part would be telling people. Jennifer had spent most of her morning on the telephone making personal calls and she was glad to talk for a moment with someone who already knew.

She told Cathy about the morning class she attended at Karmanos in preparation for chemotherapy. "I need your opinion, Cathy. In class today the nurse suggested I cut my hair short before starting treatment and I was thinking maybe
. . ."

"Jennifer, you have to cut your hair?" Cathy rubbed her forehead.

"Mmm-hmm."

"But you love your hair," Cathy instantly regretted her words.

Jennifer stared at the pile of medical forms and brochures on the kitchen counter and said, "My life is going to be very busy, and an easy hairstyle will be fun, should I become a redhead or try being a blonde?"

"Tell me, Jen, what's your natural color?" Cathy laughed.

"Boring-brown," Jennifer mumbled.

"Ah, that's too bad," Cathy teased and tried to lighten the emotional conversation by suggesting, "I think you should try sandy-haired with a touch of gold."

"Not straight-up blonde?" Jennifer was a little disappointed.

Cathy heard the landline telephone ringing in the background and asked if Jennifer needed to answer it.

"Yes, I have to hang up." Jennifer then disconnected without saying good-bye.

Cathy dialed her husband's telephone number at school hoping he would be at his desk during lunch. Jim mumbled an odd sounding hello and she asked him what he was eating.

"Today is one of my student's birthdays and I'm showing good manners as their teacher by eating their cake; after all it's part of my job." He grinned and asked how things went at work.

"It wasn't easy telling everyone about Jennifer," she told him.

"I'm sure it wasn't Cathy, but now everyone can focus their attention on what needs to be done to help her and Keith."

"I agree." Cathy felt emotionally drained.

"Listen, don't worry about fixing dinner tonight because I'm going to order pizza for the kids before you leave for church."

"I have Bible study tonight?" Cathy had forgotten.

"Yes, it's Wednesday night," Jim said.

"I don't have my homework done!"

"Write your answers down during the review," Jim teased her, as his students poured back into the classroom. As tired as Cathy was, she wouldn't miss her Bible study class, especially after going through one of the saddest times she could ever remember. Now more than ever, she needed to be surrounded by other Christians and deeply rooted in the Word of God.

> "Grace and peace be yours in abundance through
> the knowledge of God and of Jesus our Lord."
> 2 Peter 1:2

*   *   *

In less than thirty minutes, the next seven months of Jennifer's life were scheduled, and she realized she would need a special planner to help keep track of all her medical appointments. Jennifer had much to learn about breast cancer, and she wanted to be a wise and educated patient. This way if a quick decision needed to be made, she would be prepared.

She telephoned Susan Abraham because it was time to tell her.

"Hello?" Abe had taken the day off from work so he answered the telephone.

"Hello, Abe, this is Jennifer, how is Susan doing today?"

He explained that Susan was not feeling well after having a rough night, but she was awake now and doing a little better. He told Jennifer when the doctors place Susan on new medication it always takes her system a few days to adjust.

"Is she able to talk?"

"Yes, she wants to talk with you, please hold on."

Susan's throat was dry, and her voice sounded raspy. "I'm glad you called, Jennifer, how are things with you?"

"I'm sorry for not calling sooner." Jennifer didn't want to tell Susan about her diagnosis, it seemed unfair to add more to Susan's distress.

"I understand you are busy, but now tell me your news."

"Susan, I don't have good news." It took several minutes for Jennifer to tell Susan about her diagnosis and in the end, Susan cried while her husband, Abe, tried to comfort her. The news was heartbreaking and the emotional stress caused the strain in Susan's lower back to flare-up. Jennifer caught the faint sound of a soft cry over the telephone and asked if she was all right.

"Yes, I will be fine, although my back hurts some." Susan adjusted the pillow behind her and said, "Jennifer, let's pray for each other."

After they prayed, Jennifer said good-bye and promised to keep in touch with Susan. She sat alone in her living room, twirling the ends of her hair around her index finger. This was a habit she formed as a child while sitting on her grandmother's lap, rocking peacefully in the warm twilight across the Bayou. They would listen to the crickets mixed in with the harmony of peaceful rocking. The movement of the wicker chair over the creaky wooden planks on the porch to the old farmhouse, blended easily with the sweet sounds of nature.

Jennifer's thoughts carried her back in time when life was simpler and the hot summer evenings were spent sipping lemonade and catching fireflies in Mason jars. She thought of her grandmother's prize-winning watermelon patch and how Sammy, the neighbor's goat, could never resist jumping the gate to the garden. Jennifer recalled it as being the only time she ever saw her grandmother raise a broom handle to anything.

Jennifer rested her head on the back cushion of the sofa and closed her eyes. She was thinking that all the roads she had traveled in life so far had led her to this moment in time, to these circumstances, and to this diagnosis. The unfortunate medical errors which resulted in her tragic misdiagnosis last July were over and what happened could not be undone . . . *Heavenly Father, forgive me for struggling to understand.*

*   *   *

The boys raced down their driveway toward the asphalt cul-de-sac and Justin, for the first time, could out run his older brother Jacob. They were happy to have been excused from helping clear the dinner table, but noticed their dad was unusually quiet at dinner. Lately, the boys had grown accustomed to Duane talking about his work during the evening meal. But tonight when their mother, Janis, asked about his day at work, he frowned and told her they would talk later, privately. Janis watched from the front porch as her sons practiced soccer with the neighbors then she went back inside to talk with Duane. He had cleared the table and was drying his hands on the kitchen towel.

"Duane, what has happened?" she asked.

"We received bad news at work today." He leaned on the counter, folded his arms, and crossed his ankles. "One of my co-workers has been diagnosed with cancer."

"Who?"

"It's Jennifer; she has breast cancer." He raked his fingers through his hair and told Janis, "The cancer is advanced and very serious, but that's not all – Jennifer is also pregnant."

Janis inhaled sharply; she never expected to hear this sort of news. The telephone rang, but neither one moved to answer it. During the last few months Janis had enjoyed listening to the daily recap of Duane's workday. It was as if she knew his friends personally, and now she was feeling his pain. "I'm so sorry, Duane."

Tears stung his eyes as he told her about the first day he met Jennifer two years ago. He explained how she went out of her way to make him feel welcome. She made sure he knew where the test lab was and that he had someone to share lunch with – it was then he gave Jennifer the nickname . . . *Sunshine*.

Janis tore off a paper towel and handed it to him.

"I remember thinking how strange her behavior was and how out of place it seemed because no one is that nice anymore." His voice cracked.

"This is terrible, Duane, have you talked with her yet?"

"No, but I sent her an e-mail letting her know she won't go through this alone and even though her life has taken an unplanned turn, I want her to know she can count on us to help. I told her to trust in God and our Savior, Jesus Christ, who will see her through this storm."

*   *   *

Rima studied the unfinished oil painting in front of her. From several angles she viewed it and still, she couldn't determine what she did not like about it. The vantage point was aligned to be the center of the two forward-facing vehicles, which was correct. The Corvettes were penciled in at right angles, which helped to show the contrasting details from each model year. Rima stood back and eyed the painting, tilting her head from side to side. She changed her stance and concentrated on the background, thinking maybe it was not the automobiles that were the problem. She stepped back another foot and studied it more; perhaps the trees were out of proportion.

She laughed aloud and said, "Oh, glory be, it is the trees." Before the vision escaped her third eye, she mixed amber and sienna to give the tree bark, and the limbs more depth. The cobalt blue sky with smears of white cirrus clouds she left alone. The endless autumn leaves that were brushed in orange, red, and yellow, she also left alone because the vermilion hue captured the season, and the foliage was good. Rima smiled with satisfaction. She was finishing the last colorful stroke when she heard the garage door open.

Her smile vanished as she watched Bill walk in through the side door because she instinctively knew something was wrong. The color of his eyes were not the gray Rima was familiar with; the eyes she saw before her were painted in sorrow.

Life was not easy, and being a Christian by no means meant that you were exempt from pain and suffering. Sometimes bad things, even terrible things, happen to good people. The rain falls and the sun shines equally on everyone.

During these times, where do you find the strength to give the person you love terrible news? Bill understood the impact of his news was going to tear Rima's heart in two. He prayed for spiritual guidance as he walked to her side and told her about Jennifer.

"O Lord, tell me this isn't true," Rima wept.

Bill held her close as the mixture of oil paint and turpentine filled his senses.

"I must call her – "

"Sweetheart, I called and left a message earlier." He took off his glasses to wipe his tears and said, "When Cathy told us the news, she compared Jennifer's story to a modern day Job."

"Yes, Job endured great pain and suffering." Rima's eyes were burning with tears.

"That's true, but Rima let's focus on what God did for Job in the end. How God blessed the second half of Job's life more abundantly than the first because Job never lost faith or trust in God."

He told Rima about the line of people volunteering to help with meals, house cleaning, and driving Jennifer to the hospital for treatment. Bill witnessed God's hand moving today at work by sending others into Jennifer's life.

They sat on the couch and watched the sun disappear behind the farmer's vacant field across their yard. They prayed for Jennifer and her family and for those who would soon be tied together in a Christian network of faith, hope, and love.

Tonight, there were many people with bleeding hearts for Jennifer, praying for her strength to courageously walk through the gathering storms of . . . *breast cancer and pregnancy.*

~ 15 ~

Three weeks after Jennifer started chemotherapy she went to get her haircut at Variations Salon. Shari was looking forward to seeing her and wanted to make her experience at the salon as upbeat as possible. Jennifer brought a video camera to document the event for her children and Shari arranged for another hair stylist to film the appointment. She planned to focus their time on inner beauty and to remind Jennifer that one day her hair would grow back.

"Hi, Jennifer, let me take your jacket," Shari greeted.

"Thank you." Jennifer was quiet at first, but soon her apprehensions were put to rest. Shari fixed coffee while Jennifer showed the other stylist how to operate the video camera. A few moments later, Jennifer was sitting in the chair at the first station, ready for a new haircut.

Shari turned the chair toward the mirror, where both her image and Jennifer's looked back at her. She placed her hands on Jennifer's shoulders and bent to look at the reflection in front of her. "After I'm done cutting your hair, would you like me to add some blonde highlights to help offset the shortness?" Shari asked.

A slight nod from Jennifer indicated yes.

"Trust me, you'll look and feel absolutely beautiful," Shari said.

She gave Shari a thumbs-up signal, and the work began. Jennifer closed her eyes and waited nervously for the first divided ponytail to drop, instantly a heavy weight lifted from behind her right ear. She listened to the crunching sound of the scissors as they completed the second cut. Jennifer loved her long auburn curls but now they were gone. It was done and filming of the major event was over. The ponytails were tucked inside bags for Jennifer's children so two separate braids could be made for them to keep.

"We're finished." Shari whispered.

For the first time since grade school Jennifer saw the ends of her hair fall softly on her shoulders. She knew getting her haircut was a minor occurrence, especially when she analyzed the big picture that lay before her. "Cut it shorter!" Jennifer said with a smile.

"You go, girl!" Shari took out the scissors and cut another four inches off the ends.

The tense moment was over and now they made light conversation during the style makeover. Jennifer told Shari that she planned to participate in the June 5, Susan G. Komen Detroit Race for the Cure. She said her friends at Visteon had organized a team in her honor called the . . . *Jen Possible Team*.

Jennifer explained it was a spin-off from the Disney character, Kim Possible. She smiled at the confused look from Shari and then explained to her that the character, Kim Possible, is always fighting trouble and coming out a winner in the cartoon show. Jennifer said that two of her co-workers thought up the idea and even designed a team logo. Jennifer finished her coffee and asked, "Will you be at the race?"

"Yes, I never miss it." Shari told Jennifer she would be running this year in honor of her.

Jennifer smiled in the mirror and thanked Shari for her support.

"Have you gone for your first chemotherapy treatment?" Shari asked.

Jennifer frowned and opened the collar to her blouse and said, "Yes, I was given a port placement because of the swelling in my left arm at the intravenous sight. The port was necessary because it was too difficult for the nurse to locate a strong vein."

Shari concentrated on her profession while Jennifer talked and to some extent, it helped to ease the worries from her mind. In no time at all, her hair was styled and ready for coloring. As promised, to distract from the new length, Shari randomly placed foils of highlights to nicely frame Jennifer's face.

She turned the salon chair away from the mirror and walked Jennifer over to the dryer chair. Shari warmed their coffee while Jennifer started to read a book by Nancy Brinker, *The Race is Run One Step at a Time.*

Shari went into the back room to braid the cut ponytails. She secured them tightly at the ends with a sturdy band, and then placed them over a large hook. She divided the first cut into three equal parts and started the Indian artwork. It wasn't long before the emotional strain was too much and the onset of tears blurred her vision. She held the strands of Jennifer's hair in one hand and wiped her tears away with the other. Shari squeezed her eyes shut and bent her head back, trying to keep herself from crying. Once finishing the task, she tied both ends with pink ribbons and placed them in a large Variations customer bag along with a survivor t-shirt from the previous 2003 Detroit Race for the Cure.

Shari walked back into the salon with a bright smile, she handed Jennifer the gift bag and made plans to visit her during her next session at Karmanos. Jennifer thanked her and self-consciously felt the back of her bare neck. For a long time Jennifer stared at her reflection in the mirror wondering what was going to happen to the stranger she saw facing her.

Shari stood behind her. She squeezed her shoulders and Jennifer thanked her for helping her through the day. They embraced without words, and a new Jennifer Hayse stepped out onto Michigan Avenue. Her hair was short and wispy and she wondered what Keith's reaction would be this evening when he saw her for the first time.

Shari waited at the salon door and watched Jennifer bravely walk down the sidewalk as the wind tousled her short hair. Then Jennifer turned the corner and was lost from view. Shari thought about what the future had in store for Jennifer and herself.

*   *   *

Springtime always indicated a fresh start and a new beginning. Jennifer was inspired as she worked the soil beneath her hands, clearing away the dried leaves that had formed around the blooming crocuses in her front yard. Against the brick wall to her house she could see the irises she planted last year that were also trying to come back to life. She stopped and turned at the sound of tires pulling into her driveway.

"Hello, Jennifer." Mary called out to her as she walked across the lawn with two frozen chocolate shakes from the corner store in New Boston.

"Mary, you remembered my treat!" Jennifer clapped her hands when she saw the frosty drinks.

Mary gave her a hug and said, "I love your hair."

Out of habit, Jennifer felt the back of her neck and frowned, "It's very short."

"I think it looks cute." Mary handed Jennifer one of the cold drinks and took a sip of her own. "This is the best chocolate malt I have ever had," she said.

"They are tasty and I will miss this treat after we move."

"You're moving?" Mary hadn't heard the news.

Jennifer took another sip and nodded. "Yes, we need to be closer to my doctor and the hospitals."

"Where are you moving to?" Mary asked.

Jennifer said Keith made an offer on a home in Cathy and Jim's area, and they would be neighbors if the offer was accepted. "Long before my diagnosis," Jennifer said, "Cathy and I talked about being neighbors and now since my future has been rudely interrupted by cancer – " She gave a nervous laugh before she continued. "Well, relocating is the right thing to do and hopefully next month we will be moving."

"Geez, that's quick." Mary was surprised.

Jennifer shrugged her shoulders and stood. She then suggested they go for a walk and before Mary could respond, Jennifer went into the house for her jacket and two bottles of water. Mary was more than surprised at the news because there was much involved with moving, and she knew they would need a lot of help to make it possible. She bent down to pull a few weeds from along the sidewalk and was admiring the butterfly bush when Jennifer handed her a bottled water.

"That bush is one of my favorites, Mary, I hope we're still living here to see the lavender flowers bloom which attract the butterflies." Jennifer told her, "I love to watch the butterflies go through so many changes during their short lives. They start off as caterpillars, and then they withdraw into their cocoons, and finally break forth as delicately beautiful butterflies."

"They are beautiful, and they're also very fragile to go through so much in a short period of time." Mary said.

"Yes, it is a lot to go through, but then suddenly their beautiful short life is over and they die." Melancholy overshadowed Jennifer as she thought about how short life really is.

Mary thought for a moment before she said, "Even still, while the butterflies are among us, Jennifer, we are blessed by experiencing their grace and beauty."

Quietly, Jennifer stepped away. She touched the leaves on a nearby plant and then said, "The butterflies love rue and these tiny blue-green leaves will have bright yellow flowers to attract them to the plant."

Mary wiped the dirt from her hands and crumbled it around the base of the crocuses. "Jennifer, you're like my friends, Sue and Candice, who know the names of every flower, tree, and shrub in southeast Michigan."

Jennifer smiled and led the way for them to walk down the street. "How long have you been friends with Sue and Candice?"

Mary slowed her pace to match Jennifer's and said, "I knew Sue before I was hired at Ford Motor Company, which was twenty-seven years ago and I have been friends with Candice for almost seven years." She turned to Jennifer and asked, "How long have you and Cathy been friends?"

"Not long, maybe two years. We met at work." Jennifer reached for the gold chain around her neck that held a tiny glass vile and said, "Cathy gave this to me yesterday, can you see the tiny mustard seeds inside?"

Mary said yes.

"Cathy told me the mustard seeds represent my friends and the people I love, who will pray for me and spiritually support me during this storm." Although it was a painful subject, the time had come to talk openly and behind the rim of Jennifer's straw hat tears were waiting to fall. "Mary, I wonder if this is all just a bad dream."

"It doesn't seem possible, does it?" Tears began to blur Mary's vision.

"I knew something was wrong and that's why I kept going back to the doctors. I tried to make them listen, and now here I am, pregnant and diagnosed with breast cancer."

Mary slowed her pace.

Jennifer placed her hand across her midriff and said, "The only thing that I'm certain of right now is this little baby."

They turned the corner and their shadows fell before them as they walked along.

"You know, Mary, when the doctors misdiagnosed me, God knew I had breast cancer and He allowed this pregnancy to take place. This child is His plan and I could never put an end to God's plan."

Mary knew from talking with Cathy that the initial recommendation from Brandon Memorial Hospital was for Jennifer to terminate the pregnancy.

"I agree with you; this pregnancy is God's plan and as a believer, you must trust in His ability to see you through these circumstances."

They walked along in silence before Jennifer said, "You know, having this baby might be the last thing that God will ever ask me to do."

"I know, Jennifer." Mary's tears fell without warning.

"I don't know what God intends for my future, but according to medical statistics, the odds are not in my favor." Jennifer twirled the glass vile of mustard seeds next to her tiny gold cross and she said, "But, with God all things are possible."

A few minutes later they reached the end of Jennifer's driveway. They gave each other a hug before Mary opened her car door to leave. She rolled down the window and said good-bye to Jennifer before backing out onto the street. They smiled and waved to each other not realizing at the time how interlaced their futures would soon become.

~ *16* ~

During the next few weeks, Duane volunteered to organize the Jen Possible Team. Two of Jennifer's fellow engineers who designed a heart-shaped logo for the team had ordered lapel pins and t-shirts for everyone. Daily, Jennifer received e-mails, phone calls, and letters filled with prayers and emotional support. The distribution list for the Jen Possible Team consisted of more than seventy-five people.

This morning, Cathy and Mary stood outside the V.E.M.A. building, waiting in the parking lot because Jennifer was coming into work for a short visit. Her other co-workers were inside waiting in the office lobby.

"She should be here any minute," Mary said, looking at her watch.

Cathy's gaze was fixed westward down Commerce Drive. "I'm sure she will be here soon. I spoke with her last night and she was feeling fine, although she was a little preoccupied at the time because Keith was in the middle of shaving her head."

Mary shot a surprised look at Cathy.

"Sorry, but I wasn't sure if you knew." Cathy shielded her eyes from the bright sun and said, "Jennifer said, she wanted to shave her hair off because the chemotherapy attacks and kills cancer cells, but in so doing it also destroys the hair

179

follicle cells which make the hair fall out and when this happens, it hurts."

Mary creased her brows and asked, "When her hair falls out, it hurts?"

"Yes, the hair follicles have nerve endings that are sensitive and consequently it hurts, she said it feels like a throbbing toothache." Cathy crossed her arms and said, "Jennifer keeps in touch with Susan who gives her additional information on what to expect during treatment."

Jennifer pulled into the parking lot and parked in the open spot next to the picnic table. Mary and Cathy felt their stomachs tightened from sadness when they saw her. This wasn't going to be easy for them, but it was going to be harder for Jennifer.

She opened the car door and stepped into the warm sunlight, wearing a pink scarf tied securely around her head. Mary was sure Jennifer had lost weight in the last few days and her appearance was very pale, indicating she was not feeling well. But she continued to smile as she carried with her a plate of homemade chocolate brownies for everyone.

"Hi, Cathy and Mary!" No matter what her circumstances, Jennifer always tried to be pleasant and happy.

"Oh, thank you Jennifer, I love your brownies!" Cathy cheered.

They walked into the front lobby where, as planned, everyone was waiting. The doors opened, and one at a time people from the engineering department stepped forward to greet her. Mary and Cathy stood off to one side, their hearts filled with emotion as Jennifer visited with all her co-workers. Cathy's eyes brimmed with tears, and in an effort to ease the tension, she whispered to Mary, "I don't think there are enough brownies to go around, do you?"

"No, we should hide them for later." Mary also tried to smile.

It was several minutes before the noise and commotion settled down, and then everyone formed a semi-circle around Jennifer. Duane stood at the front door with Al, Bill, and Kathy. As Mary looked on, she clearly remembered it was less than a year ago when she entered this lobby and met Jennifer for the first time – how quickly things have changed.

Jennifer was thanking everyone for establishing the Jen Possible Team when someone asked if she would be able to walk with the team during the Race for the Cure.

"I hope so," she said. This was the first time Jennifer had to live within the confines of medical treatments and appointments. She stood on her tiptoes, trying to look over the crowd and asked, "Where is Cathy?"

"Right here," Cathy raised her hand and stepped forward.

"I have two announcements." Jennifer clapped her hands and waited for Cathy to join her before she said, "Keith and I are moving to Plymouth. We bought the house behind Cathy and Jim!"

"Praise God!" Cathy stretched her arms to the ceiling.

"And one more thing – " Not everyone knew she and Keith were moving, so Jennifer waited for everyone to stop talking before she said, "This morning the obstetrician called me."

Stillness came over the gathering as everyone held their breath.

She placed her hands on her midriff and announced, "It's a girl!"

*   *   *

It had been a busy day and Jennifer took a long nap after visiting with her co-workers. It was now late at night and there was much to do. She stood in her kitchen smoothing the wrinkled crayon drawing Nicholas had given her last year for Mother's Day. She taped it carefully to the kitchen cupboard, and then, next to the window, she placed last year's handmade card from Natalie.

In less than two weeks, it would be Mother's Day again, and Jennifer couldn't stop her thoughts as they drifted into the future. She would have three children next year and she wondered what sort of celebration would take place in the spring, 2005.

Earlier in the day, Cathy had helped her clear out a few personal items from her workstation. They were things that Jennifer wanted to bring home with her, and after opening the box and removing her children's Mother's Day gifts from last year, she reclosed the lid. There was no point in unpacking as they would be moving in two weeks. She handed the box over to Keith so he could reseal it with tape.

At the same time, Jennifer reminded Keith about the news reporter who telephoned earlier and requested that she be interviewed on a health segment for the evening news. Once again, she asked how he felt about her being interviewed by a local television news station.

"I don't know Jennifer, everything is happening so fast and the last thing I want is for you to become overwhelmed." He looked around their home at piles of clothes and stacks of boxes. "There's a lot to do here and you are – "

"I am what?" she asked.

He taped the box closed and with a thick black pen he marked it for storage in the basement. He slowly exhaled and his shoulders slumped in frustration. He carefully said to her, "Jennifer, you're very sick and setting time aside to be interviewed for local television and newspapers might be too much stress." He capped the pen and placed it on the counter. "Besides, why do you want to be on television?"

"The reason I want to be interviewed is because my story might help other women in knowing they too could be misdiagnosed at an early age." Jennifer told him, "I want others to learn through my experience. I want women to be aware of the warning signs of breast cancer. Maybe if I would have known last July – ”

Keith went to comfort her. He reached out to stroke her long hair but stopped, the memory of its touch was still fresh in his mind. He laid his hands on her shoulders and drew her into his arms and whispered, “This is not your fault.”

“Exactly, Keith, this is *not* my fault and that’s why other women need to know about my story.”

“Is it really that important?” He wanted to understand how she felt.

“Yes, because we’re supposed to help others, and I believe telling my story will help someone.” She told him, “Look at how many people are helping us move, plus look at all the people who are participating in the Race for the Cure on my behalf. There are a lot of people who are helping me, but I’m not physically able to help others in return.”

“No one is expecting you to help.” He taped another box closed.

“But don’t you see, Keith? I can help others by sharing my story and spreading the need for awareness. More importantly, if a woman feels there is something wrong, she shouldn’t be passive, she needs to be bold and get her doctor’s attention.”

Keith stretched his arms to the ceiling and walked over to the couch. He sat down and released a tired yawn. He crossed his feet and placed them on the coffee table. Jennifer sat next to him; she too was suddenly tired. He placed his arm over the back of the couch and said, “You’re serious about being interviewed, aren’t you?”

“Yes, I am very serious and I want you to support my decision. I want to shout my story from the rooftops, I want everyone to hear it because I don’t want anyone else to go through what we’re going through, Keith.”

"You have a valid point." He placed his hand over the tiny swell of her midriff. "I agree with you, Jennifer, I don't want anyone else to go through this needlessly. If you want television crews camped outside our house for the next six months, then so be it."

"Thank you." She kissed him tenderly.

Simba purred at their feet, the children were upstairs asleep and it past eleven o'clock at night. The house was in shambles, boxes were strewn everywhere and their future became more uncertain with each passing day. Very soon, time spent alone as husband and wife would be hard to find and even more precious.

*   *   *

Several weeks later, Cathy and Duane, sat in Senate Coney Island monitoring the front door for Jennifer. Once again they reviewed the list of volunteers to help with moving and were satisfied enough people would be available to help.

"My head is spinning." Cathy rubbed her temples.

"This will work, Cathy, don't worry." Duane was looking over the menu and said, "We have three trucks, six men, plus all the women – we can do this!" He clenched his fist in victory.

"I suppose so," said Cathy, appreciating his confidence, "I promised Jennifer I would help, and now she's literally going to be in my backyard; this is a special blessing."

"I agree it is special Cathy, and God will provide a way for all of us to help Jennifer."

"There she is." Cathy waved to her. "Ah, Duane, I feel so bad for her."

"So do I, but we must not show our concern." He pulled out the chair next to him and Jennifer sat down.

"You guys look terrible, is something wrong?" Jennifer tried to ease the tension with her smile. She knew it was awkward and disheartening for them to see her this way.

"Oh, you're too funny, Jen." Cathy slightly grinned.

"How are you doing, Sunshine?" Duane asked.

"I'm doing okay, but most of the time I feel lousy after a treatment, then a few days later when my white blood cells rebound, I feel much better." She sipped ice water because coffee was beginning to lose its appealing taste. "Before my sessions, the doctors administer steroids which keep me awake, but that's okay because it gives me oodles of energy to pack things for moving."

"We have plenty of people scheduled to help out, so please don't overdo things," Duane told her.

"Is Saturday, May 16, still the moving day?" Cathy, along with many others wanted to confirm the date.

"Yes, Keith gave me the thumbs-up signal before I left this morning, so it's official."

"Good, and you'll be able to move into the house without any major cleaning either," Cathy said, while eating her salad.

Duane finished his sandwich, and said, "We have a team scheduled to paint your home on Pond View Drive once you move out."

"I am so blessed." Jennifer had barely eaten her lunch. She talked about work and how she missed being part of the engineering teams. She missed the way things used to be, the way she thought things were supposed to be. A moment or two passed and she asked them, "Do you have time for a short walk before going back to work?"

Duane and Cathy could never say no to Jennifer, especially now.

When they were through eating Jennifer explained, "One of the drugs I'm taking is known for heart toxicity, so the doctors recommend that I exercise to keep my heart muscle strong."

Duane stretched in his chair and yawned; he had eaten too fast.

Jennifer placed her hand on her midriff and chided him, "Duane, if I can walk, surely you can walk along with me!"

They casually laughed and followed Jennifer to the register. While leaving the crowded eating area, Cathy noticed more than one person staring at Jennifer. The fifth month of her pregnancy had forced her petite frame into maternity clothes and anyone could surmise that not only was she an expectant mother, but she was also a cancer patient.

Cathy and Jennifer walked outside while Duane stood in line to pay the lunch bill. Jennifer was tugging with the zipper to her jacket when Cathy began to laugh at her comical attempt. "Jennifer, your jacket is too small. You'll never get it zipped."

"Wow, that's strange I could zip it just last week." As hard as she tried, Jennifer could not get the metal ends to meet.

"Here, you can wear my jacket." Duane said, shedding it for her.

"Thank you," she smiled.

Duane carried Jennifer's jacket in his hand as they walked along the sidewalk behind the restaurant and through the colonial neighborhoods of Dearborn.

"Jen, you set the pace and the distance," Cathy said.

After they walked two blocks, they came around the corner of the street and a strong gust of wind caught them by surprise. Jennifer quickly grabbed at her toppled scarf. The moment was strained and the heartache from Duane and Cathy was evident.

"I'm sorry my illness is upsetting the people I love." Jennifer walked between them with both feet on the sidewalk while Cathy and Duane straddled one foot on the cement and the other on the grass. "It seems everywhere I go there is a trail of people staring at me, like during our lunch. I know everyone is thinking exactly what I'm thinking." She slowed her pace and said, "They're thinking . . . *'How could this happen? Especially with today's medical advancements and modern technology'?*"

As he listened to her, Duane felt the sting of tears behind his glasses.

Jennifer told them, "There are times I want to speak up and say, 'I agree with you – how could this happen'?"

Cathy stopped walking and directly asked, "Jennifer, I don't believe anyone can completely understand your feelings, but help us to understand a little by telling us what you're praying for."

Jennifer thought for a moment and said, "First off, I admit there are times when I struggle with my feelings, but I can tell you that I'm praying for three things." She gazed through the barren tree branches to the blue sky, and placing her hand over her abdomen said, "Number one: I pray for a healthy baby girl!"

Duane and Cathy nodded in agreement.

"Number two: I pray for a miraculous healing." Tears filled her eyes before she said, "Number three: I pray for God's divine grace to see me through this terrible storm."

*　　　*　　　*

Sue drove in from Chicago to spend Mother's Day with her daughter, Nicole, her sister, Pam, and her friend, Mary. Her first stop was always at Mary's house because she and Mary were early risers and they could visit while everyone else slept. Today would be no different as Sue arrived at Mary's house for breakfast before seven o'clock.

After eating, they continued to sit at the kitchen table and visit. They talked about everything; how their loved ones were doing and how their jobs were going, when Sue asked, "I think about Jennifer all the time, Mary, how is she doing?"

"She is coping well with the chemotherapy treatments and for now she only has a few mild side effects, but she is tired most of the time. The medical staff at Karmanos is taking excellent care of her needs and Jennifer speaks very highly of her doctors."

"It is wonderful that she can go through treatment while pregnant. I'm sure her obstetrician specializes in high risk pregnancies?" Sue asked.

"Yes, and her doctor said the baby's development is normal," Mary sighed.

"It is difficult to understand God's will Mary, and at times like this we need to pray for increased faith in order to trust in His sovereign plan for Jennifer and her baby." Sue folded her hands on the table and said, "Although, I can't imagine being in Jennifer's situation."

"I can't, either."

Sue waited before asking, "Mary, what if this were happening to our daughters, to either Nicole or Jessica?"

"It certainly would be a dynamic test of our faith."

"Yes, it would."

While the thought of helping others through the storms of life lingered in her mind, Mary asked, "Did I tell you that Jennifer and Keith are moving next week?"

"In the middle of all this turmoil, they're moving?" Sue was surprised.

Mary nodded and told Sue about the conversation that Jennifer had with Cathy, regarding the house in Cathy's backyard where the Herders lived, and how Jennifer had envisioned she and Keith living in that home.

"Believe me Sue, Cathy was speechless because the home that Jennifer pointed to was actually going up for sale in a few days, but the real estate agent hadn't placed the home on the market." Mary smiled at the look of surprise on Sue's face and from across the kitchen table, Mary held her hand in the air saying, "Scout's honor, the house wasn't listed yet so the next morning, Keith called the realtor and they scheduled an appointment to look at the home. It wasn't long afterwards when Keith and Jennifer decided it was the right thing to do and they made the Herders an offer." Mary snapped her fingers.

"Isn't it awesome to witness God providing for others?" Sue loved hearing of His miraculous presence in everyday lives.

"Yes, it is wonderful and there is a list of volunteers from Visteon that are going to their home in New Boston next Saturday morning to help them move." Mary stacked their breakfast dishes and carried them to the sink.

"I'm sure you were first to volunteer." Sue placed the cereal back in the cupboard.

"No, I won't be able to help out because Jessica and I are leaving for New York with the Dakota Senior Choir next weekend."

"That's right, Jessica is graduating this year, isn't she?"

*　　*　　*

It was the first of June when Keith and Jennifer began to settle into their new home, and the number of boxes to unpack became less with each passing day. Jennifer was feeling better now that she was closer to her friends and her doctors. It was Wednesday evening and Shari had invited her to the mid-week service at Northridge Church, and she was excited to be going.

"Keith," she stood behind him at the computer desk, "the children are ready for bed and Shari will be here in a minute."

"Are you feeling well enough to go to church?" He watched her reflection in the white glare of the computer monitor.

"Yes," she patted his shoulders.

Natalie snuggled on the couch with her favorite blanket, and Nicholas was climbing onto Keith's lap. At the sound of the doorbell, Jennifer kissed everyone good night, took her Bible from the bookshelf and locked the front door behind her.

In the driveway, Shari held open the car door, and Jennifer climbed into the back seat. Jeff put the car in reverse as Shari introduced them.

"It's nice to meet you," Jennifer said in her musical voice.

Jeff looked in the rearview mirror and smiled; he was surprised at Jennifer's healthy appearance. Although her scarf and hat covered the side effects of chemotherapy, she otherwise appeared to be remarkably healthy, both physically and emotionally. Ten minutes later, Jeff pulled into the church parking lot from North Territorial Road. They stepped out of the car and joined the others who were walking toward the main entrance.

"Jennifer, is it all right with you if we sit in the balcony?" Shari asked as they entered the modern building.

"Yes, the balcony is fine." Jennifer took the program sheet handed to her and placed it inside her Bible.

They found seats in the center close to the upstairs railing. They stood as the worship team came out, and Jennifer clapped hands in rhythm with the Christian music. She was joyfully singing and praising God while being filled with the presence of the Holy Spirit.

That evening's message was centered on the subject of learning how to pray. Everyone was asked to turn their Bibles to the beginning verses in Luke, Chapter 11, and the pastor began teaching the congregation how to pray effectively, focusing on The Lord's Prayer.

Like many Christians, Jennifer memorized the prayer as a child, but never realized the powerful design of the words within the prayer. With the mind of an engineer she jotted down in order the components necessary for effective praying.

First, begin with honor and praise to God; obedience to His Will; asking for God's provision; repenting of sins; asking for forgiveness; avoiding temptation; and closing with praise and giving thanks. Jennifer folded the program sheet and placed it inside her Bible right by the Gospel of Luke.

As the worship music filled the church, everyone was asked to stand and repeat The Lord's Prayer aloud. In one hand Jennifer held her Bible; and with the other, she held Shari's hand. In turn, Shari held tightly to Jennifer, knowing from experience what the rest of the year would have in store for her and Keith. Shari faithfully prayed for their unborn child, the precious baby girl that Jennifer was guarding . . . *with her own life.*

Blushing Knockout Rose
Summer of 2004

~ 17 ~

It was a sleepless night for Kathy since an unsuspecting fever had kept her newborn, Lydia, awake all night. It was six o'clock in the morning before the fever broke and Lydia was resting peacefully, but now it was time for Kathy to get ready for work.

Three hours later, Kathy couldn't stop yawning as she walked down the hall toward Duane's desk. She wanted an update on what the plans were for the Jen Possible Team during Saturday's Race for the Cure.

Duane was reading an e-mail from Jennifer when Kathy stepped into his workstation. He said hello and then read aloud the last sentence Jennifer wrote. '*Statistically I will have to live longer than Moses to repay everyone for their kindness!*'

"Leave it to Jennifer to talk statistics." Kathy stifled another yawn while reading over his shoulder.

"You must not have gotten any sleep last night, is Lydia teething?" Duane asked.

"I think so because she has been up the last three nights in a row with a small fever." Kathy yawned again.

"Stop it; you're making me tired." Duane laughed.

"Hey!" Cathy waved to them and when she got close enough to see Kathy's dark circles, she teased, "Whoa boy, you look tired."

Kathy nodded yes, and Duane asked, "Is Jennifer ready to become a TV star today?"

"Mmm-hmm, a reporter is interviewing her this morning at Karmanos and they plan on using the news clip to promote the Susan G. Komen Detroit Race for the Cure this year." Cathy confirmed the information.

*   *   *

Keith stood next to Jennifer in the treatment room at Karmanos doing his best to stay out of everyone's way. Little did he realize when they discussed this event two weeks ago, that it would ever actually happen.

"Are you cold or just nervous?" he asked Jennifer, noticing her leg bounce.

"I'm nervous and cold." Jennifer watched the medication slowly drip through the intravenous tube and into her system. She raised his hand to her cheek and then softly placed butterfly kisses on his fingers.

"Jennifer, I'm very proud of you." Keith rubbed her back being careful to avoid touching her left arm or shoulder because lately she was in constant pain from the swelling. "What you're doing is more than any woman I know would do for her husband and children."

The television crew worked quietly around them.

"I don't know where you get your inner strength." Keith had not realized he spoke the words aloud until the nurse, Danielle, smiled at him.

"My strength comes from my faith in God." Jennifer said, wishing he had a clearer understanding of God's love for all His children.

Danielle monitored the medication and checked Jennifer's port. She nodded in the direction of the television camera and said to Jennifer, "I see your pretty face is going to be on the local news station today."

Jennifer nodded and sipped cold water from a plastic cup.

Keith watched as the nurse's ebony hands skillfully administered the anti-nausea medication and the stark contrast between the two flesh tones made Jennifer appear very pale. The cameraman tested the flood lights, and while checking the station's video equipment he asked if Jennifer and Keith were ready.

"Yes." She smiled, and they began to film her live chemotherapy session.

The reporter was professional and asked only a few more questions after the filming was complete. WDIV Channel 4 News would show a voice-over video clip of the treatment procedure on the evening news. Danielle was camera shy and had left without a trace of her profile on film; viewers would only see her loving hands. A short time later the treatment room was empty and Keith helped Jennifer down from the examining table.

Jennifer took her clothes from the side locker and told him, "I need to use the restroom."

He walked ahead of her to turn on the light. She told him she would be all right, but he stayed close by since he knew it was an emotional time for Jennifer. Moments later from behind the closed door he heard soft whimpering and knew she was crying. He understood her feelings because their circumstances were difficult to comprehend.

*   *   *

The uncared-for picnic table was covered in cobwebs, but it didn't bother Duane, he sat down anyway. In front of him was yesterday's *Detroit News* paper with an article written by Lila Lazarus: "*Young mom discovers cancer hits all ages.*" He read it twice before Cathy and Mary joined him outside for lunch.

He handed the paper to Cathy, and Mary asked her to read it aloud. After finishing, Cathy gave it back to Duane and said, "Jennifer certainly does want other women to know that age should not be a factor when diagnosing breast cancer."

"Yes, and I'm glad she's taking this opportunity to tell others," Duane said.

Mary asked, "Duane, please read once more what Jennifer told the news reporter about her prognosis?"

He scanned the newspaper column and read aloud, '*Jennifer knows the prognosis is not good.*' Sadly, he refolded the newspaper and set it aside.

*   *   *

Early on Saturday morning, June 5, the Jen Possible Team met at Comerica Park in preparation for the Race for the Cure. All seventy-five members grouped together in a vacant parking lot near the starting line. The team banner was assembled and everyone was wearing matching t-shirts that were bright orange with white orbiting circles displaying the Visteon company logo.

Cathy retied her tennis shoes while her husband, Jim, focused his camera. Their children, Rebecca, Ryan, and Emily, stood close by watching their dad enjoy his hobby of photography. Jim snapped a picture of Duane who was taking a picture of the large crowd. Then the two men grinned at one another through their camera lenses and snapped photographs of each other.

Janis secured the racing form on the back of Jacob and Justin's t-shirts. Kathy made sure Lydia was strapped safely into the baby stroller and she reminded her older daughter, Rose, to stay close by. Kathy was happy to spend the morning with her daughters, walking for a cure.

Al carried the empty t-shirt boxes over to the dumpster while he debated on whether he should walk or run in the race. Mary watched her teenagers, Christopher and Jessica, trade sunglasses. Duane was talking on his cell phone waving toward the east entrance to the parking lot, while he directed Keith and Jennifer to their location on Woodward Avenue.

Stepping out of the car, Jennifer was greeted by the sound of applause that brought tears to her eyes. She held tightly to Nicholas' hand as he tugged on his Tigers baseball cap and looked up at her. He sensed everyone was clapping for his mom. Keith placed Natalie in the wagon and stood next to Jennifer so Duane could take their photograph. Although he was smiling, Keith was certain it was going to be a long and very emotional day.

Jim stood close at the front of the crowd with his camera poised and ready to snap Jennifer's profile at the perfect moment. She wore a pink-and-white print top with white Capri pants and under her pink hat she wore a bandana and incredibly . . . *she was so happy.*

The amount of people that came to show their support helped to lift Jennifer's spirits. She waved to everyone just as Jim snapped her picture and captured a portrait of her that everyone would soon treasure. Moments later, the 2004 Detroit Race for the Cure started. Keith held Jennifer's hand and pulled the wagon behind him that carried their children, Nicholas and Natalie.

*   *   *

Four days before the race, Shari made arrangements for Jennifer to participate in the day's closing ceremony. Lila Lazarus was the spokeswoman for the event, and she planned on interviewing Jennifer and to give the Team Spirit Recognition Award to Jennifer's co-workers. When the race was over, Keith pulled the wagon under a spot of shade near the grandstands, and seated on the bleachers among the survivors, was his pregnant wife. He joined the crowd's applause as Jennifer was introduced and once again, she was before the watchful eye of the camera. As Lila talked briefly about breast cancer awareness and early detection, Jennifer stood next to her and nodded in agreement. Jennifer smiled at the women in the bleachers with hope in her eyes when one of the survivors spontaneously jumped up and blew Jennifer a heartwarming kiss. Jennifer's response was radiant; her smile widened and her cheeks glowed, like a Blushing Knockout rose.

Everyone noticed the woman's spontaneous action and Lila turned to give Jennifer an embrace, and then the crowd rose to their feet in applause. It was obvious Jennifer and her unborn child deserved a moment of special tribute, and the ladies cheered even more when Jennifer wiped her tears and placed her hand over her heart. The clapping soon faded as Lila spoke into the microphone thanking everyone for their support, and then she asked Jennifer to say a few words.

As she looked out at the group of survivors, Jennifer was filled with emotion. She searched for Keith and found him under a tree and he pointed to the wagon that held their sleeping children. Her co-workers waited patiently for her to speak and then, with a shaky voice that was filled with love, Jennifer proclaimed to metro Detroit . . . *"I am lucky – God has blessed me so much!"*

*   *   *

The following week Jim sat in his living room and downloaded the photographs from the race day onto his computer. His respect and admiration for Jennifer was growing every day. He studied her face, the sparkle in her eyes, and her inner glow that radiated toward others. He knew Cathy would want to see the picture, so he placed a printed copy of it on her Bible and then went outside to mow the grass. Cathy stood silently next to him in the driveway and watched him fill the lawn mower with gas.

"What are you thinking about?" he asked.

"I'm thinking about Keith," she sighed. "I was sitting on the back porch a minute ago watching him work outdoors, and I couldn't help but wonder how he is doing."

"I wonder how he's doing too, because this must be hard for him." Jim primed the motor before pulling the cord. "I saw him talking with Duane at the race last Saturday, but for the most part, Keith appears to be content with keeping to himself."

A puff of white smoke coughed through the engine's exhaust. He pushed in the choke until the motor settled and the smoke disappeared. Jim lined the wheels of the mower with the edge of the sidewalk and started cutting the grass.

Cathy walked into her backyard and watched Keith bring out a plastic Cinderella dollhouse onto his patio for Natalie. He wondered if it was the same one he stored in the garage last winter. He examined the paint and the new labels. He swung open the tiny front doors that now moved with ease and he was convinced; it was not the same dollhouse.

Cathy cut across her yard and cheerfully asked him from the edge of his patio, "What are you looking for?"

He didn't turn at the sound of her voice but instead, he tilted the roof of the toy toward him so he could inspect the back. "Jennifer bought a new dollhouse before we moved, didn't she?" he asked Cathy.

"It sort of looks new, doesn't it?" Cathy stood next to him.

"It is new." He turned to Cathy and said, "Jennifer isn't home right now, she's back at the old house with Rima."

"Yes, I know, I came over to visit with you, not Jennifer."

He didn't comment or show any interest in her visit, and he began working on another project.

"How do you like your new home?" Cathy asked.

"It's all right." He kicked at the warped boards on the wooden portion of the deck.

An awkward moment of silence passed before Cathy asked, "Keith, how are you coping with everything, I mean are you doing okay?"

His voice was quick and his words were filled with anxiety. "I'm not sure what you mean, Cathy, are you referring to how I'm coping with two mortgages? Or are you referring to how I'm coping with the stress of my wife having cancer and expecting another child?" The words were said before he could stop himself.

Cathy knew what a difficult time this was for his family. She understood his situation and therefore, she was not offended.

Keith rubbed the knot in his stomach and was quick to apologize, "I'm sorry, Cathy, I didn't mean to lash out at you."

"You don't need to apologize." She knew he was facing a multitude of issues. She glanced over and saw Jim mowing under their swing set. She slightly turned at the sound of Keith's voice.

"Cathy, I want to thank you for all your help." A weary smile of gratitude crossed his face.

*   *   *

Out the corner of his eye, Jim watched Cathy as she quickly cut across the yard. She walked through the patio doors and went directly into the den where her Bible sat next to the computer desk; she knew exactly which scripture she needed to read. The Word of God was her comfort and as a Christian, she must give completely to others the love of Christ. Cathy understood her reward was in knowing her work for the Kingdom was not done in vain.

The colored photograph on her Bible came into focus from across the room. The picture of Jennifer showed a radiant smile and a flawless complexion. With tears blurring her vision, Cathy studied the photograph and realized if it were not for the bandana and the pressure sleeve bandage on Jennifer's left arm, no one would guess the woman in the photograph was seriously ill.

Cathy held the picture next to her heart and prayed . . . *O Lord, you know our petitions before we ask, and I humbly pray that You will bring a multitude of believers into Keith's life. Make them steadfast Christians who will give unselfishly of their time and never grow weary of helping him. I pray his eyes, ears, and heart will be opened to see You working in Jennifer's life. Amen.*

*   *   *

A week after the race, Mary sat at her kitchen table looking over the guest list for her daughter's graduation party. Jessica wanted the celebration late in the summer before her friends left for college. Earlier that morning, Mary had met her friend, Candice, and they talked about the graduation party and how things went at the Race for the Cure. Candice had saved the article about Jennifer from the *Detroit News* and had given it to Mary. They discussed the emotional stress that was facing Jennifer and Keith as a young married couple.

It was hard for Mary to describe to anyone the calm and gracious spirit Jennifer continuously maintained. Although Mary knew there were times when Jennifer privately spoke of her sorrow to Jesus, on the outside for everyone else to witness, Jennifer demonstrated God's love and grace.

Candice had asked her how Jennifer would be able to cope with a newborn baby after her mastectomy, and oddly enough, this was the same question that had kept Mary from countless hours of sleep lately. Tears filled Mary's eyes as she circled Jennifer's name on the party list . . . *Dear God, how can I plan a party for my daughter when Jennifer is fighting for her life and the life of her unborn daughter? There are many unanswered questions, please show me how to be of service to Jennifer, in any way I can – and may it all be done for Your glory. Amen.*

Mary stood and paced the kitchen floor. She was seeking answers to her prayers because there were many what-ifs surrounding Jennifer's circumstances. She reminded herself that God is in the midst of this storm and that He will provide for everyone whom He placed into Jennifer's life at this time. Once again the emotional weight of Jennifer's circumstances lay heavily on her shoulders. The telephone rang, and she answered, "Hello?"

"Oh, Mary, what's wrong?" Sue knew by the sound of her friend's voice that she was upset.

"Sue, I just can't stop thinking of Jennifer and her situation," Mary cried.

"Yes, it is sad, but I believe that God has placed you into Jennifer's life right now for a very special reason."

Mary let out a deep sigh, lately she also felt that God was preparing her in some way to respond to a special need for Jennifer.

Sue's cat, Harley, jumped onto her lap for attention and she calmly stroked him while explaining, "From my perspective, Mary, I see that God has surrounded Jennifer with Christian support. He is giving everyone an opportunity to participate in His plan, and it's wonderful to see

Christians who are obedient to His call and are willing to help Jennifer."

They talked for a long time, and before ending their telephone call, Sue told Mary that she would not be able to attend Jessica's graduation party. She and her husband, Bill, had previously booked a Harley-Davidson motorcycle tour of Europe and it was during the same week of the party. "I'm sorry, Mary, but we will be riding through the mountains in Austria when you are cutting the graduation cake."

"Oh, don't be sorry, I'm happy for you because this'll be a chance of a lifetime, Sue."

"I knew you'd understand." Sue continued and said, "Oh, by the way, did I tell you my sister, Pam and her husband John, purchased two new Harley's?"

"No, you didn't tell me." Mary smiled.

"Pam and John bought the bikes a week ago for their twenty-fifth wedding anniversary – isn't that cool?"

~ *18* ~

Several years ago, Jennifer and Keith went through the process of securing legal guardians for their children. As with any couple, it was a huge step and they were happy when the documents were finalized. But unfortunately, during the last two days those arrangements were altered. Soon after the children's guardians heard of Jennifer's diagnosis and the news of a third child, they began to reconsider their prior commitment to Keith and Jennifer. However, they waited until now to bring the matter up.

The guardians had unexpectedly dropped by over the weekend and immediately the purpose for their visit was clear. Jennifer realized there could only be one reason for their social call because the couple rarely kept in touch anymore. It was not long before they awkwardly approached the subject and asked to have their names removed from the documents. Now, in light of her illness, the urgency to secure another couple as legal guardians was Jennifer's only priority.

It was the third week in June and Jennifer was six months pregnant. She leaned against the cyclone fence while she watched Nicholas play hide-and-seek at Red Bell Preschool. She followed his navy shirt coming and going from behind the wide oak trees. In the far corner of the school yard, Natalie was building make-believe castles in the sandbox with children her own age. It was hard for Jennifer not to think about her children's future and because she loved them so much, she lingered a moment longer, watching them play.

Jennifer spiritually asked . . . *Dear Lord, why are You allowing this added turmoil along with everything else in my life right now?* Sadly, there was no putting off what needed to be done today, so she turned away from the fence and walked toward her car.

The night before, she and Cathy had prayed for a positive outcome to the unfavorable situation that was blindly thrown into her path. However, that didn't stop the nagging question from repeating itself in her mind . . . *Forgive me, but isn't my burden heavy enough?*

Jennifer was terribly hurt and concerned over the legal provisions for her children. But in spite of it all, she refused to walk away from her source of strength. She knew there was a reason for this additional upheaval, and she would place her trust in God. Her left hand automatically twirled the mustard seeds around her neck.

*   *   *

Rima sat next to Bill at the picnic table while Cathy sat across from them. Cathy was grateful they hadn't asked why Jennifer desperately needed to talk with them this morning. She was certain she wouldn't know how to explain the dilemma as her own head was still spinning from the disturbing news. All three friends waited and placed their faith in the promises of scripture. They knew when two or more believers were gathered in His name, His presence would be among them.

Jennifer arrived and walked toward them, thankful they were sitting in the shade. It was odd meeting her co-workers in the parking lot of where she used to work. Bill gave her a hug and she leaned over to give Rima a kiss on the cheek. They asked if she would like to go for a walk, but she declined, explaining it was better for her to sit in the shade and relax. The dark circles under her eyes were evidence of how tired she was today.

Before she began to explain the situation, Jennifer apologized to Bill and Rima for placing them in such a delicate position. She hoped that once she explained her circumstances they would understand and not feel she was asking too much of them. She told them that no matter what their decision was, it would not change their friendship or the love they had for one another.

Bill reached beneath the picnic table and held Rima's hand. Life was not easy, and it is during the hard times, not the joyful times, you discover who your loyal friends are. Cathy was uncomfortable, but she knew Jennifer welcomed her moral support and wanted her to stay and listen.

*   *   *

At first, Jennifer's voice was soft and calm, but toward the end of her story it was filled with emotion and strain. Once she was through, she inhaled sharply and asked Bill and Rima to become the legal guardians for her children.

Bill and Rima sat close to each other. They were at a loss for words but not at a loss on how to silently communicate. Bill gently squeezed Rima's hand and waited for her response. Within seconds she squeezed his hand in return, and their decision was made without a single word spoken.

Cathy broke the long uncomfortable silence and said, "When Jen told me about this, the first thing we did was pray and we know you will also spend time in prayer before you – "

Bill held up his hand to stop Cathy from saying anything more and with spiritual confidence he said, "Yes, Jennifer, we'll be the legal guardians for your children."

"What?" Cathy was stunned.

Jennifer clapped her hands and cried aloud, "Thank you, Jesus," as the heavy weight was lifted from her shoulders.

Cathy reverently whispered, "What an awesome God we serve."

Rima reached out and took Jennifer's hand across the splintered wood of the picnic table and said, "Jennifer, thank you for this honor."

*　　*　　*

It was a serious decision, yet it was made without a moment's hesitation. An hour later, Bill and Rima were driving along the country roads, enjoying the beautiful afternoon and the smooth ride of the Corvette. They had just pledged to be the legal guardians of three children, and they hadn't yet celebrated their first wedding anniversary.

Bill came to a stop at the crossroads, down-shifted into first gear, and before taking his foot off the brake while the roar of the engine engulfed them, he smiled at Rima. "Doesn't God work in mysterious ways?" he asked.

She said yes and folded back the loose windblown strands of black hair that had escaped her long braid.

"Would you like to go out for lunch and celebrate?" Bill suggested.

"Absolutely, let's celebrate."

His foot eased off the clutch as he shifted into first gear, and in no time they were sitting in their favorite restaurant. After the waitress took their lunch order, Bill said, "Rima, you made me proud to be your husband today."

"Why thank you, William, and did you notice that Jennifer asked us to be the guardians of her three children, not just Nicholas and Natalie?"

Bill nodded.

"Lord knows I pray every night for Jennifer's unborn child." Rima refolded her napkin and stared at her lunch plate. "It amazes me how Jennifer remains joyful under her circumstances."

"She does so because she is a living example of God's grace," he said.

"Bill, do you realize that Jennifer's mastectomy is scheduled two weeks after her delivery and then she will undergo five weeks of daily radiation." Rima's eyes flooded with tears and she asked, "How will she manage to go through all this with two children and a newborn?"

"Don't worry. God will place it on someone's heart to help care for Jennifer and the baby."

*   *   *

The chemotherapy unit at Karmanos, although busy, was a restful and quiet place. Jennifer's attending nurse was an expert in his field and she felt blessed every time he administered her medication. "Will any of your friends be coming to visit you today, Jennifer?" the nurse asked.

"Mmm-hmm, I will have two friends visiting with me today: Shari and Mary."

"That's nice because friends help to make the time go by faster." After checking the drip from the IV bag, he left the treatment room just as Shari walked in.

"You're getting so big, Jennifer!" She kissed the top of Jennifer's pink scarf and said, "How are you and the baby feeling today?"

"We are doing fine." Jennifer placed her hand on her midriff.

"Would you like me to get you anything to drink before I sit down?" Shari offered.

"No thanks." Jennifer sipped ice water.

Shari brought with her a large assortment of magazines for them to browse through during the next few hours. Jennifer was so grateful that each one of her friends brought something unique and special into her life. Shari sat down and started to look for the dog-eared pages she had marked the day before.

"We're going to do three things today, Jennifer. First, we will enter a sweepstakes contest, and then we'll learn how to redecorate your attic, and next we'll search the pages for store coupons." Shari was there to keep Jennifer's mind off her illness.

As the morning faded, they discovered the sweepstakes contest deadline expired two months ago. Shari laughed and threw the magazine away. Next, they debated whether or not they would use their attics even if they were nicely decorated. The rest of the time was spent quietly cutting coupons and soon Jennifer was tired, and Shari recognized the signs of weariness.

"Let me get you some fresh water." Shari walked down the hall to the small cafe and bought a chocolate bar, hoping Jennifer would enjoy it after her session. Years ago, Shari remembered experiencing a metallic taste during and after chemotherapy, and she also noticed Jennifer no longer drank coffee. Shari suspected that coffee too, was more than likely leaving an aftertaste so she decided against buying anything. She returned to the treatment room where she found Jennifer fast asleep.

*   *   *

The hospital was very busy and people of all ages, nationalities, and walks of life came through the building because for the most part, cancer has no boundaries and it shows no discrimination when selecting its victims. It was likely to effect in some way, large or small, almost everyone's walk through life.

Today was Mary's first visit to Karmanos Cancer Institute and she had no problem in finding the treatment room where Jennifer waited. She slowed her pace as the somber reality of walking into a hospital's chemotherapy unit struck an emotional chord within her. Mary was fortunate to be healthy and she seldom went to the doctor's office, but the sudden reality of being among other people who were seriously ill was heartbreaking. Oddly enough, Mary was experiencing feelings of guilt about her own health when she saw Jennifer, who was pregnant and undergoing cancer treatment. Shari recognized her standing near the doorway and motioned that Jennifer was asleep. She pointed to the side door, and Mary walked over to meet her there.

"It's good to see you again," Shari said.

"It's good to see you too, Shari, how is Jennifer doing today?"

"She is struggling with her feelings today because unfortunately reality has a sneaky way of settling into your thoughts during a treatment session."

Mary glanced Jennifer's way and sighed, "Yes, I can imagine." She stepped aside so another patient in a wheelchair could enter the room. "I haven't seen Jennifer in three weeks and it's good to see that the baby is growing."

"Yes, Jennifer is so petite that in the beginning it was hard to tell she was pregnant, but now her pregnancy is noticeable."

While Jennifer slept, they visited for a short time in the corridor and Mary thanked Shari for staying with Jennifer in the morning. After saying good-bye, Mary walked into the treatment room and sat in the vacant seat next to her young co-worker.

Mary was alarmed at Jennifer's pale color and the fragile hands that rested on her swollen midriff. Her pink scarf was lopsided, revealing the scalp that she tried so hard to conceal. Over the past several months Mary would share her times of sorrow with Sue and Candice, but she only demonstrated strength and encouragement to Jennifer. She wanted Jennifer to know that she was strong and capable of helping her carry this burden. It was half past two on the television screen when Mary looked at the remaining fluid in the IV bag and estimated Jennifer's treatment was almost complete.

Less than an hour later the nurse came back to disconnect the tubes from Jennifer's port, and although she was awake, Jennifer didn't move, she kept her eyes closed. The nurse rolled the metal stand aside and placed it against the wall where it stood waiting for the next scheduled patient. He told Mary that Jennifer could rest for another fifteen minutes before he would need the chair.

Jennifer remained still, and it was true what Shari had said earlier, Jennifer was struggling with her emotions today. Tears fell from her closed eyes and Mary placed a calloused hand over Jennifer's delicate one. She reached for a tissue, wiped Jennifer's tears and said, "Don't cry, Sweetheart, I'm here for you."

~ *19* ~

It was a humid Saturday afternoon in the middle of August and the guests came to Jessica's graduation party as quickly as the clouds covered the sunshine. Two years ago it rained for Christopher's party and now it was about to rain for Jessica's. What were the odds? The tables were safely under the outdoor tent and decorated with balloons and crepe paper trimmings. Christopher was directing traffic in the street courtyard while Jessica greeted her friends.

"This must be the place," Cathy said, pulling alongside the curb.

"Mmm-hmm, this must be Mary's house!" Jennifer clapped her hands and placed her straw hat over her scarf and said, "My hat isn't too big, is it?"

Cathy tossed her sunglasses on the dashboard and smiled, "Not at all, Jen, as a matter of fact, you look like a movie star."

"Really, which one?" Jennifer was feeling wonderful today.

Jessica nudged Christopher to come with her as she walked out to meet her special guests.

"Hi, Jennifer and Cathy!" Jessica was happy they came.

They hugged the graduate and gave her their congratulations.

Jennifer held onto her hat as she tipped her head back to look at the handsome football player standing in front of her.

"Christopher!" She sang out his name.

He welcomed her with open arms and held her as if she were a fragile baby bird.

"It's so nice to see you again." Jennifer held his hand and said, "Your mother talks about her children all the time and it feels as if I know you and Jessica, personally."

"That's true, Mary sure does like to talk about you guys," Cathy winked at the two young adults.

"Oh yeah, what does Mom say about us?" Jessica asked.

"Trust me, she only says good things." Jennifer's eyes sparkled.

As soon as they stepped into the foyer of the house, Christopher remembered to fill the cooler with ice, and Jessica was pulled away by one of her girlfriends. They left Cathy and Jennifer in the living room feeling a bit awkward because this was their first time visiting Mary's home.

Cathy set her purse on the table and Jennifer looked to her left, she smiled at the man and woman in the den, next to the foyer. Candice was showing Walt the photographs Mary took of her trip to Alaska when she stopped and realized the guest smiling in her direction had to be Jennifer. Candice returned the smile, but her heart was filled with empathy for the young mother.

Christopher came back and handed Cathy and Jennifer a glass of punch and said, "Make yourselves comfortable and I will let Mom know you are here."

"Oh, please don't worry about us because we know Mary is busy," Jennifer said.

"Jen, come over here and take a look at this, will you?" Cathy interrupted them and drew Jennifer's attention to a collection of antique keys displayed on a hidden wall in the living room. "What do you think the meaning is behind all these keys?"

Jennifer carefully studied the assortment of tarnished locks and antique keys, but couldn't come up with an explanation.

From inside the kitchen, Mary heard the familiar voices of her co-workers and she walked into the living room to say hello. As she approached them, she overheard Cathy say to Jennifer as she looked around, "Wouldn't this be an awesome place to recuperate after your surgery, Jen?"

The reason Cathy brought up the subject was because they had talked on the way over to Mary's house, about what Jennifer's plans were for recuperating after the baby's delivery and her mastectomy. Jennifer was honest and told Cathy she had not made any plans yet because she was leaving the arrangements in God's hands.

Mary stepped forward to say hello, and they both turned in her direction.

"I love your home," Jennifer said.

"I do too, Mary, but please explain these keys." Cathy was overly curious.

"Oh, that's such a long story," Mary grinned.

"Please tell us about them, we love your stories," Jennifer said.

Mary hesitated, but then began by sweeping her hand over the collection and explained that first off, no two keys are exactly alike because each one is unique and serves a different purpose. Some of the keys are used for opening jewelry boxes, pieces of furniture, or front doors. While others were railroad boxcar keys, hotel keys or even jailhouse keys. Mary said that not one of the keys could perform the work of another because they all had their own special design and unique purpose. She indicated the largest key which was displayed in the middle, and said, "This key represents God in our lives, and the two locks on either side of it represent my children and their spiritual lives."

The younger women gave her a quizzical look.

Mary smiled and did her best to explain, "All these keys represent God's spiritual blessings and promises to His children." She pointed to the nearest key and said, "For instance, this key is for love, this one friendship, this one wisdom, this one faith, and this one is for trust."

She continued by pointing at many of the other keys and recited more of God's blessings which were equally available to her children, and of course to all of God's children. "You see, all the keys will easily fit into the lock, but the lock will only turn when you have complete faith and trust in the Master Key; only then will the door be opened to you."

"Whoa!" Cathy was surprised at the spiritual comparison.

Jennifer took one of the keys from its hook and asked, "I think I understand Mary, each key serves a special purpose for its Owner, correct?"

"Yes, we all play a special role in God's universal plan," Mary answered.

Jennifer replaced the key on its hook.

Mary held her breath for a brief moment before saying, "Jennifer, I'm glad you were able to come visit my home today because I wanted you to see where I live. I pray your visit today will help you decide on what I am about to offer you."

Jennifer blinked, tilted her head, and shrugged her shoulders at Mary.

"I'm not sure if you have made any arrangements yet Jennifer, but if you have not, I would like you to come and stay at my home after your delivery and during your recovery from the surgery."

Cathy glanced from Jennifer to Mary then back again to Jennifer.

"Mary, do you mean it?" Jennifer asked in a hushed voice.

"Yes, of course, that's if you haven't made other arrangements," she said.

"Actually Mary, I have nowhere to go and I would love to come and stay with you."

"Well then, it's settled, but let me warn you about one thing," Mary smiled. "You can trust my ability to take care of you and the baby, just beware of my ability to cook!"

Jennifer had prayed God would provide her with a tranquil place to rest. She had asked God for a house of refuge where she could regain her strength and bond with her infant daughter and now Mary's front door was open to her. Jennifer held the key in her left hand and Mary's home . . . *would be her home.*

*   *   *

The following Saturday morning, Candice backed into Mary's driveway with an SUV filled with baby furniture, clothing, bottles, toys, and blankets. She was happily delivering to Mary everything Jennifer would need for the baby while recuperating. Candice had borrowed the items from her niece, Stephanie. Mary helped unload the items and in no time her home was transformed into a makeshift nursery.

"I'm so grateful for your help Candice. This is a huge relief knowing things are now ready."

"You're welcome Mary." Candice closed the vehicle doors and asked, "When is Jennifer's due date?"

"She is due the second week in September, but the doctors are very anxious for her to go into labor, they feel the sooner the better."

"Do you think they'll induce labor?" Candice asked.

"I think so, but Jennifer doesn't want them to because she wants a natural delivery," Mary said.

"She is remarkable."

They walked back inside and Mary looked around at the crowded house now filled with baby furniture. Candice followed her gaze and asked, "Are you ready for this?"

"To tell you the truth, Candice, I've been too busy to even think about it." Mary poured them coffee.

"Well, maybe this will help." Candice gave her a daily devotional written by Max Lucado called, *Everyday Blessings*. "Turn to today's date, August 21." Candice sipped her coffee and admitted, "I already peeked at what it says."

Mary found her reading glasses and read the passage marked for that particular day. It was taken from John 2:3, which was Jesus' first miracle, the wedding at Cana in Galilee. Mary read what the author had written, "*Mary was not alarmed over the situation because she knew Jesus would handle things.*"

"So, there you have it," Candice said, "God will handle things for you and Jennifer by making her recovery a peaceful event."

Mary placed her reading glasses down and said, "Candice, thank you for this devotional and all you have done to help. Jennifer will be very grateful because she wants to use her recovery time for bonding with the baby and healing physically." Mary sighed, "She starts radiation three weeks after her mastectomy."

~ 20 ~

It was early on Wednesday morning and time for their scheduled walk. Cathy knocked on Jennifer's patio door and said hello through the screen. After awhile she knocked again, but still there was no answer. She walked along the garage to the front door and was relieved when she looked through the window and saw Jennifer sitting at the computer.

"Come on in," she called out.

Cathy stepped into the living room and for the first time, it struck her how different Jennifer looked now, as compared to when they first met. Jennifer was wearing glasses instead of contact lenses. She wasn't wearing her scarf because it was lost somewhere in the kitchen, and she hadn't bothered putting on any make-up yet.

Cathy hid her feelings of anguish; she glanced at the computer screen and asked, "What are you researching?"

"Statistics on infant birth trauma for induced labor because my doctor wants to schedule me for delivery, but I want to go into labor naturally."

"Why does your doctor want to induce labor, is something wrong?"

"Not with the baby, but they are concerned about me going through the physical stress of labor." Frustrated, Jennifer moved her chair away from the desk and said, "I can't find anything on the Internet."

"Do you want me to try?" Cathy offered.

"No." Jennifer's thoughts were foggy and she wondered why Cathy was at her house so early in the morning.

Cathy recognized her look of dismay and gently reminded her, "Are you ready to go for a walk?"

"Sure, I'll be ready in a minute," Jennifer now remembered.

"Would you like me to make you some coffee?" As she walked into the kitchen, Cathy noticed a basket of laundry and several piles of toys scattered across the family room floor.

"No, thanks." Jennifer was in the kitchen searching for her scarf.

Cathy concealed her look of surprise at the disorder surrounding her. She picked up a board game from the floor and said, "I've noticed you haven't been drinking coffee lately, Jennifer, did the doctor's recommend cutting back?" She placed the game on a bookshelf.

"No," Jennifer yawned. "Coffee tastes funny lately along with chocolate because the medicine from chemotherapy alters your sense of taste, you know." There was a noticeable edge of sarcasm in her voice.

"No, I didn't know," Cathy murmured.

"Here it is." Jennifer put on her scarf and handed bottled water to Cathy. "I'm tired this morning because I was up most of the night with leg pains, so we should only go for a short walk."

They stepped outdoors and Cathy said, "I remember getting leg cramps when I was pregnant with Ryan."

Jennifer looked straight ahead and said, "I don't think being pregnant is the reason for my leg cramps, Cathy. I think something else is causing the cramps along with the increased swelling in my left arm." She waited a moment before she told her, "I found a fourth lump in my left breast last week, which means the cancer is growing – instead of dying."

Cathy's steps faltered, she immediately lost her stride and had to regain her footing, her voice cracked when she asked, "What did your doctors say?"

"They have changed the date of the mastectomy from the first week in October to the third week in September," Jennifer said and kept on walking.

"I'm sorry to hear that, Jen." Cathy whispered.

"It is sad because this means I won't be with my family on my birthday, and everyone knows how much I love to celebrate birthdays, especially my own. Instead of celebrating this year, I'll be at Mary's recovering from my surgery, and on top of everything else, Cathy, this might be my last birthday."

"Jen, please don't say . . ."

Jennifer held up her hand and said, "I have to accept that possibility, Cathy." She was not upset she was simply stating the facts, the statistics. "I also have to make a decision concerning the delivery, but it just doesn't seem fair to force my daughter into this world because after all, none of this is her fault."

"No matter what your decision is Jennifer, in my books you are every woman's hero!" Cathy gently hugged her because Jennifer seemed particularly fragile today. "You have gone through so much, and I think for this decision, you should make the choice that is best for you."

"I have gone through a lot, but it's not on my own strength that I have done this, Cathy." Jennifer softened her tone.

"Yes, I know your strength is through God's grace, however not everyone in your position would have listened and obediently done His will."

They walked in silence and passed several houses before Jennifer said, "Keith and I need to make our decision this morning."

"I think of Keith often, how is he doing?"

"He's privately handling things in his own way," Jennifer chimed with a soft laugh.

"It would be foolish and inconsiderate for anyone to say they understand how Keith must feel," Cathy stated.

Just then a neighbor walked toward them with his dog. But once he saw Jennifer, he nervously cut across the street to avoid saying hello. Jennifer watched him, and after he was out of hearing distance she said, "You know, I went to high school with him, and he used to talk with me all the time, but now he doesn't even stop to say hello anymore." She tightened her scarf and said, "I suppose my appearance makes him uncomfortable, because I'm sure he doesn't know many women his age that are pregnant and have breast cancer."

"It is sad when people don't know how to cope with someone's illness." Cathy half-turned and watched the man carelessly run away.

They walked back toward their homes and Jennifer talked with Cathy about Susan Abraham. She told Cathy they had a chance to visit a few times and that Susan was starting to recover nicely from her surgery and radiation.

Susan was informative and had personally explained many things to Jennifer, mostly about what she could expect during her recuperation after surgery. Susan gave Jennifer some helpful facts about the side effects from radiation and although thankful, Jennifer was sad to have two friends, Shari and Susan, mentor her through the stages of cancer treatment.

*   *   *

Bill selected a cheeseburger and a bag of chips from inside the cafeteria at work. Kathy waved to him from across the cashier's line, pointing to a corner table where she would save him a seat.

"Where is everyone?" Bill asked before he sat down to join her.

"It's the week before Labor Day and most people go on vacation before their children go back to school." Kathy cut into her salad.

"It's already September?" Bill didn't wait for a reply. Instead he opened the bag of chips and asked, "How are things with your family?"

"Very busy. My children, Rose and Jacob, will be in school all day this year – hurrah!"

Bill shook his head in disbelief at how fast Kathy's children were growing.

"That leaves our youngest, Lydia, at home soaking up all the parental attention. She's a blessing to our family because she brings more joy and laughter to our household." Kathy smiled knowing her third child was special. "How are things with you and Rima?"

"Very good, thanks." He finished his soft drink and said, "Rima has offered to help Jennifer with caring for the baby while she goes through radiation." It was heartbreaking for him to say the words: *Jennifer and radiation* in the same sentence.

Kathy knew it was upsetting and encouraged him by saying, "Bill, you and Rima have been a blessing to Jennifer."

"Well Kathy, we're in a unique position to offer this sort of help and not everyone can offer to babysit, although Duane and Janis have offered too."

"Yes, I know and I heard that after Jennifer's surgery on September 23, she and the baby will be staying with Mary for a while."

"Yes, I heard that was the plan." Bill crumpled the empty bag of chips and said, "God has given all of us an opportunity to help, and I think caring for Jennifer after her surgery is a job that Mary will handle with wisdom and love."

Sedum Angelina
Autumn of 2004

~ 21 ~

W ednesday, September 8, Keith turned the car off and
watched others walk through the sliding doors into
the hospital emergency room. He rubbed his face with both
hands, and then wrapped his arms around the steering wheel.
He closed his eyes, leaned forward, and rested his head on
his wrists. His thoughts were reeling as his concerns over
the future were crashing into each other like the space games
he played on the Internet . . . *What if something happens to
Jennifer and I can't cope with the future?*

There were too many what-ifs, and the familiar churning
of his stomach started again. He reached into his pocket for
another antacid tablet. He looked across the front seat at
Jennifer and although her eyes were closed, he knew she
was only resting. He respected her decision for refusing a C-
Section and opting for induced labor instead, but at the same
time he didn't want her to suffer through labor needlessly.
He glanced at his cell phone, it was only nine o'clock in the
morning, and he wished the day was through.

"Are you nervous?" Jennifer asked with her eyes still
closed.

"Not at all, are you?" He didn't want to worry her.

"Not at all." She didn't want to worry him, either.

"Well, let's go then. Can you carry your own suitcase?" he teased.

The hospital staff greeted her at the door and she sat comfortably in the wheelchair that was waiting for her. She recognized each of their familiar faces from the past nine months. Jennifer was wheeled through the glass doors and down the hallway. Keith walked behind her carrying her overnight bag while Jennifer's eyes followed the signs marked . . . *Labor and Delivery.*

* * *

Keith paced outside the treatment room while the nurses prepped Jennifer and in a few moments, they were through. The IV drip to induce labor was administered, and everything was set into motion as her vital signs started to register on the diagnostic equipment. He was grateful that Jennifer and the baby were being closely monitored.

Keith stood in the doorway and watched as Jennifer rested. He recalled how during the last nine months each passing day had been unpredictable. Again, he contemplated his future and what it might be like someday if Jennifer were not with him and their three children. He turned away and walked toward the drinking fountain. He took another antacid, checked his cell phone for the correct time, then turned and went back to be with his wife.

"I thought you might have left and gone back to work," Jennifer smiled.

"I thought about it," he kissed the tip of her nose, "but since I'm such a wonderful guy, I decided to stay and keep you company."

A sharp pain raced across her midriff, and Jennifer instantly started blowing out in short rapid breaths. She held his hand as he timed the contraction on the large overhead clock and forty seconds later, she relaxed.

"Whew, that was fast and strong," she said, surprised.

"This may not take long," he said.

"By seven o'clock this evening our baby will be born," Jennifer prayed.

"I think it will be sooner." He wiped the tiny beads of perspiration from her brow as tears clouded his vision.

Their miracle baby was born just before five o'clock, weighing a healthy six pounds and ten ounces. Jennifer rested peacefully in a private room. Down the hall, Keith stood at the nursery window, amazed at the tightly wrapped pink bundle. He watched the nurse place the name card above the cradle . . . *Baby Girl, Hayse.*

*   *   *

The next afternoon, as Shari walked down the hospital corridor she avoided the temptation to stop at the nursery; instead she visited Jennifer first. She untwisted one of the silver stars from the pink gift box she was carrying, setting it free to bounce in the air. The present sparkled, and she knew it would make the baby's mother smile.

Jennifer sat on the edge of the hospital bed with her feet dangling several inches above the linoleum floor. Her head was bent low and she was softly talking on the telephone. Shari was beyond the doorway before she noticed that Jennifer was crying.

The sound of footsteps caused Jennifer to look up in surprise. Her glasses were lopsided as she struggled to wipe the tears from behind the plastic frames. Shari started to leave, but Jennifer patted the space next to her on the bed, indicating she wanted her close by. Shari placed the gift on the food tray and stepped aside as she busied herself with watering the flower arrangements. She tried not to intrude on the private telephone conversation.

Shortly, Jennifer ended the call and reached for a tissue. Shari was in the bathroom adding fresh water to the bouquet of pink Gerbera daisies and white carnations from the Jen Possible Team. Shari placed the flowers near the window and straightened a pile of magazines before sitting on the edge of the bed to hold Jennifer's hand.

"Did you see the baby?" Jennifer asked between sniffles.

"No, I wanted to see her mommy first."

"She is beautiful Shari, and I'm thankful no surgery was necessary."

"Okay, then why are you crying?"

"I'm crying over Keith." Jennifer took off her glasses to wipe her eyes.

"Don't worry about Keith, he'll be fine, Jennifer."

"I'm not worried about him." She blew her nose and said, "I'm crying because we are in a disagreement over the baby's name."

Shari took the used tissue from Jennifer's hand and teased, "Nine months wasn't long enough for the both of you to decide on a name?"

"Shari, I've known since my first visit to Karmanos what I wanted to name the baby." Jennifer sipped ice water.

"My guess is Keith wants a different name?"

Jennifer nodded while she rubbed her hands.

Shari moved out of the way and said, "You seem cold, why don't you get under the covers?"

Jennifer raised her feet onto the bed and said, "I don't like arguing because it makes me nervous."

"I get nervous when I argue, too." Shari placed an extra blanket over Jennifer's legs and sitting down on the edge of the bed, she asked, "Would you like my opinion?"

"I would love someone else's opinion because I'm tired of making decisions." Jennifer was exhausted.

"Okay, here is my point of view; you have gone through months of stress, Jennifer, not only nine months of pregnancy, but also several months of chemotherapy." She tucked the blanket around Jennifer's feet and added, "And before that you spent eight months of uncertainty with the first group of doctors in trying to make them listen to your health concerns."

Jennifer nodded because she knew it was all true.

"Girlfriend, you have been on an emotional roller coaster ride!" Shari stood up, placed her hands on her hips and asked, "What do you want to name your daughter?"

Jennifer's face beamed, she gave one soft clap of her hands and said, "I want to name her Angelina which means: *Angel from God.*"

"How special." Shari immediately agreed with Jennifer's choice, but to be polite she asked what name Keith preferred.

"Natasha." Jennifer pouted at the thought.

Shari took the pink gift and gave it to Jennifer announcing, "This is for Angelina!" While Jennifer opened the gift for her daughter, Shari thought of the thriving plants that grew along the walkway to her garden at home. The brilliant yellow foliage reminded her of soft young pine trees. It was lovely to look at, soft to the touch, and it was called . . . *Sedum Angelina.*

* * *

The week after Jennifer was released from the hospital she asked Cathy to take her shopping. Between having Angelina and her scheduled surgery, Jennifer wanted to celebrate Natalie's birthday. Cathy massaged the side of her neck since today the pain was close to unbearable. She reached into the cupboard for extra-strength Ibuprofen. She stood at the kitchen sink and let the cold water run while she uncapped the bottle. She took two tablets and quickly swallowed them with a glass of water.

Across the yard she saw Jennifer reach for one of the many prescription bottles that lined her windowsill. Cathy watched through her window as one by one Jennifer took her prescribed medication. Cathy turned off the faucet, grabbed her purse, and walked out the front door.

She drove to Jennifer's house, and in the short distance of two streets, she prayed for physical and emotional strength for the day. It was heartbreaking to watch her friend suffer, and the emotional strain was manifesting itself physically within Cathy. The pinched nerve and the accompanying muscle spasms in her neck had never before been this intense.

Jennifer was outside, ready to leave when Cathy pulled into the driveway and she could tell from where she stood that Cathy was in pain. Cathy held her neck at a peculiar angle and was turning her entire torso to open the car door. Jennifer was glad she knew exactly what she wanted to buy for Natalie and that would make the shopping trip easier.

As planned, two hours later they were home, the birthday gifts were wrapped, and they were outside relaxing in Cathy's backyard. They were enjoying a fresh pot of coffee while Rima watched Angelina.

"Thanks for your help today, Cathy." Jennifer now drank coffee out of pure habit.

"It was my pleasure and what can I do tomorrow to help out with Natalie's party?"

"I don't want you to do anything except come over at four o'clock with your daughters, Rebecca and Emily."

"There's nothing I can do to help?" Cathy questioned.

"No, a few of the neighborhood moms have offered to make a cake and bring the ice cream, and some other ladies have offered to stay during the party to help me out."

"That was very thoughtful." Cathy finished her coffee.

Jennifer set her cup down on the table and said, "Yes, I am very lucky."

Cathy's throat tightened and she couldn't respond because Jennifer's faith and outlook toward the future astonished her at times. She continued to gently rock in her lounge chair.

Jennifer leaned forward and held Cathy's attention with her eyes saying, "I know it's difficult for you to watch me suffer when you know the pain I'm enduring." Jennifer waited before continuing, "Cathy, please listen because I want you to believe me when I say – *I am lucky*." She took Cathy's hand and said, "God has blessed me with your friendship, and I value your dedication in helping me."

"I know you do, Jen." She stopped the rocking motion of her chair.

"But Cathy, I think my circumstances have become too much of a burden for you to carry right now."

She stared at Jennifer, her mouth agape.

"Just listen to me for a moment, because you need to step outside of my life and get some rest." Jennifer patted her hand and smiled, "I'm putting you on a medical leave of absence from my life."

"You're doing what?" Cathy was stunned.

"Yes, as of today you are officially on medical." Jennifer finished the last of her coffee and when Cathy began to protest, she broke in and said, "In a few days I'll be staying at Mary's house with Angelina and while I'm gone, I want you to focus on yourself. Meaning, I don't want you to call me or visit me, do you understand?"

Cathy considered what Jennifer was saying, and perhaps she was right because her emotional involvement was starting to affect her physically. Cathy knew it and so did many others. Her work partner, neighbor, and friend sat across from her and waited.

"Okay, I agree, but only while you're at Mary's."

Jennifer laughed and gave Cathy a thumbs-up.

*   *   *

Keith was upstairs in what Jennifer called her sewing room and what he referred to as his office. The pile of mail from their health care provider was left unopened for too long and Keith dreaded the stack of anticipated paperwork. Nicholas and Natalie were asleep and Jennifer had just finished feeding Angelina. He watched her shadow down the hallway as she changed the baby's diaper and put her down in the crib. He listened as she sang to their infant daughter, "You're such a pretty little girl."

Jennifer left the door ajar to her daughter's room with the small lamp on the dresser softly glowing. She came down the hallway and saw him sitting at the desk. She whispered from the doorway, "Hey, stranger."

Keith said hello without looking up at her.

Jennifer walked in and sat down at her sewing machine. The tiny, odd-shaped room was intended by the builder as a fourth bedroom, but for now it served as a catch-all room. She sat sideways in the chair and watched him open the mail; she knew the majority of it contained her medical bills.

"How are you feeling?" Keith asked as he shuffled through the envelopes.

"Good, how are you feeling?" She loved him so much.

"Good." He was good if she was good.

They sat there listening to the stillness that filled their home.

"I received an interesting phone call today from Karmanos," Jennifer said brightly.

That caught his attention. He turned in the swivel chair toward her and cautiously laced his hands behind his head then asked, "Good news?"

"Yes," she quickly said. "It's good news about the hospital's annual banquet for Michigan Breast Cancer Survivors."

"Oh." Keith returned to opening the mail.

"The hospital is celebrating the Tenth Annual 'Heroes of Breast Cancer' this October and I have been selected as this year's recipient of the *Geri Lester Courage Award!*" Jennifer enthusiastically clapped her hands.

Keith stopped opening the mail and stared at her.

She waited for his response, which was a split second too late, resulting in hurt feelings as she cried, "Why aren't you happy for me?"

Keith was tired, and it took a moment before her news registered in his overwhelmed mind. "Whoa, don't cry, Jennifer." He reached over to her and showed his prize-winning smile before saying, "I'm very happy for you because Karmanos has picked the most deserving *'Hero'* I know of."

"Do you mean it?"

"Yes, of course I do." He patted her knee and asked, "Are you going to be on television again?"

She wrapped her arms around him and admitted, "I suppose so."

"My wife, the TV star."

The sound of a tiny cry came from down the dimly lit hallway. They held their breath and the whimpering soon stopped. Angelina was a good baby.

"What time is your doctor's appointment tomorrow?"

"The first test is eight o'clock sharp since the doctors want new scans and blood work done before my surgery."

Keith ignored the involuntary cramping in his stomach. Jennifer stood to leave since she was tired and knew she needed to sleep while the children slept. She closed the door softly behind her.

~ 22 ~

On September 23, Keith paced the hospital's surgical waiting room from one end to the other. It had been several hours and still there was no word on how Jennifer was doing. He compared the time on the overhead television set with his laptop and the time was correct. He never anticipated her surgery would take this long.

Moments later he looked through the glass doors and was relieved to see Dr. Bouwman walking toward the waiting room. The surgeon made eye contact with Keith and motioned for him to step out into the hallway for privacy. Keith's shoulders dropped as he listened to the post operative report. Their conversation lasted several minutes before Dr. Bouwman clasped Keith's shoulder; he firmly shook his hand and then quickly returned to his medical duties.

       *   *   *

Keith would give anything to go back in time. It was less than a year ago, he was happy – they were happy. Everything was perfect then, but now things were horribly wrong and what he just heard seemed impossible to comprehend. He walked back inside the waiting room for the surgical nurse to come and take him to Jennifer's bedside. Dr. Bouwman said he would be able to see her for a little while, but not for very long.

Keith closed his eyes and watched the fireworks go off inside his mind. He pictured Jennifer sitting next to him on the park bench, her long auburn curls blowing softly in the heat of the Florida breeze. Jennifer was so happy and he remembered how her eyes sparkled when she told him she was pregnant.

He recalled everything about that night: the outfit she wore, the silver shoes on her feet and how they played a flirtatious staccato medley when she walked. He remembered the position in which he was sitting and how his feet were firmly planted on the yellow brick road when she told him. It seemed make-believe now, was this all a fairy tale or was this real?

He took a magazine from the end table and squeezed it into a tight circle. He sat with his legs crossed and tapped it aimlessly against the sole of his left shoe. He inhaled deeply as the alarming outcome of Jennifer's surgery penetrated his thoughts.

During her mastectomy, the surgeons discovered an auxiliary arm of the breast tissue, and this piece of breast tissue had worked its way upward, and had settled underneath her left arm. During the last nine months, it adhered itself to the wall of the brachial artery, using the artery as its source of blood supply – its source of life.

The auxiliary piece of breast tissue was now a malignant tumor that was in a precarious and dangerous position. It was intertwined with nerve endings making it extremely difficult, if not impossible, to be removed. Their hope of hearing a cancer-free outcome after the surgery had vanished with this news.

After months of chemotherapy treatment, suffering, and waiting, and after all the medication and doctors appointments, Jennifer still had cancer. Keith hurled the magazine across the empty waiting room. The pages unraveled one at a time and silently fluttered to the floor. Keith wanted to ask why this had happened, but no one was there to answer him, in his mind he had been forsaken and to Keith, there was no one he could turn to in . . . *heaven or on earth.*

*   *   *

Cathy was the first to know, and once again it was she who ultimately notified the Jen Possible Team. Their hearts, along with their hopes, were shattered as they learned the prognosis was not good for Jennifer. Many prayers were said as people everywhere cried out to the Lord for Jennifer and her family.

Shari leaned against her patio door and gazed out at the backyard. Her eyes burned with the sensation of tears. The news left her stunned since she could hardly believe the unexpected turn of events. She and her husband, Jeff, had met for lunch earlier in the day and before returning to work, he asked her to call as soon as she had any news. She left a message on his voice mail, telling Jeff that the surgery was not as fruitful as they had hoped.

It was nine years ago when Shari was a patient in the same hospital and on the same surgical floor, but the outcome was much different when the surgeon spoke with her husband after her surgery. At that time, Dr. Bouwman shared good news with Jeff and he gave them a very good prognosis for their future.

Yet here she was today, preparing to go back to the same hospital ward to give support and comfort to a young woman she had only known for seven months. Shari was ready for the overnight stay and had dressed casually in a comfortable jogging outfit. Inside her tote bag was a sweater, a few magazines, some note paper, and of course, her Bible.

*   *   *

The light shined softly over Jennifer's hospital bed and Shari was told that Jennifer would be asleep most of the night. Shari glanced across the room and was thankful the second bed was unoccupied. She was thankful not only for the privacy, but more so for the fact that another woman was not going through the recovery stages of a mastectomy.

She walked over to the far side of the bed rail so she could see out of the room and into the hallway. She wiped her fallen tears. She prayed for strength as it was she who volunteered to take the evening watch over Jennifer. As she closed her eyes her mind drifted back to when she was the one lying in bed, recuperating. It was a time, no matter what her age, when a woman wanted her mother to be at her side.

Shari was blessed that her mother had stayed with her the night of her surgery and throughout the following week. Until this very day, her mother was still there for her, long after recovery; however, not all women were that fortunate.

Just like before in the maternity ward, Shari again moved the hospital blanket higher across Jennifer's shoulders. Shari knew Jennifer would want to be covered up because she loved being warm and cozy. Jennifer had soft tufts of hair growing back into place, but for how long Shari could only speculate. She noticed how young Jennifer looked. Shari felt a stranger would hardly guess Jennifer was old enough to be a wife, let alone a mother of three children.

Shari slid her right hand under the tips of Jennifer's fingers; she leaned over the bed railing and whispered to her fellow survivor, "This is what we call the *circle of survivorship,* you live through it, you learn from it, and then you pass it on to others. You see, if we had never been diagnosed with breast cancer, we would never have met each other and Jennifer, you have been a blessing to me from God." Shari took several short breaths before she continued, "You are a little gift that came my way as a result of this dreadful disease." She squeezed Jennifer's hand.

They were sisters-in-Christ and sisters-in-survivorship, and their precious bond would lead them through the storms of cancer. For one day we will all be made whole again to live in God's Kingdom without suffering or pain, without tears and without breast cancer.

*   *   *

When they came home from church the following Sunday the telephone was ringing. Jessica ran for the receiver while Christopher and Mary waited, wondering if it was Keith.

"Hello?" She turned to them and shook her head; it wasn't Keith. "Yeah, Mom is right here, Sue, hang on a minute." Jessica handed the telephone to her mother.

Mary covered the mouthpiece and told her children to get ready for work; she then walked outside onto the deck to sit in the cool afternoon breeze.

"I prayed for you this morning in church Mary. How is Jennifer doing?" Sue asked.

The trees in Mary's backyard were starting to turn color as another season was approaching. She turned the patio rocking chair toward the sun and told Sue about the unfortunate outcome from Jennifer's surgery. It was difficult communicating the sad news.

After several minutes, Sue asked, "Mary, are you saying this tumor lived through several months of chemotherapy?" Sue didn't wait for an answer before saying, "Jennifer's cancer must be very aggressive. Did you visit with her in the hospital?"

"Yes, Cathy and I went to deliver her flowers along with Bill and Kathy. It was awful, Sue, Jennifer looked very pale. She has gone through a lot, and I don't know how much more of this she can withstand."

"Oh, Mary, I'm sorry."

"Jennifer knows her treatment was not successful and she has to start over."

"This is tragic Mary, and I can't imagine how she must feel."

"How can she go through this all over again?" Mary cried.

"Please don't worry because God will provide Jennifer with the strength to endure more treatment," Sue said.

Christopher and Jessica were standing at the screen door, listening to their mom. They wanted to say good-bye before going into work, so they stepped outside and stood next to her.

"Sue, the kids have to leave, and I need to hang up because Keith should be calling any minute."

"I understand." Sue stroked her favorite cat, Harley.

Mary ended the telephone call and gave each one of her children a warm embrace.

"Mom, we have never seen you cry this much, ever." Christopher's eyes were gleaming with tears.

"I know, but these circumstances are very sad and extremely unusual." Mary dabbed her nose and said, "It seems as if Jennifer is constantly under attack from Satan."

Jessica leaned on the deck railing and her eyes were filled with tears as she remembered the cheerful woman she met at her graduation party just a few weeks ago. She found it difficult to describe to others her own age the inner beauty that was simply, pure Jennifer. And when asked, Christopher told Jessica that people have to know Jennifer inwardly in order to appreciate her courage and faith. Mary smiled at him and then placed her arm around her daughter's shoulder and held her close to her side. She kissed Jessica's temple and walked with her down the deck stairs and toward the driveway.

"Come on, Sweetheart, I don't want you to be late getting into work this afternoon." Mary wiped her face with her open palms and said, "Look, the sun is shining and it's a gorgeous day. It's Sunday, the day the Lord has made." She took her son's hand and told him, "We need to place our trust in God and not be overcome with sadness."

"You're right, Mom, especially while Jennifer is staying with us because she'll know the reason why we're crying, and that would only make her feel terrible," he said.

There were times when her son's maturity and foresight amazed Mary.

Jessica finished tying her tennis shoes and said, "But, it's hard to smile when your heart is breaking."

~ 23 ~

Jennifer was relieved to have the mastectomy behind her, to have Angelina in her arms, and to be out of the hospital. For now, her objective was to regain her strength so she could continue to fight. She sat peacefully in the warm sunshine at the kitchen table, and while Mary fed Angelina, Jennifer enjoyed a bowl of homemade soup.

"Where are your children?" Jennifer asked.

"They're at work and won't be home until later this evening." Mary wiped the formula from Angelina's little mouth.

Jennifer placed her napkin on the table and relaxed in the chair. The warmth of the afternoon sun was making her drowsy. Mary watched Jennifer's movements and was grateful to see her using both arms.

"Would you like more soup?" she asked her.

Jennifer smiled at her baby and said, "No thank you, but I think Angelina needs to rest."

Mary whispered to the sleepy infant, "Your mommy wants you to take a nap, and I think maybe your mommy should take a nap, too."

Jennifer agreed, and before placing the baby in the bassinet, Mary brought her to Jennifer's side. She leaned over to kiss her daughter on the forehead. Mary then placed her in the bassinet and covered her with a light blanket.

"Okay, you're next." She helped Jennifer into the bedroom where Mary drew the blinds closed and eased Jennifer onto the bedspread. She laid the afghan over her shoulders and asked, "Do you need any pain medication?"

Jennifer moved her head from side to side, indicating she was fine.

"Can you reach this?" Mary moved a glass dinner bell to the edge of the nightstand.

Jennifer smiled and said yes.

"Good, because when you're ready to get up or if you need something, just ring this bell, and I will come and help you."

"Thank you." Jennifer quickly drifted off to sleep.

*   *   *

For the next few days, the Richardson household was quiet, and Jennifer made exceptional progress toward recovery from her surgery. God's presence was with her and her tolerance for pain was remarkable. Jennifer's courage was beyond explanation, and the love she gave to Angelina was immeasurable. Never before had Mary witnessed such selflessness. It was clear Jennifer possessed motherly love and wisdom beyond her years. Yet something else took place that had changed Jennifer from within, her level of faith and understanding was far deeper now than before.

All in all, the makeshift family of five, blended by God's loving hands, managed quite well during the temporary living arrangements. Everything she could have possibly wanted was at Jennifer's disposal, and Angelina was cared for to the point of being spoiled. Everyone lavished her with love and attention. Jessica marked on the kitchen calendar several "Spa-Time's for Angelina," and with her mother next to her, Jessica would bathe, powder, and pamper the newborn baby. Angelina was indeed an angel from God.

Christopher quietly tiptoed around a household occupied with females. His six-foot-two, husky frame was unmistakably noticeable everywhere he went. Yet it was his gentle hands and kind heart that were first to react when the cries from Angelina sounded throughout the small home.

Jennifer was pleasant, cheerful, and extremely grateful. It was difficult to comprehend that in less than three weeks she had delivered a baby and underwent extensive radical surgery. Each day a trace of color brightened her cheeks, and the ability to do small things on her own gradually returned.

Mary continuously thanked God for His provision over Jennifer and the baby while under her care. She recognized the power of prayer and knew others were also praying, asking God to protect her household. And yes, Angelina was awake every three hours wanting to be fed, which kept everyone very busy; however Jennifer's needs were minimal. What Jennifer wanted most was to spend time in prayer and in Christian fellowship with Mary and they did so without ceasing.

Jennifer rocked her daughter while talking about God's plan for her own life. She told Mary of her personal testimony and at what age she had surrendered her life to Christ. Jennifer was twenty-six years old when she began a personal relationship with Jesus. She told Mary that as a child she would listen to her Grandmother Catherine read her stories from the Bible. It was during those tender years when a tiny seed of faith was planted in Jennifer's heart.

Mary knew Jennifer was filled with God's grace and the powerful balance between faith and survival were monumental to Jennifer. Her will to survive was second only to her desire in accomplishing God's purpose for her life . . . *whatever that might be.*

*   *   *

Early in the evening, on September 29, Jessica finished frosting Jennifer's pink birthday cake. A white lopsided heart was outlined in the center, and in the middle the number thirty-three was written. There were three gifts stacked near a wicker basket that was filled with eighty-five birthday cards, all of them where for Jennifer.

Christopher gave a gentleman's whistle when Jennifer walked into the kitchen because today she was feeling well enough to be dressed and out of her bathrobe. She was wearing a blue flower print blouse with khaki slacks. She had taken off her glasses and was wearing contact lenses, and a small touch of blush was applied to her cheeks.

Jessica sang from the table, "Happy Birthday!"

Jennifer gave Jessica, who was a head taller than her, a warm embrace and said, "My birthday cake is beautiful!"

"I hope it tastes better than it looks," Jessica admitted.

"Is this all for me?" Jennifer asked, looking at the table.

Christopher turned to his mother with a look of bewilderment and with his eyes he asked; *"Doesn't Jennifer know how special she is?"*

While Mary warmed the baby's bottle she said, "Jennifer, it has been wonderful having you and Angelina in our home."

"Mary, I'm happy we became friends, but I'll never be able to repay you for your kindness."

"I don't expect you to ever repay me, Jennifer, because this is what Christianity is all about." Mary took Angelina from the bassinet and said, "Besides, this little one has been a blessing to my family."

Christopher pulled out a chair for Jennifer and said, "Sit down and open your presents!"

Jennifer untied the pink ribbon from the first small box and inside it there was a butterfly brooch, and on its wings sat a tiny gold angel. "What a perfect gift." She placed her hand over Christopher's and thanked him.

Next, Jessica gave Jennifer her gift. It was a wind chime with a cross in the middle. Jennifer waved the pipes, and the jingle caused Angelina to turn from Mary's arm and gaze toward the direction of the sound. The last gift was from Mary; it was a glass angel carrying in her hands the September birthstone, a dark blue Sapphire.

"Do not forget to entertain strangers, for by so doing some people have entertained angels without knowing it."
Hebrews 13:2

*　　*　　*

Later that evening, everyone was gone except for Jennifer and Angelina, and when Keith rang the doorbell, Jennifer waved for him to come inside. He crossed into the living room and sat next to her on the couch. He missed his wife and was happy to see her looking well and rested. He said hello and wished her a happy birthday. Jennifer asked about Nicholas and Natalie and Keith told her they were fine but they missed their mommy, terribly. They leisurely talked about everyday things and an hour later, when there was nothing more to say other than the obvious, it was Jennifer who brought up the subject.

"My appointment at Karmanos is Friday morning at eight o'clock."

Keith remained silent as he stretched his arms across the back of the couch.

"I don't think Dr. Bouwman is going to have good news for us." Jennifer's tears began to fall and she continued, "If the tumor under my left arm is inoperable, then what else can be done for me, Keith?"

"I don't know, Jennifer, we just have to wait and see." He stared at the ceiling.

She turned sideways to face him and said, "Keith, do you understand this might be my last birthday?"

"Come on, Jennifer, don't say that." Yet, Keith understood the truth behind her words.

"I desperately wanted to be cancer-free after the mastectomy." She laid her head on his shoulder and wept.

*   *   *

Two days later, at five o'clock in the morning, Angelina fell back asleep after finishing her morning bottle. Mary watched the sunrise through the family room window and wondered if Jennifer had slept well last night.

The evening before, they sat together in the den until after eleven o'clock. Jennifer read aloud to Mary all the birthday cards she had received and before going to bed, Jennifer placed them back into the wicker basket, except for one.

Susan Abraham's card stood alone on the coffee table and on the inside she wrote congratulations on the birth of Angelina along with words of encouragement for Jennifer. Susan told Jennifer that during her own cancer treatment, she realized how precious each day was and that no matter what the day brought to simply rejoice and be happy in it. Susan noted Psalm 118:24 at the bottom of the birthday card.

A few hours later the sun was shining and Jennifer was finishing her breakfast while Angelina continued to sleep. Mary placed inside the car Jennifer's backpack which was filled with medical notes and diagnostic procedures to carry with them to Karmanos. She was certain it was going to be a long day and when she came into the kitchen from the garage, she found Jennifer crying at the table. Mary ran to her side and asked, "Jennifer, what's wrong?"

"Today isn't going to be a good day, Miss Mary, I just know it." Jennifer cried and wiped her tears with a napkin.

"I don't want to go and see Dr. Bouwman because I'm tired of hearing bad news."

~ 24 ~

It was after dark before they returned home from Karmanos. Jennifer was emotionally stunned and physically drained. Mary led her into the bedroom and Jennifer hardly allowed her shoes time to drop to the floor before she curled up on top of the bedspread. Mary covered her, drew the blinds closed, and softly shut the door.

Throughout the course of the day, weakness overtook Jennifer's mind and body and now she was completely distraught. During her surgery, the discovery of the hidden tumor was more devastating, more critical, than anyone had imagined – except for Dr. Bouwman, her surgeon.

Mary walked into the kitchen and opened the cupboard to reach for a bottle of Tylenol. She leaned against the counter and covered her mouth with both hands, stifling her cries of sorrow. The day was beyond her comprehension, and she could not believe the drastic aftermath from Jennifer's surgery. In her mind, Mary kept hearing the medical option given to Jennifer that day and it seemed a choice that was beyond the human scope of endurance . . . *Dear God, Jennifer has gone through so much, how can she make this choice?*

Jennifer had been coping remarkably well with the emotions of postpartum blues after her labor and delivery. Additionally, two weeks later she underwent the traumatic surgery of a double mastectomy. Again, she was dealing remarkably well with all these devastating changes in her life, but the choice placed before her today seemed terribly unfair.

As a young and loving mother, Jennifer was not able to hold Angelina to her breast and nourish her the way she did Nicholas and Natalie. The natural bonding and nurturing God designed for motherhood was cruelly taken from Jennifer and Angelina. In light of all this, Jennifer still had to make another life-altering decision. After talking with Dr. Bouwman, she understood that another operation was the safest option regarding the malignant tumor under her left arm, but it came with no guarantees of increasing her chances of survival because with or without additional surgery, Jennifer's prognosis was terribly grim.

The doctors discussed the tumor under her left arm and its precarious location. There was no doubt the tumor was dangerously intertwined and tangled amongst the nerve endings that traveled down her left arm. The surgeon's remorse was evident as he explained to Jennifer that the medical recommendation was to amputate her left arm.

*   *   *

On October 5, two weeks after her mastectomy, Jennifer walked on stage at Penna's of Sterling Heights. Once again she was in the camera lens of the media as local radio hosts and television personalities jointly presided over the formal dinner benefit.

Jennifer spoke with Lila Lazarus who was the emcee for the evening's fashion show segment at the Tenth Annual 'Heroes of Breast Cancer' awards ceremony. Shari Franko was also there and she lovingly applauded as Jennifer stood at the podium to receive her award. Jennifer was honored to be the recipient of the Geri Lester Courage Award because for many years, Geri played a key role in providing educational services to the metropolitan Detroit area. Jennifer's closing words to her speech were no surprise to anyone as her message was always clear . . . *"If you suspect something is wrong, get a second, even a third opinion."*

* * *

The next few months were exhausting and physically draining for Jennifer. Since the tumor was untouched by previous chemotherapy, a more aggressive combination of medication was being administered. Her system was under attack, and understandably, this left her with very little energy and minimal strength. Besides the cancer treatment, she was going through rehabilitation after the mastectomy because she needed to increase the range of motion in her left arm before radiation could begin.

The Jen Possible Team membership spread throughout the city of Plymouth like the wings of a butterfly. The many volunteers included Jennifer's neighbors, public school teachers, business owners, and local churches. Everyone began to offer their support and prayers.

Cathy handled all the school and daycare schedules for Nicholas and Natalie. She coordinated with neighbors in helping to drive the children to dance classes and Cub Scout meetings. Bill and Rima alternated weeks of babysitting with Duane and Janis in keeping Angelina at their homes, both day and night.

* * *

It was mid-November when Mary came to spend the day with Cathy at Jennifer's house. Jennifer slept restlessly on the sofa bed in the family room while they picked up the toys from the living room floor.

"Jennifer is spending most of her time sleeping." Cathy spoke in a hushed voice to Mary. "The tumor in her arm is causing a lot of pressure on her nerve endings, and she is taking pain medication now that she avoided taking while she was pregnant."

Mary ran her fingers through her hair and said, "This is not good, Cathy."

Just then, Cathy was about to say something when Angelina woke from her nap. Mary took her from the crib while Cathy warmed a bottle, but the sound of the infant crying woke Jennifer from her rest and she started to move.

"Jen, we'll take care of Angelina, you don't need to get up," Cathy told her.

Nevertheless, Jennifer swung her feet over the side of the mattress and said, "All I do is sleep." She searched for her bandana under the pillow and blindly placed it over her scalp. "Who else is here, Cathy?" She looked for her glasses.

"Hi, Jennifer," Mary answered.

"Hello, Mary." She got up and slowly walked into the downstairs bathroom.

Cathy handed a clean baby outfit to Mary so she could change Angelina after feeding her. A few moments later, Jennifer shuffled into the kitchen and sat at the table.

Cathy opened the refrigerator and asked her, "Would you like spaghetti or baked chicken for lunch?"

"Neither," Jennifer yawned.

"You have to eat something, Jen." Cathy stood with the refrigerator door open.

"Everything I eat leaves me with a funky metallic aftertaste," Jennifer frowned.

"Are you using plastic utensils?" Mary asked.

"No, why?" Jennifer was puzzled.

"It helps reduce the aftertaste, remember?"

On cue, Cathy rummaged through the kitchen drawers for a plastic fork and spoon. She brought out a box, laid it on the table, and reheated the leftover spaghetti.

The telephone rang and Cathy handed Jennifer the cordless receiver. It was the pharmacy needing to verify her prescription. "Yes, this is Jennifer Hayse, and the prescription is for me. When can my husband pick it up?" Jennifer was becoming agitated as she drummed her fingers on the table while shaking her head back and forth. "Why not?" she bluntly asked the person on the other end of the telephone line and with her left hand she twirled the mustard seed pendant around her neck.

"Fine, what time will the prescription be ready?" She was not happy.

Cathy and Mary exchanged worried glances.

Jennifer tossed the telephone on the table and said, "Nothing is easy anymore."

"I'll run to the pharmacy for you, Jennifer," Cathy offered.

"No, you can't because I have to go myself in order to sign for it."

"That's odd; what kind of insurance do you have?" Cathy asked.

"It's not my insurance company." Jennifer explained, "The prescription is for morphine, and because it is a controlled substance, the pharmacist can only release it to me."

Mary cradled Angelina in her arms while Cathy sat next to Jennifer.

"I can't tolerate the pain in my arm any longer," Jennifer stated in a tense voice, "and you might as well know that I can't climb the stairs without an oxygen mask." She tried not to notice the look of shock on their faces.

Mary and Cathy felt terrible as the words *morphine and oxygen* shipwrecked their hope.

*   *   *

It was the beginning of November and Shari was grocery shopping. She took the next available cart and made her way down the first aisle of Kroger before she dialed Jennifer's cell phone.

"Hi, Jennifer, don't look outside because I'm not in your driveway."

"That's good Shari, because I'm not home." Jennifer was grateful for the many times Shari would stop by the house, just to check on her.

"Where are you then?" Shari asked.

"I'm at Kroger with Angelina."

"So am I! What aisle are you in?" Shari looked around.

"I'm in the produce aisle," Jennifer said, as she looked for Shari.

"Stay put and I'll be right there." Shari wheeled the cart down the next two aisles and spotted Jennifer right away with Angelina sleeping peacefully in her car seat. "Oh, she is beautiful, Jennifer." But the smile on Shari's face disappeared when she saw the portable oxygen kit next to the sleeping infant.

"Yes, she is beautiful." Jennifer appreciated the compliment.

"I'm so happy to see you Jennifer. How are you doing?"

"I could complain, Shari, but it won't do any good." She moved her cart along.

"Go ahead and complain if you want, I will understand." Shari reached for the lettuce and asked Jennifer if she needed any.

She said no. She only needed milk and some baby food, and as they walked along they caught up on recent news. They turned down the infant food aisle, and before Shari could help, Jennifer reached for a box of baby cereal, and without thinking she used her left hand. Wincing in pain she closed her eyes. Shutting off the flow of tears, Jennifer instantly squeezed her left shoulder with her right hand. It was because she was left-handed that she automatically reached for things with the hand she used most often. "Careful, please let me get it for you." When Shari placed the box in Jennifer's cart she saw the agony etched on her face and asked, "Will you be all right?"

Jennifer gave her a slight nod and although she did the exercises prescribed for her rehabilitation, there were times when she overexerted herself and the result was a muscle spasm in her shoulder. "Cancer is such an inconvenience," Jennifer said with frustration.

She told Shari she was getting used to the numbness in her fingertips that was caused by the nerve blockage, but even so, she often strained her shoulder when trying to extend her left arm over her head.

Shari helped her through the cashier line and out into the parking lot. She placed Jennifer's groceries into her SUV and belted Angelina in place, who was now awake. "I'll follow you home Jennifer to help you unpack," Shari offered.

"No, that's okay because I have to stop at the pharmacy and besides, Cathy is coming over for a short visit. She will be there to help me and if not, these few groceries can stay in the car until Keith gets home."

Shari hugged her and waved good-bye as she watched Jennifer pull out into traffic. The pain on Jennifer's face as she reached for the cereal box had frightened Shari because she knew the pain was not a sign of recovery.

October Glory
Winter of 2004

~ 25 ~

It was the week after Thanksgiving when Al walked toward the engineering conference room. The meeting was scheduled for nine o'clock and everyone was sitting down waiting for him. Al walked in, glanced at his agenda, and then abruptly said, "We have a lot to cover this morning, so let's get down to business." He didn't say hello or look directly at anyone, which was very unusual because Al was such a respectful manager.

His employees followed his lead as he set the tone for the meeting, and after delegating several new assignments, Al closed his planner and brought out a separate sheet of paper. Everyone could sense that something must be wrong.

"We have good news from Susan Abraham," he said. "She is finished with her cancer treatment and Susan hopes to return to work in the next few months."

The room cheered and he added how grateful the Abraham family was for all the prayers and cards that were sent to Susan. He checked his notes and then waved in Cathy's direction.

"I want to give everyone an update on Jennifer. I talk with her daily and see her often. She wants to make sure everyone knows how much she appreciates all we've done because she understands we are extremely busy with our personal lives, yet we have found the time to help her family. Additionally, I would like to say that none of us have a boat load of free time on our hands, either." Cathy gave a nervous laugh before she continued, "However I look around this room, and I see many of the same faces at every event held for Jennifer and she thanks you!" The color in Cathy's cheeks darkened and she became more serious. "Jen is not out of the woods yet and she wants all of you to know that she loves you and it saddens her to tell you that she will not be returning to work."

Duane glanced across the table at Mary while Bill drummed his fingers on the arm of his chair.

"Jennifer wants you to know she appreciates your support." Cathy tucked her hair behind each ear and said, "For those of you who may not know, she is undergoing a second round of chemotherapy followed by radiation, all in the hopes of killing, or at least reducing in size, the aggressive tumor under her left arm."

"What if the second attempt at treatment fails?" someone asked.

"Jennifer is praying it will work because to her, the only medical option at this time is not feasible. She plans to send an e-mail to everyone before Christmas which will explain her circumstances in further detail. As always, Jennifer wants to remain open about her cancer, her medical condition, and her treatment."

Cathy placed her elbows on the conference table and crossing her arms in front of her, she said, "Jennifer is very ill, she still has cancer, and the tumor is causing her a great deal of pain and she wants more than anything for all of us to continue praying for her."

Al waited until Cathy was finished before he began again by saying, "I know this is the Christmas season, and it's supposed to be a joyful time of year, and I would like more than anything to end this meeting with good news, but unfortunately I cannot."

Everyone glanced about wondering what was going to be said.

"Kathy Walsh – " Al stopped anticipating there would be interruptions.

"Kathy?"

"What has happened to Kathy?"

"Quiet down everyone and just listen." Al lowered his hands and said, "Kathy has rearranged her work schedule to coincide with doctors appointments for her baby daughter, Lydia, who is in the hospital."

The group of engineers braced themselves for more unhappy news.

"Last week over Thanksgiving, Kathy's husband, Bob, noticed a small bump on Lydia's tailbone. They took Lydia to see the family doctor who referred them to a surgeon. The pediatric surgeon ordered an ultrasound which showed the lump not to be cystic. Consequently, Lydia was immediately admitted to the hospital."

"She's only a baby," Duane murmured.

"The following day an MRI confirmed it was a tumor, and Lydia underwent surgery a few days ago to have it removed."

"Will she be all right?" Mary asked.

"I believe so, but let me read what Kathy wrote." Al adjusted his reading glasses and read from her e-mail, *'The tumor was found to be a malignant germ cell tumor, and since the margins were not clear, the doctors have recommended chemotherapy.'*

"Chemotherapy for a small baby?" someone asked.

Bill cleared his throat and said, "I talked with Kathy this morning and Lydia is home right now, but she will be going back to the hospital tomorrow to begin her treatment. Lydia will stay in the hospital for the next two weeks, but she is expected to be released on Christmas Eve." Bill waited before adding, "Kathy did say that the chemotherapy will start up again the first of the year."

Al explained that Kathy would be available for any work-related issues, but he asked that everyone first go through Bill to resolve things and only if necessary, Bill would contact Kathy.

"Is there anything we can do?" Duane asked.

Bill answered him, "No, she wants everyone to keep their focus on helping Jennifer. Kathy jokingly told me that she doesn't want the Jen Possible Team to fall behind while she's out of the office."

*   *   *

The 2004 Christmas season melted as quickly as a light dusting of snow will melt in the warmth of the sun. It was now three weeks into the New Year and Jennifer sat among storage boxes in her living room where she was placing holiday ornaments back into containers for the following year. She reminisced over past holiday celebrations in her life, beginning when she was a child to a young teenager, and now as a wife and a mother. She placed the Disney ornaments into their velvet boxes – how many of these keepsakes did she have and who would take care of them if she were not here next year?

The clock kept ticking, the months on the calendar kept turning and with each new day she found herself slipping further into the unyielding grip of breast cancer. The recent test results confirmed what she already suspected; her cancer was growing – it was now categorized as . . . *Stage IV*.

There were multiple large masses identified in her recent CAT scan and going through radiation and additional chemotherapy simply was not enough. The tumor in her arm, although smaller in size, was still active; it was shrinking, but it was not being destroyed. Last week the final results from the radiology department were given to Dr. Bouwman at Karmanos and Jennifer knew without asking the report was still in favor of radical surgery to amputate her left arm.

At the sound of the doorbell, Jennifer stood to let Mary inside, but she didn't stay in the foyer. As she walked away from the cold outside air, she warned her, "Watch your step, Mary, because Simba is somewhere underneath these boxes." On her way back to the couch Jennifer moved one of the Christmas boxes hoping to find the cat, and sure enough Simba darted between Mary's feet and went down the basement stairs.

"That is one big cat!" Mary jumped out of his way.

"He is getting fat, isn't he?" Jennifer gave a weary shrug.

Mary glanced around the living room. There were open boxes everywhere leaving little room to stand. "Where do you want me to begin?" she asked while rolling up her sleeves.

"You can hand me the ornaments from the top of the Christmas tree." Jennifer pointed and said, "Then I'll find the matching gift box for each one either in here, or over there in the dining room."

Mary knew she would need to identify things, so she felt for her reading glasses inside her sweater pockets.

Jennifer watched Mary bring down a few of the ornaments when she suddenly became frustrated and overwhelmed with the task. "I shouldn't have put up so many decorations, but I wanted this year to be special – " She sniffled and reached for another Disney character and said, "Because next year I may not be here for Christmas." Suddenly, Jennifer dropped the ornament onto her lap and she began to tremble with uncontrollable sobbing.

Mary quickly went to her side and with mounting tears of her own, she said, "Jennifer, please don't say such things."

She crouched down near the couch and placed her hand on Jennifer's knee.

"Oh, don't pay any attention to what I say, Mary, because my hormones are swinging drastically ever since the mastectomy." Jennifer had told Mary months ago the surgery had thrown her system into early menopause.

"Let's work on putting away the Christmas ornaments later," Mary said, taking the box from Jennifer's grip and holding her hands. "Right now I think you should tell me what's troubling you."

Jennifer slumped back into the couch and her shoulders sagged under the heavy weight of emotional stress. Again, Mary wondered how much more of this storm Jennifer could endure. She held tightly to Jennifer's hands and listened while she explained the results of her recent CAT scan.

"I prayed God would use radiation to perform a miracle," Jennifer wept.

Mary felt sick to her stomach and didn't know what to say because everyone had been praying for the same miracle.

"I want to know the reason for my suffering!" Jennifer cried aloud and took the colorful scarf off her scalp. She roughly wiped away her tears. She crossed her legs and tucked her feet under each knee. "I want to know – " she sobbed. "Why, all of this – " her breaths were short and quick. She swept her hands over her chest and pointed throughout her home at the disarray and disheveled life she was living. The magnitude of her feelings were so intense that they prevented her from completing her own thoughts. She slammed her tiny fists onto her bent knees and shouted, "I want to know what possible good-thing there is behind my suffering?"

There it was – the stone wall Jennifer had built around herself began to crumble and her tears fell like rain. With short, rapid intakes of breath she filled her lungs and exploded with verbal emotion, "*I have sacrificed so much!*"

Her cries echoed throughout the house and Mary had to raise her voice in order to be heard, "Jennifer your suffering has had great significance!"

"But I didn't do anything to deserve this!" She bounced her head several times against the back of the pillowed couch. Her hands were still clenched into tight fists.

Mary sat next to Jennifer, cradling and rocking her as they both cried. Mary knew verses of scripture, and she would share them with Jennifer later, but for now she simply let her cry.

*   *   *

Hours later, the ornaments were stored away in the basement, and the house was somewhat neater. Jennifer and Mary were sitting in the kitchen sharing coffee and scriptures from the Bible. Jennifer was calmer and felt much better. She listened to Mary say, "Jesus suffered unspeakable pain, and He did nothing to deserve His suffering, Jennifer."

"Yes, I know, He suffered so much for all of us." Jennifer slowly rocked back and forth.

"Jennifer, listen carefully to what I'm about to say." Mary waited for Jennifer's full attention before she continued, "I'm not in your situation, therefore I'm unable to completely understand how you must feel, but I know the Word of God and I trust in Our Lord when He tells us that as believers we must share in His sufferings." Mary swallowed the lump in her throat and said, "We are called to believe in Him and to suffer on His behalf, like the Apostle Paul explains here in Philippians 1:29, 'For it has been granted to you on behalf of Christ not only to believe on him, but also to suffer for him'."

"Cathy quoted the same verse to me yesterday." Jennifer wiped her tears.

They continued to sit, knee-to-knee with the open Bible on Mary's lap. Jennifer squeezed Mary's hand and said, "Find another verse for me, please." Jennifer bowed her head.

"It takes an abundance of faith to understand this Jennifer, but the first book of Peter 4:12 reads, 'Dear friends, do not be surprised at the painful trial you are suffering, as though something strange were happening to you. But rejoice that you participate in the sufferings of Christ, so that you may be overjoyed when his glory is revealed'."

Jennifer released a long sigh and slowly refilled her lungs.

"Jennifer, the Word of God says not to be afraid when we suffer, but to be strong and remain faithful." Mary leaned over and kissed the top of Jennifer's bowed head.

"To persevere and continue running the race," Jennifer whispered.

"Jennifer, look at me please." Mary waited to make eye contact with her before she said, "Only God knows the reason for your suffering and the explanation belongs to Him alone."

"Oh, Miss Mary, I know you're right and every day I ask the Holy Spirit to increase my faith." She wiped her tears with a fresh tissue.

Mary closed the Bible and asked her, "Do you realize how much my faith has grown since I've met you and witnessed your walk with Jesus?"

"What do you mean?" she reached for another tissue.

"Jennifer, you have shown me the true meaning of selflessness and you gave me a glorious opportunity to demonstrate Christ-like behavior to my children when you came to my home with Angelina and stayed with us."

"Really?" she asked, unknowingly.

"Sweetheart, you are dramatically impacting the lives of those who come in contact with you and many people have become stronger Christians because of your testimony. Believe me when I tell you that our faith has been magnified by witnessing your walk with Jesus."

"I thank my God every time I remember you."
Philippians 1:3

~ 26 ~

Rima was comfortable and she loved holding Angelina while listening to her husband talk. She prayed that one day soon God would bless her marriage with children of her own. Bill kept her informed about Kathy's daughter, Lydia, and her gains toward a speedy recovery, he told Rima, "Little ones are so resilient, they bounce back quickly from illness, or so I've heard."

"I've heard the same, Bill." She kissed Angelina's forehead.

"Kathy certainly has been an example of strong faith during this crisis." Bill admired his friend and co-worker.

"Is the extra workload too much for you, William?"

"No, because Susan will be coming back to work next month and she will help with Kathy's assignments. After that, things should be back to normal."

Angelina suddenly woke from a sound sleep, and her cries filled the entire room. "Oh, what's the matter baby girl?" Rima cradled her in an effort to coax her back to sleep.

Bill continued to say, "Susan was helping Kathy before, and she has plenty of work experience, so it will be a relief to have her back in the office." He raised his voice over Angelina's cries and asked, "Do you want me to warm up the rest of her bottle?"

"Yes, sir, I do." Rima smiled at how strong-willed Angelina was and as soon as her little fingers grasped the warm bottle, the house was filled with peace.

"She certainly is a determined baby." Bill stroked the soft brown waves covering Angelina's head and thinking of the infant's mother, he said, "The news from the radiologist must have been devastating to her folks."

"O Lord, it breaks my heart knowing Jennifer is getting worse instead of better, what will she do next?"

"I don't know because Jennifer is opposed to the recommended surgery since there are no guarantees that amputating her arm would increase her chances of survival." With a cloth diaper he wiped the formula from Angelina's tiny mouth.

*   *   *

Cathy dialed the last number in her phonebook hoping to find a last-minute babysitter for the afternoon. Although her husband, Jim, wanted to go with her, it looked as though he might have to stay at home with their children. A few hours ago, Cathy's mother was taken to the hospital in an ambulance and was being admitted for a thorough medical evaluation.

Cathy took her parka from the hall closet and told Jim she was going for a short walk because she could always think more clearly when walking. By the time she reached the end of the driveway, her thoughts had turned to prayer . . . *Dear Lord, why today of all days?*

Today was her mother's birthday and after listening to her step-dad's shaky description of her mother's medical condition, Cathy was more than mildly concerned. Several times in the past Cathy answered late-night telephone calls responding to her mother's health, but this time things were different.

Cathy's steps were quick, and before she realized it, she turned the corner onto Mayflower Drive where Jennifer's front door was only four houses away . . . *please be home, Jen!* Cathy leaped over the steps and had barely finished knocking when Jennifer opened the door.

"What's wrong?" she asked.

"Will you pray with me?" Cathy was out of breath.

Jennifer drew her inside and sat with her on the stairs. Cathy sank down to the first step and said, "Jennifer, it's my Mom, and this time it's serious because she's been admitted to the hospital."

"Where are Jim and the children?"

"They're home, but we can't find a babysitter so I have to go to the hospital alone." She stopped to catch her breath.

"I'll get my coat and go with you," Jennifer said.

"No, I can't ask you to do that," Cathy protested.

"Why not?" Jennifer thanked God for this opportunity because this morning when she woke, she asked God to show her how she could be of help to someone in need and now her prayers were answered.

Cathy didn't know what to say when she noticed that Jennifer was dressed in blue jeans and a sweater. It was odd because Cathy had become used to seeing her in a bathrobe and slippers, yet somehow today she was dressed and feeling well.

Jennifer zipped her coat and said, "Cathy, God led you to my doorstep today, and He is giving me a chance to offer you support in His name, won't you please let me help?"

*   *   *

Three hours later, the doctor stood in the hospital waiting room explaining that Cathy's mother had suffered a Grand Mal seizure. The doctor said her mother would be staying in the hospital for the next couple of days, sedated and resting.

Knowing everything was under control, Cathy decided to leave since her step-dad would be spending the night at the hospital to be with her mother. Cathy and Jennifer took the elevator down to the cafeteria; they were hungry and tired.

Halfway through their meal Jennifer noticed Cathy reacting to the painful stiffness in her neck and asked, "Did you see your neurologist last week?"

"I sure did," Cathy sipped her pop.

"And?"

"He told me to reduce the stress in my life."

"That's easy to say, however life seems to be full of stress," Jennifer commented.

Cathy felt the sting of remorse because no matter what her circumstances were, Jennifer's were tenfold; she offered to change the subject. "Let's talk about happy things."

"Okay, next week is my wedding anniversary," Jennifer blushed.

"Congratulations, how many years?"

"We've been married twelve years and we're planning a quiet dinner at home this year because I never know when it's going to be a good day for me, so it's best not to plan things."

"I can't imagine how difficult – " Cathy's incomplete sentence hung in mid-air she tried another approach. "Jen, you look remarkably well for someone who – " The awful blunder was too obvious to ignore.

"That's all right, Cathy, even the doctors say I look exceptionally well for someone who is seriously ill." Her voice was kind, and sooner or later the subject needed to be discussed, so Jennifer took the first step. "Cathy, we need to have an honest conversation, without pretense, about the likelihood of my not surviving the battle with breast cancer."

Cathy sighed and moved her plate aside. She wanted to speak honestly and after several minutes of private conversation between the two of them, she asked Jennifer if she was spiritually prepared for eternity.

"Yes and no," she replied.

"You are spiritually, but not physically?" Cathy guessed.

"Yes." Jennifer placed her elbows on the table and said, "You would laugh Cathy, if you knew how many times a day I repent for the smallest things, even simple things that a year ago I wouldn't have recognized as sin."

"Can you give me an example, like what for instance?"

"Okay, yesterday I repented for sleeping too much and for moving too slowly, all of which resulted in a wasted day."

"Oh, I think under your circumstances that would not be a sin."

"No, I think it would be a sin because I slept more than necessary, and wasted too much time *before* I was diagnosed with cancer, and that was a sin." Jennifer was extremely calm when she said, "I live with the daily reminder that whatever I just did might be the last time I ever get to do it."

"Are you referring to certain things or everything?"

"Everything Cathy, take for instance right now having dinner with you." A gentle smile came across Jennifer's face. "For all I know, this might be our last meal together." After a long silence, she said, "Cathy, I want you to know that I'm prepared to die. However my prayer is that God will first grant me time to adjust to missing everyone – and that especially means you."

"I won't ever be able to say good-bye to you, Jen." Cathy allowed her tears to fall.

*   *   *

Keith was working late and he had missed stopping for lunch earlier. He looked through his desk drawers for snack food, but didn't find any, so he walked down the hall toward the vending machine. He opened a bag of chips and rested against the nearby coat rack. He drank from a can of diet pop and telephoned Jennifer so he could wish her a happy anniversary.

"Hi, Keith." Her soft lyrical voice was more noticeable when she spoke to her husband, especially on their wedding anniversary. One of the things he loved most about his wife was her voice; it was a soothing remedy for all his ailments.

"Happy Valentine's Day." He tilted his head back and emptied the last of the crumbs from the bottom of the chip bag.

"Happy anniversary, too." She stood at the sink and took the last of her midday medication.

"How are you feeling?" It was a routine question now and he wondered how many other husbands asked their wives daily how they're feeling.

"This morning was rough, but I'm feeling much better now."

"Good." Keith didn't want to tell her he would be late for dinner because a potential buyer wanted to look at their old home on Pond View Drive which was still for sale. "Umm, Linda called me this morning from the real estate office."

"Oh?" Jennifer leaned against the doorframe to the dining room and glanced at the table. It was set with two place settings of their good china, cloth napkins and silver candlestick holders. In the middle of the table was a framed photograph of their engagement picture with Keith's arms wrapped around her waist. It was autumn, and they were leaning against a magnificent maple tree bursting with color as October Glory filled the silver frame.

"Do you remember the couple who looked at the house last week?" he asked.

Jennifer didn't reply. She didn't like where the conversation seemed to be going.

"Well, they want to look at the house again tonight and they might make us an offer to purchase the home."

*   *   *

Although Jennifer was disappointed, selling their other home was important, perhaps even critical at this point. She prayed for the couple and that God would bless them with the finances necessary to make the purchase, and what a gift it would be for her and Keith to have one mortgage. She looked at the clock and prepared an evening bottle for Angelina.

Jennifer was no longer in pain due to the prescribed morphine she was taking, but nevertheless, the tumor had caused severe irreversible damage to her left arm. She experienced continuous tingling in her finger tips, and often the entire length of her arm was in a constant sleep-like stage. She no longer trusted its strength, so she learned to adjust her lifestyle and to do things differently.

Angelina slept comfortably on a mattress pad that was laid over the family room carpeting, and all her baby items were placed in low stacking bins on the floor. Jennifer sat on the floor and gently rolled Angelina over while she softly sang out her name. She was five months old and sleeping through the night which was a blessing.

Jennifer blew soft puffs of warm air onto the baby's cheeks. This had become a little secret gesture, a routine of sorts that only mother and daughter knew about. It was Jennifer's way of identifying herself to her child because Angelina had many loving caregivers, and each of them had their own way of showing affection. Jennifer wanted a signature way, a unique language of her own that identified her as someone special – the child's mother.

She moved closer to the side of the mattress to change the baby's diaper. Jennifer leaned over, and with her right arm, lifted Angelina onto her lap. She cradled her in the comfort of her crossed legs, and Angelina gave her mother a beautiful smile.

*　　*　　*

It was a twenty minute drive to New Boston, and Keith was already thirty minutes late in meeting the real estate agent. He wanted to sell the house and hoped the potential buyers didn't want to linger, at least not tonight. The nagging thought kept entering his mind . . . *What if this is our last wedding anniversary?*

Driving into the old subdivision brought to mind lost dreams and goals that were now out of his reach. He was reminded of how quickly their lives had turned around when Jennifer was diagnosed. He parked on the street in front of their home, as there were two other vehicles in the driveway. All he wanted to do this evening was sign a purchase agreement and quickly leave.

*　　*　　*

It was past eight o'clock in the evening and with heavy eyelids, Jennifer was trying her best to stay awake. She nodded off several times before she got up from the couch to turn on the lamp. Their anniversary dinner was on the stove, and if Keith didn't come home soon, she would place it in the refrigerator for tomorrow night.

At the kitchen sink she poured a glass of water to swallow her nightly medication. With the cover of darkness from outside, the kitchen window served as a mirror. She stared at her reflection, wondering if the real Jennifer, the beautiful bride from twelve years ago, would ever return. She asked herself . . . *Would this be our last time together on Valentine's Day?*

She focused on clearing her mind, but her thoughts drifted to the telephone voice message left by the doctor's office earlier that morning. A decision needed to be made very soon regarding her progress, and she was asked to come in for an evaluation of her treatment.

Jennifer's doctors wanted to send her medical records for a consultation review at the Cancer Treatment Centers of America, and the nearest location was in Zion, Illinois. She wasn't certain whether this was good news or bad news. She meditated on the scriptural reference to Zion – it was an immovable, unshakable mountain and her faith needed to be like Zion.

Out the corner of her eye, she caught the circling of headlights dance across the walls of the family room meaning Keith was home, and he would be hungry. She turned on the stove and started to reheat their dinner. She was glad Nicholas and Natalie were spending the night with school friends. This way she could discuss her treatment without any interruptions.

"I'm starving, and dinner smells great." Keith took off his jacket and laid it across the kitchen chair.

"Good, I'm glad you didn't stop for fast food."

"Not a chance." He kissed the side of her neck and said, "I'm getting used to such easy access to your neckline."

"Good, because when this is over I plan on keeping my hair short, very short." She turned to face him.

"How much time do I have before we sit down for dinner?"

"You have plenty of time." She knew he wanted to shower and change his clothes before eating.

He laid a rectangular black box with a tiny silver bow on the counter. "No peeking!" He warned her as he took the stairs two at a time.

The candles were melting, and the wax was beading precariously under the twin flames. Dinner was over and Keith wished he hadn't eaten so much. Their plates were set aside, and Jennifer was eager to open her present. She was glad last year they decided to exchange only one gift on their special day. Keith picked the even years to buy a gift, and Jennifer was in charge of the odd years; hers would be next year.

"I'm surprised you have waited so patiently, Jennifer." He handed her the gift.

"Thank you!" She leaned over to kiss him.

She opened the box slowly – determined from now on to absorb every precious moment. Inside was a delicate gold herringbone bracelet with three midnight blue Sapphires, and each dark stone was separated by sparkling crystals.

"Sweetheart, this bracelet represents my three girls whose birthdays are all in the month of September." Keith fastened the clasp onto Jennifer's delicate wrist and ran his fingertips over the stones, and pointing to each one, he said their names, "Natalie, Angelina, and their beautiful mother, my wife."

"Keith, how romantic." Jennifer felt loved. "I'll never be able to top this gift next year."

"I only want one gift from you next year," his voice cracked.

"Oh?" She asked while admiring her bracelet.

"Yes, the only gift I want is for you to be cancer-free on our next wedding anniversary." His vision blurred as he blinked away his tears.

Jennifer held his hand and said, "I promise Keith, I will do everything in my power to be healthy and cancer-free by February 14, 2006."

In the fading glow of the candlesticks, they smiled and gave each other their trademark salute . . . *a victorious thumbs-up!*

Noble Fir
Spring of 2005

~ 27 ~

ᗢᘔᘖᗣ

S ue and Mary stood in the far corner of the parking lot
away from the rowdy crowd so they could talk in private. It was past midnight and the surprise birthday party was
almost over. The weather in Michigan was always unpredictable and today was no exception. It was mid-March, St.
Patrick's Day, and the temperature was unseasonably warm.

The party's last song sounded loudly through the ampli-
fiers as the voice of Bob Seger was heard over the roar of
departing Harley motorcycles. The lyrics from the song
titled, "Against the Wind," voiced Sue and Mary's thoughts .
. . *It seemed like yesterday, but it was long ago.* The rain had
stopped earlier in the evening leaving a mist that saturated
the air with the strong aroma of nature from Boulder Lakes
Golf Course.

"My brother-in-law, John, outdid himself for Pam's 50
Birthday." Sue commented.

"It was a wonderful party, Sue, but I suspect he got a
little help from you," Mary said.

The music continued to play.

"No, actually John did most of the planning. He wanted
to surprise Pam, but you know my sister – I think she found
out about the party anyway!"

"Whether she knew about it or not, Pam had a great time," Mary laughed.

"Pam always has a great time." Childhood memories of her younger sister drifted through Sue's thoughts . . . *and the years rolled slowly past.* Life was precious, and the time spent showing those we love, how much we appreciate them, was never wasted . . . *I found myself further from my home.*

Sue shook the musical cobwebs from her thoughts and asked Mary about Jennifer.

We were young and strong . . .

"Starting next week she begins a new treatment phase at the Midwestern Region Medical Center in Zion."

"She's going to the Cancer Treatment Center of America?" Sue asked.

I'm still running . . . against the wind.

"Yes, the clinic is in Zion, Illinois," Mary said.

"Hmm, that's not far from where I work," Sue commented.

There were oh so many roads . . .

Mary gazed out at the golf course watching a heavy mist take shape across the fairways. Her mind began to drift thinking about the emotional ride it was to be helping Jennifer.

I began to find myself searching for shelter . . .

"Maybe CTCA will have the answer that Jennifer is seeking," Sue said.

"She has gone through so much already."

"Yes, she has and it must be hard for you Mary, and for everyone else to witness her suffering."

"Watching her suffer is very difficult, but sometimes the hardest part is dealing with personal guilt."

Sue frowned and asked, "I don't understand what you mean?"

I've got so much more to think about . . .

Mary hesitated before she admitted, "Jennifer's suffering makes me feel guilty."

"Why?"

"I feel guilty because I'm healthy, and Jennifer isn't."

"Mary, I believe God has blessed you with good health so you can help Jennifer."

Well, I'm older now and still running . . . against the wind.

They could have talked until daybreak, the way they used to years ago when life was simpler and time was on their side, but the music had stopped playing, and their lives were much different now. The parking lot was almost empty and the crowd was nearly gone. The last motorcycle pulled out onto Fairchild Road, and the party was over.

*   *   *

Kathy's daughter, Lydia, finished chemotherapy and her last scanning showed no trace of cancer in her little body. Kathy was grateful and thanked God for His tender mercy. She was now back to work and gradually fell into the familiar routine. She joined her co-workers in the cafeteria for lunch and sat next to Susan who was telling everyone that Jennifer had left that morning for Illinois.

Duane added, "Jennifer will spend three days at the Center while the doctors evaluate her medical status. She wants to start treatment there by the end of March."

"As a surprise," Bill said, "we're flooding the Illinois Beach Resort will telephone calls and messages for Jennifer so at night when she returns to her room, she can listen to prayers from familiar voices. Maybe it will help to make her out of town stay less lonely."

"I think that's a great idea." Again, Kathy inwardly thanked God for Lydia's health report.

"Jennifer will be going to Zion every twenty-one days for three day treatment sessions." Cathy said while finishing her lunch. "While Jen is gone, the moms in her neighborhood have offered to help Keith with Nicholas and Natalie." She nodded toward Duane and Bill and said, "Angelina will alternate staying with the Hardys and the Lanyons."

"Excellent job, everyone has kept the Jen Possible Team afloat!" Kathy said.

"Just barely Kathy, but Duane will explain everything." Cathy left and returned to her workstation.

Kathy watched her walk away and asked, "Is everything all right?"

"Cathy is under a lot of stress since her mom was hospitalized," Duane answered.

"What happened to Cathy's mother?"

"She had a Grand Mal seizure and was in the hospital a long time, but she's home now."

There was a dark cloud hovering over the Jen Possible Team. Everyone felt it and recognized the attack was from the Archenemy. It was an evil attempt to lure them away from helping Jennifer.

Several minutes passed before Duane lightened the mood and asked, "Kathy, did you hear that Al has announced his retirement?"

"No, when is he leaving?" A lot had taken place in the office while Kathy was away.

"Al plans on leaving next week. Don't worry, we saved you a ticket to the retirement party," Susan said.

*   *   *

Shari looked over the crowd of people at Detroit Metropolitan Airport. She was looking for Jennifer and was anxious to hear about her trip to Illinois. She spotted Jennifer inside the terminal talking on her cell phone. Shari waved hello and Jennifer ended the call, as she wheeled her suitcase into the aisle.

"You look good, Jennifer. How did things go?"

"Fine, I'm scheduled for a PET scan on March 31 and for the time being, the oncology team at CTCA is not recommending surgery on my arm."

"I pray that's good news." Shari took Jennifer's suitcase and opened the door for them to walk outside. "How do you like the medical staff?"

"I was impressed with everyone I met, especially Dr. Robert Levin, who is the Chief of Medical Oncology and Dr. Ranulfo Sanchez, who is a Surgical Oncologist." Jennifer described the modern facility, the personnel team and their professionalism; she prayed this would be the final lap of her race toward recovery.

*   *   *

Al Partington had mixed emotions over his decision to retire after working thirty-eight years in Detroit's automotive industry, but he knew it was time to take the magical step. Today, one at time, he would be saying farewell to his team of engineers; he clicked his pen open and shut while waiting for Mary to arrive in his office.

"So tell me Al, how do you feel?" Mary asked as she closed the door behind her.

"I feel wonderful riding off into the sunset." He laughed and started to open the manila folder on his desk, but hesitated and then pushed it aside. "Mary, when you first came to my section, I realized it was a major adjustment for you because you had worked with the same group of people for over twenty-five years. Then suddenly you were back to being the new-kid-on-the-block." He adjusted the pile of paper in front of him and said, "I want to tell you how much

I have appreciated your organizational skills and hard work. Your expertise certainly helped to make my job easier."

Mary smiled; she admired Al and appreciated his gratitude.

"But more than your work performance," Al cleared his throat before saying, "I want to commend you for all the gracious work you have done for Jennifer."

As always, Mary was uncomfortable when anyone offered her compliments.

Al noticed her uneasiness and explained, "We have all played unique roles in helping Jennifer, but you stepped in and filled a special void in her life."

Mary understood what he meant, but she chose to shine the light on others, "The credit goes to all the members of the Jen Possible Team, because everyone in your group has put forth extra effort in helping Jennifer."

"Yes, everyone has contributed to this extraordinary experience." He looked out his third-story office window at the busy streets of Dearborn and said, "I will miss working with such a high caliber of engineers."

"We have all followed your example, Al." Mary and everyone else would miss him.

After pausing he asked, "I heard you'll be going with Jennifer to Illinois. When do you plan on leaving?"

"We leave in two days and Jennifer is very nervous about the trip."

"I imagine she is and it's my understanding that the results of her PET scan will determine whether or not the cancer has metastasized."

"That's correct and Jennifer will know the results of her scan before she leaves CTCA."

"I'm glad you'll be there Mary, because Jennifer shouldn't go through this alone, especially if the doctors present her with discouraging news."

"If one falls down, his friend can help him up.
But pity the man who falls and has no one to help him up!"
Ecclesiastes 4:10

~ 28 ~

I t was three o'clock in the afternoon and Mary watched Jennifer sleep in the chair across from her at CTCA. Earlier that day, Jennifer saw the nutritionist and spent time with a counselor in the Work Life and Stress Management Department. Then after lunch, they met Dr. Sanchez, whom Jennifer instantly liked. He was a kindhearted physician who treated her with compassion.

It had been a busy day and Mary was thinking about closing her eyes to rest when the lobby receptionist asked her, "Are you with Jennifer?"

"Yes, I am," Mary said and Jennifer stirred at the sound of her friend's familiar voice. Mary waited for her to wake up and then quietly said, "Jennifer, it's time for your PET scan."

The technician stepped into the hallway and waited while Jennifer got her things. Mary stood to give her a hug and before leaving the lobby Jennifer stopped to say hello to a young boy across the row of seats. He was about the same age as Nicholas, and Jennifer offered him a piece of peppermint candy. He smiled and thanked her. Mary had noticed earlier how much the boy resembled Nicholas; in fact, they could have been twins.

The toys he was playing with were called Transformers, and they were great for the active imagination in young boys.

He concentrated on what he was building, and in no time he was flying his design through the air. He smiled at the lady sitting in the waiting room across from him.

"These toys are awesome!" he said. A few seconds later he purposely crashed the object and it disassembled onto the table. In a huff, he left the wreckage there and sat back in his chair; he was tired of playing and tired of waiting.

He was dressed in faded blue jeans with a white short-sleeved shirt that engulfed his small frame and the tips of his ears were covered with sandy brown hair. He kicked at the air with his scuffed tennis shoes. The lace on his right shoe was too long and every time it passed the left shoe in mid-air, the plastic covered ends would snap against his rubber sole. One lace was brand new, and the other was old and faded.

"You've been waiting a long time, haven't you?" Mary sympathized with him.

He looked over his flying shoes and nodded his head.

At first Mary hesitated, but then decided it would be all right and asked him, "What is your name?"

"Dylan James." He spoke his name proudly as if he were Abraham Lincoln.

Mary smiled at him.

"And my last name is Potter." Then he shouted for everyone to hear, "Dylan-James-Potter!" Dylan kicked his feet with each separate pronunciation and laughed, "It rhymes, doesn't it?"

Mary creased her forehead and mouthed the words in exaggeration. He caught her look of concentration and waited eagerly for her response. She smiled inside, knowing his name didn't rhyme but she wouldn't dare disagree. "Yes, it does rhyme."

He smiled at her and turned his thoughts and actions back to playing with his toys. Mary wondered what sort of storm was blowing through his young life that brought him to a cancer treatment center. It was obvious Dylan was used to spending time alone, waiting for whomever he was with to be treated at the clinic.

He tossed his toys into a worn cloth bag with the outline of a large tree and the silhouette of a child playing with an airplane. It was the logo for Cancer Treatment Centers of America. The faded tote bag was further indication that this was not Dylan's first visit to CTCA.

"Come on, Dylan, we have to go." A frail voice sounded from down the empty hallway.

"I'm coming!" He stepped around his chair and waved in the direction of the voice.

Mary heard footsteps and then a young woman walked into the waiting room and Dylan smiled at her. She was in her mid-twenties and she couldn't have been more than five feet tall. She was pale and very thin, and her artificial hair was dyed black with streaks of orange. She wore a sleeveless tank top and black jeans with scuffed tennis shoes. The lace on the left shoe was brand new and too long. It snapped back and forth against her right leg when she walked.

"Hi, Mom," Dylan said.

"Hey Buddy." In her hand she carried an oversized manila folder containing x-ray films and stuffed into her jean pocket were prescriptions for several types of medications. She hoisted her oversized purse onto her shoulder and with her free hand she took hold of her son.

As they walked out of the waiting room and toward the elevator, Dylan held tightly to his precious belongings – his mom and his toys. They stopped in front of the large steel doors and waited for the sound of the bell. Just before the doors opened, Dylan looked back down the hall to the lady sitting in the chair. He smiled at her, and Mary smiled back at him, watching as the matching laces to their tennis shoes stepped onto the elevator.

Time goes by slowly in a hospital, especially when you're waiting for a loved one, and eventually the minutes blend into hours. People come and people go all day long from the cancer institute, some of them are sick, some are caregivers, and some are survivors. Dylan James Potter was there today with his mother for reasons beyond his control; he wasn't a patient, a caregiver, or a member of a support team, but he was a survivor in a different way because he was surviving the tragic circumstances of . . . *his mother's cancer*.

*   *   *

Mary and Jennifer woke up early the next morning to a moderate wind gusting outside their hotel, but despite the weather, a walk on the beach was their plan. Jennifer took off her scarf and tucked it inside her jacket pocket. Although it was rare for her to expose the raw truth of her illness, she wanted to feel the freshness of the breeze. She and Mary walked beside the water and their footsteps quickly disappeared behind them with the splash of each white-capped wave. Jennifer turned to face Lake Michigan with her eyes closed and her face lifted toward heaven. Mary stood next to her, and with the toe of her shoe she nudged a stone from its sandy hiding place.

"I don't think today is going to be a good day," Jennifer stated.

Using her hand, Mary bent to release the stone from the sand and asked, "Why, is there something you haven't told me?" Mary stayed low on bended knees while she brushed the sand from the flat side of the stone.

"No, I tell you everything, Miss Mary," Jennifer smiled.

Her appointment with Dr. Levin was at one o'clock and he planned to review with her the results of yesterday's PET scan. Jennifer wondered if CTCA could provide her with any hope.

Mary stood and placed the wet sandy stone she had unearthed inside her pocket. She tried to hide her feelings, but she, too, felt that today was not going to be a good day.

"Let's not cry today, Mary, no matter what the test results are. Let's pray instead of crying." Jennifer reached over and squeezed Mary's hand.

Far above the sound from the crashing white capped waves God heard their prayers . . . *Heavenly Father, bless us with spiritual courage today as we learn the results from yesterday's scan. Be our constant companion throughout the day. We love You, Jesus, because You first loved us. Amen.*

"Mary, thank you for remembering my grandmother's prayerful ending."

"I would have liked to have known your grandmother," Mary said.

They turned around and walked toward the patio outside the hotel lobby.

"You remind me of Grandmother Catherine," Jennifer smiled.

"Oh, is it because of my gray hair?" Mary laughed.

"No, no, no." Jennifer covered her mouth and giggled because of what she was about to say. "No, actually you remind me of Grandmother because she loved to talk just as much as you do!"

Mary stopped and in a false show of offense, she placed both hands on her hips.

Jennifer laughed at her friend's bad acting skills and exaggerated stance. She said, "Oh, believe me, that's a compliment!" She shaded her eyes from the sun and took Mary by the elbow. "My grandmother loved to tell stories about real people who attended her small church or about those who lived in her hometown. But always in her stories, Grandmother compared their lives to a character in the Bible, whether they were deemed righteous or unrighteous people."

They reached the patio and Mary sat facing the sun with her feet propped on an extra chair as she listened intently to what Jennifer was saying.

"As a child, my favorite story was about Marcelon who owned a fish market where Grandmother did most of her shopping." Jennifer tied the scarf around her head. "Grandma compared his life to the Apostle Peter because Marcelon loved Jesus and he loved to fish, but I always felt sorry for poor Marcelon."

"Why?"

"Because he never married and had children." Jennifer brought out her camera and snapped several quick photographs of Mary.

"How many pictures do you have?" She was now accustomed to having her picture taken by Jennifer.

"I have a lot, Miss Mary; I carry my friends with me so I can visit with them anytime." Jennifer put the camera back in its case and sighed, "I don't want to leave, but we better catch the next shuttle bus to the hospital."

*　　　*　　　*

Jennifer was correct in knowing the day was not a going to be a good one. Her scan from the previous day uncovered a new tumor on the left side of her heart. It was near her lung and was in a dangerous position for radiation. After hearing the results her eyes filled with tears, but she did not cry and before leaving the clinic, she telephoned Rima. Jennifer asked her to make the arrangements for babysitting Angelina throughout the end of summer because she would be coming back to Zion for several months of additional treatment.

Jennifer was spiritually prepared to fight the next phase of her battle with breast cancer. Her faith in God was strong, and in this she never waivered. She would continue to soar as if on the wings of an eagle, determined to finish the race God set before her and not to become weary.

It was past midnight before Mary got home to Macomb Township after dropping Jennifer off in Plymouth. She tossed her jacket over the kitchen chair when she heard it clunk against the wooden leg. She searched the pockets and found the stone from earlier that day on the beach. Mary took it to the sink and wiped away the few remaining grains of dry sand.

At first glance the stone appeared to be narrow and smooth – just the right kind for skipping across the water. Although after examining it more closely, she found it was thick and too heavy for skipping – its hidden appearance was deceiving.

The visible side of the stone was a smooth slate gray surface, but underneath it there were layers of deep crevices and heavy lines which gave the stone a three-dimensional appearance resembling mountains and valleys.

In the dim light of her kitchen, Mary compared the two sides of the stone to Jennifer's life. On the outside, you saw Jennifer's delightful personality, her lyrical voice, and a constant beautiful smile, and many people would unknowingly conclude that she was facing a minor or temporary illness.

However, those who knew what Jennifer was going through, and the mountains and valleys she had climbed, are the people who clearly saw the other side of the stone, the other side of Jennifer. Once again, Mary was reminded of how precious it was to witness God's grace in Jennifer's life.

She wiped away the last grains of sand from the deep grooves on the stone and walked from the kitchen into the den. By the dim shadow from the outside lighting she sat down in the wicker chair by her desk. Mary was reminded of how fragile life was and how appearances and assumptions regarding someone else's life can oftentimes be wildly incorrect.

She thought of how sad it was to watch Jennifer schedule more chemotherapy treatments at Zion. With a heavy heart, she opened her Bible to Psalm 23 and read how sometimes we walk through green pastures and beside still waters while other times we walk through valleys of darkness in the shadow of death. Yet, in spite of our surroundings, we are to fear no evil because the . . . *Good Shepherd is always beside us.*

*   *   *

Cathy worked hard and was almost finished with the schematics for the module launch scheduled for next week. She stopped working long enough to contemplate the photograph of Jennifer from the Race for the Cure that she had tacked on the wall inside her workstation. She shook her head in an effort to clear her thoughts and once again concentrated on the deadline she had to meet for shipping next week.

"Are you busy?" Kathy knocked and asked from the doorway.

"Yes, but I could use a break, come on in." She pressed the save button on her laptop and asked Kathy how Lydia was doing.

"My family has been truly blessed – Lydia is doing great."

"Amen," Cathy agreed.

"Her hair is growing back and it looks very cute, so I'm tempted to keep it short."

"Jen said she was going to keep hers short, too." Cathy pushed the bangs out of her eyes, thinking of how much everyone's life has changed during the past year. "I meant to tell you that Susan stopped by Jennifer's house for a visit on Saturday."

"Oh?"

"Yes, I talked with Jennifer after she left, and Jennifer wants to celebrate Susan's recovery by having a party for her." Cathy's eyes burned with tears and she admitted, "I'm not near as humble a Christian as Jennifer because I can't say that I would be as gracious as she by wanting to celebrate someone else's recovery."

"I know how you feel Cathy, and I know for certain that Susan struggles with her emotions and how difficult it was for her to visit with Jennifer."

"We are very happy for Susan and we'll celebrate her victory, but at the same time we're filled with sorrow for Jennifer," Cathy sighed.

*   *   *

At home, Jennifer watched a short documentary on her computer about butterflies and the four stages of their short, but miraculous journey through life. She watched as the video clip went from the hatching of tiny eggs that clung to the sturdy branches of a Noble Fir right into the caterpillar stage. Next, it showed the transformation of the chrysalis to the emerging butterfly.

Many times Jennifer would compare her life to a butterfly, because she felt surrounded in a cocoon going through a metamorphosis of her own. She felt a transparent change was approaching and it would soon be time for her to emerge from God's swaddling wrap, and spread her wings to dry in the warmth of His Son. In the process, she would become what God had intended her to be long before she was born, and somewhere within her heart the flicker of awareness flamed and she knew . . . *His plan for her life.*

Then, right before her eyes the butterflies broke free from their silky nests. She watched as they flew across a field of wild flowers up toward the sky. They drifted until she could see them no longer.

"I'm glad we went to Rima's birthday party today." Keith startled her when he walked into the spare room and said, "She and Bill were happy to see you."

"They were happy to see us, Keith, not just me," she emphasized.

He sat down and stretched his hands over his head and asked, "Where did you find time to make soap and a bracelet for Rima's birthday present?"

"It was hard finding the time Keith, but it's important to do special things for those we love."

He placed his right ankle over his left knee and asked, "Did you tell Bill and Rima what the doctors discovered on your latest PET scan from the hospital?"

Jennifer told him yes, because from the beginning it was her decision to be open and honest with everyone about her illness. She felt it was the best way to deal with the unpleasant circumstances.

She took a bite of cookie and he asked, "What are those?" He twisted one of the dark molasses cookies in the air. "We've never had these before and now they're all over the house. When did you start buying them?"

"Those are ginger snaps and Shari told me they might help ease the nausea caused by chemotherapy. Go ahead and try one, Keith, they're good for you." The disagreeable look on his face made her laugh.

"They're hard as a rock," he said. After a mouthful of chewing he asked, "Will you be coming to bed soon?" He brought her to her feet and wrapped his arms around her.

She responded to his touch and held him close, wondering how much weight he had lost in the last few months. She knew that stress had a way of affecting his appetite. She turned off the lights and followed him into their bedroom.

~ 29 ~

Cathy held Angelina's hands as her tiny bare feet mimicked walking between Cathy's sandals. They practiced through the dining room and into the living room where Nicholas dodged their movements so he could watch his favorite cartoons. They went around the foyer and the kitchen twice, waiting for Jennifer to finish her telephone call.

Jennifer met them by the staircase and told Angelina, "You're so pretty!"

She was ten months old and smiled at the musical sound of her mother's voice. She bounced in Cathy's grip, urging her to keep moving, so they continued and Jennifer followed.

"You look nice today, Jen. Do you have plans to go somewhere?" Cathy asked.

"Yes, I have a busy day planned and today is Keith's birthday. Mary offered to come over and bake a cake for him, and since she will already be here, I asked her if she would watch Nicholas and Angelina so I can attend Natalie's dance rehearsal." Jennifer waved the brown hair away from Angelina's eyes and explained, "Because I may not be able to attend the dance recital on Friday night."

They were back in the kitchen and Cathy noticed the prescription bottles along with a notepad by the telephone. She asked, "How are things going with your treatment?"

"I was just talking with one of the nurses from CTCA." Jennifer cleared the table so they could visit and asked, "Have I told you about Sarah?"

"No, you haven't."

"Sarah is a kindhearted nurse who spends extra time talking with me about my treatment and medication. Yesterday was her day off, but she e-mailed me information about the new drug the doctors have prescribed for me." Jennifer waited to make eye contact with Cathy before she said, "It appears the time has come once again for me to take a different approach regarding my battle with breast cancer."

"What do you mean?" Cathy wondered if Jennifer was referring to surgery on her arm.

"You know the news was not good during my last visit to CTCA, right?"

"Yes, you told me," Cathy gripped her empty coffee mug.

"I'm sorry Cathy, but it's hard for me to remember who I have told and who I haven't told," Jennifer rubbed her forehead.

"It's okay, Jen." Cathy sensed there was hesitation in Jennifer's words, so she asked, "Are the doctor's recommending surgery to your arm?"

Jennifer slowly shook her head.

"Whew, that's a relief!" Cathy sat back in her chair.

"No, not really," Jennifer's voice broke with stress.

"I don't understand, isn't that good news?"

Jennifer sighed, "No, because amputating my left arm at this point would serve no purpose." Jennifer had accepted this fact.

Cathy couldn't hide the sadness she felt, she was stunned and at a loss for words.

"The physicians at both hospitals, Karmanos and CTCA, agree on the next step for my treatment." Jennifer reached over and took Cathy's hand and smiled. "I'm lucky because there are teams of doctors that are consulting with Bethesda on my case study and they will devise the best medical plan for me to pursue."

Cathy's eyes burned with unshed tears.

"I don't want you to be sad," Jennifer said calmly, "because it makes me feel terrible when I see the people I love become upset and hurt over my illness."

Nicholas ran into the kitchen, complaining about Angelina taking the television remote out of his grip. The sound of the toddler's bare hands and knees came crawling across the kitchen floor. "Oh, never mind, I'll figure out where she left it," he said with a huff.

Angelina sat and played with the cat, Simba, who never complained.

Jennifer turned her attention back to Cathy and said, "Right now I'm waiting for my insurance company to return my call so I can ask questions about my healthcare coverage for bone marrow and stem cell transplants." Jennifer waited for her reaction.

Cathy blinked several times and then inhaled deeply while she listened to Jennifer explain the rest of the details.

Jennifer said, "My health care insurance will cover a portion of the procedure if it is performed in the United States." She paused and watched Angelina tease Simba. "However, my doctors are recommending treatment outside the United States." Angelina crawled over and climbed up to her knees and Jennifer whispered to Cathy, "I think a trip to a foreign country is in my future."

*   *   *

Later that afternoon, Mary arrived to stay with the children and Jennifer left to attend Natalie's dance rehearsal. Since Jennifer was scheduled to return to Zion the following morning, and she never knew for certain how she would feel after she came home. She didn't want to miss her chance to watch the rehearsal in case she could not attend Friday night's performance.

Nicholas was playing with Ryan in the backyard, Angelina was taking a nap, and Keith's birthday cake was in the oven. Mary was in the dining room folding laundry when she dropped one of the socks on the floor, and bending to reach for it she noticed a photo album on the bottom shelf of the hutch.

A cameo picture of a beautiful bride holding a bouquet of white roses framed the outside cover of the book. Mary lifted the album from the shelf for a closer look and found it hard to believe the bride on the cover was Jennifer. She wiped a thin layer of dust off the portrait and stepped over to the light by the window.

She leaned against the window pane and turned each page of history while picturing in her mind how romantic the Valentine's Day wedding must have been. Jennifer's hair was a rich amber color styled in long curly ringlets. Her bangs were full and softly rested just below her brow line, and she wore a white lovely ballroom style wedding gown.

A faint trace of Jennifer could still be seen in the image the camera lens had captured years ago. Her smile was filled with joy, and her laughter could be heard through the glossy colored photographs. On one of the pages Keith stood next to Jennifer near the altar where the background appeared to be a quaint old-fashioned chapel. In the photograph they were young, nervous, and obviously very much in love. As Mary turned the pages from almost thirteen years ago, she came to know a special part of Keith and Jennifer.

The traditional last page was of the bride standing at the foot of the altar. The back of her train was cascading down the steps, and Jennifer was half-turned toward Keith. His hand was stretched out to meet hers, offering to bring her into his world and the talented photographer snapped the picture moments before their fingers touched.

Mary carefully placed the wedding album back on the shelf thinking, today as a married couple, Jennifer and Keith have climbed more mountains and walked through more valleys than most couples twice their age. She could only imagine the strain a serious illness, such as cancer, might possibly have on a marriage.

*   *   *

Mary turned at the sound of the garage door opening, and seconds later Natalie ran inside the kitchen, but she forgot to close the screen door. Simba took advantage of the error; he saw his chance to step out for a night of prowling and he was gone in a flash. Jennifer stood at the foot of the driveway as he ran like a tiger across the street and into the neighbor's backyard.

Jennifer knew it was the last she would see of Simba for the next few days. She soon gave up looking for him and went inside the house. She walked over to the stove and began stirring the spaghetti sauce on the back burner while Mary placed Angelina in the high chair.

Jennifer said over her shoulder, "Natalie's rehearsal was wonderful and it was great spending a few hours chatting with the other moms, just doing something ordinary, something normal for a change."

"I'm glad you enjoyed yourself." Mary placed animal crackers on the tray in front of Angelina and then helped herself. She held the open box in Jennifer's direction and Jennifer had some, too.

"I'm going to try to make Natalie's dance recital." Jennifer chewed the tasteless cracker and said, "I should be feeling all right, but the Race for the Cure is the next day, June 11." Jennifer lowered the flame on the stove. "Everyone has done so much for me, and I want to show my appreciation by attending the event again this year."

"Jennifer, maybe you shouldn't over-exert yourself."

Jennifer paused wondering if Cathy had mentioned the bone marrow transplant to Mary. "Did Cathy tell you?"

Mary nodded, "Yes, and a bone marrow transplant is a huge step."

"I know." Jennifer covered the sauce and said, "I will need everyone's prayers in making this decision because seeking treatment outside the United States is now my only option in fighting this battle."

"Everyone is praying for you, and if this is God's plan for you to leave the country, then we will do everything we can to help you."

"God continues to provide for me and I am so lucky," she sighed.

"God is watching over you, Jennifer." Mary gave her a hug and assured her, "You can depend on the Jen Possible Team and know that we will always be here for you."

~ 30 ~

A few days before the 2005 Detroit Race for the Cure, Shari was outdoors helping her husband, Jeff, clear out the winter debris from their garden, when the telephone rang. Without looking up, Jeff knew Shari would drop the rake to answer the call. He respected the time she freely gave to help others coordinate the major event. Shari jumped over the pile of leaves, let the rake fall from her hand, and on the last ring she picked up the receiver. "Hello?" she said.

"Hi, Shari, are you busy?" Jennifer asked.

"Not at all, what can I do for you?" She took off her garden gloves and left them in the back room.

"Can you tell me if Duane picked up the participant packages for Saturday's race?"

"Yes, he stopped by the salon last week and took everyone's packet except for yours and Keith's. Would you like me to drop them off at your house tonight?"

"No, you better not because I'm in Zion for treatment and I won't be home until Wednesday evening." While talking with Shari, Jennifer was beading a bracelet for her favorite nurse, Sarah, in the oncology department.

"I was wondering if you were going to participate in this year's race or not," Shari stated. She knew there was a possibility of Jennifer having a bone marrow transplant.

"I would like to." She counted the beaded crystals on her tray and searched for a fancy silver one to break up the pattern.

"Everyone will understand if you can't participate," Shari said.

Jennifer took off her glasses and laid the tray of beads at the foot of her hospital bed. There was a pause on the telephone line while Jennifer reached for a tissue. Shari walked outdoors onto the patio to stand in the warmth of the afternoon sun while she listened to Jennifer explain the options for treatment. Like everyone else, Shari felt it was a serious choice, but if God brought Jennifer to it, then God would see her through it.

After talking it over with Shari, Jennifer felt better. She put her glasses back on and was determined to find a special silver bead. Changing the subject, she said, "Shari before I forget, guess what Keith told me the other night?"

"What?" Shari smiled at the noticeable change in Jennifer's voice every time she talked about her husband.

"He thought of a great name and idea as a team theme for the race," she smiled.

"Oh, what name and idea did Keith come up with?"

"Mrs. Potato Head!" Jennifer laughed, "You would have to know Keith in order to appreciate his sense of humor, so let me explain." She found the perfect silver bead and said, "You see, Angelina is always confused over my never-ending appearance because one day I have on my glasses and the next day I wear my contacts lenses. Then I might wear my wig, but the next day I don't and sometimes I wear a scarf, when other times I wear a hat – do you get it?"

"I know what you mean, interchangeable parts and behavior," Shari smiled because she did understand.

They talked for a while longer, and after the telephone call ended, Jennifer felt renewed. She threaded the last pink crystal bead onto the wire for Sarah's bracelet and now she could add her personal touch to the unique piece of jewelry. She held a tiny silver cross between her index finger and thumb, she prayed for all the nurses, but especially for Sarah because she was compassionate and thoughtful. She brought the cross to her lips then strung it carefully onto the wire; and in everything Jennifer does . . . *she does it all for His glory.*

*   *   *

Three days later, Jennifer kicked off the bed covers and threw her pillow onto the floor. The bedroom window was open letting the cool night air fill the room, but she was sweating horribly. The bed sheets were soaked, and her nightgown clung to her body. She jerked her head toward the bedroom door. Her eyes were open, but it took a moment for her to realize she was home and not sleeping at the cancer clinic.

Can't anyone hear the baby crying? She leaned on her elbows and listened again for the sound of crying, but suddenly it was gone and she wondered if she was dreaming. Keith was next to her sound asleep and the house was silent. She let her bare feet hit the carpet then steadied herself before standing.

There it was again, the sound of an infant crying. Her head snapped back in the direction of the hallway. She thought she heard Angelina whimpering and the soft cry filled her maternal instincts. She hurried down the hallway across the upstairs landing and into her daughter's bedroom.

The nightlight cast a shadowy glow over the entire room. Her hands reached into the crib only to find it empty, and she was overcome with sudden fear. Her heart was racing, her temples throbbed, and she felt dizzy, but there it was again – a baby was crying, and Jennifer tasted fear racing up the back of her throat.

She ran down the stairs turning on every light switch as she circled the interior of her home. She raced into the living room just as Simba darted out from behind the curtains. The gray movement startled Jennifer; she quickly skirted out of the cat's way and stumbled back onto the arm of the sofa. She was fully awake now and remembered that Angelina was staying with Duane and his wife, Janis. She listened carefully and realized the crying noise came from outside the front window where Simba was napping. Jennifer soon discovered the neighbor's female cat was paying a visit and desired Simba's male company.

Several minutes passed before her mind reorganized itself, and she became aware of the pricking needle sensation across her chest cavity. Immediately she understood the reason why she woke up terrified. It had been months since she had experienced the phantom pains. She remembered how often they used to occur and the persistent discomfort that accompanied them. She refused to make the emotional mistake of touching her chest because she was awake and she knew her breasts were gone.

She wandered into the kitchen and looked at the stove clock; it was three in the morning. She went to the cupboard and twisted the cap off the prescription bottle, and phantom or not, she felt the imaginary pain and wanted it to stop . . . *Dear Lord, how much more time do I have?*

Jennifer leaned against the counter as her thoughts examined the last few days. The nausea from her recent chemotherapy treatment was awful. It had left her weak and light-headed. She took all the anti-nausea medication allowed, but it still wouldn't release its sickening grip on her stomach.

On top of that, she was hardly well enough to attend Natalie's dance recital on Friday night, but she did anyway. The following morning, the day of the race, Jennifer thought she was feeling better. However, when Keith loaded the children into the wagon and they found the Jen Possible Team, the uncontrolled vomiting sensations returned.

Jennifer paced the kitchen floor. She desperately wanted to experience a normal life again by having fun with the people she loved; laughing and socializing once more. It seemed the only people she associated with lately were medical professionals, health insurance personnel, or pharmacists . . . *Dear Jesus, please forgive me, but I miss being an engineer – I feel so unproductive.*

It was just before dawn when she tossed the prescription bottle onto the kitchen counter and watched it roll behind a stack of medical bills. She dropped her head into her hands and wept as she rocked back and forth crying . . . *I'm so tired, Dear God, I don't feel like I can do this anymore.*

Several minutes passed before a striking memory came into focus behind her closed eyes. Soon, she stopped rocking and her hands dropped to her side. The tears rolled down her face as she grasped the edge of the counter, and through blurry vision she looked toward heaven as the image of Jesus carrying the cross to Calvary was clear in her mind . . . *Dear Lord, forgive me, because after all you did for me – how dare I complain about breast cancer?*

The teams of physicians working diligently to advise Jennifer were from Zion, *the mountain of hope in Jerusalem,* and Bethesda, *the healing pool inside the city gates.* Remembering all of this, Jennifer raised her hands in worship crying aloud, "My God, You reign!"

"Hear my prayer, O Lord; listen to my cry for mercy.
In the day of my trouble I will call to you,
for you will answer me."
Psalm 86:6

*   *   *

Late Sunday night, Janis finished giving Angelina a bath and since she was teething, having a routine at night seemed to help her fall asleep faster. Janis and Rima kept in close touch with each other making sure they did things uniformly, so the baby was accustomed to a routine no matter who was taking care of her.

Duane washed his hands at the kitchen sink and called for his sons, Jacob and Justin, who were watching television. They came into the dining room to help stack the dirty plates before placing them on the kitchen counter.

"How long is Angelina staying with us, Dad?" Justin asked.

"She'll be here a few days," Duane answered.

"Jennifer didn't feel good at the race yesterday, did she?" he asked.

Jacob stopped to listen because he didn't think she was feeling well, either. He knew she had cancer, but to him she never really looked or acted very sick. Until yesterday, he was used to seeing her happy, but things were different now.

"You're right, Jennifer didn't feel well yesterday and that's why your mom and I asked you boys to pray for her this morning in church." Duane hung the towel over the kitchen rack and said, "Do you both understand how sick Angelina's mother is?"

Jacob was emptying the garbage and he waited for his younger brother to answer the question, but Justin kept silent.

"Okay, boys, we need to talk about what's happening with Jennifer." Duane stretched his long legs out in front of him and leaned against the kitchen table. "We don't know what God's plan is for Jennifer, but we do know that whatever happens, whether it be good or bad in our eyes, it will be perfect in His eyes."

The brothers knew the wisdom their dad was speaking, yet it was hard to understand how it could be a good thing for Jennifer's health to continue on its downward spiral.

Anticipating their thoughts, Duane said, "I know it's hard to understand that her illness could ever be a good thing, but this is when our faith and trust in God are tested."

"Jennifer's so nice. I've never known anyone who smiles as much as she does." Justin's eyes pooled with tears. He added, "She thinks about other people all the time."

"I think when she does nice things for other people, it must take her mind off her own problems," Jacob said, thoughtfully.

Duane didn't interrupt them because he wanted them to speak openly.

Justin compared mother and daughter by saying, "Jennifer is like Angelina, she tries to always be happy and never have any downtime."

Several minutes passed and Duane was about to speak up when Jacob said, "It would be hard not to cry all the time if I were Jennifer." He twisted the cap to the pop bottle on and off while he talked. "I mean, it has to be hard for her to think about dying."

There it was: the word Duane hoped they would understand.

"Yes, it is hard for Jennifer because the doctors have told her that her cancer is getting worse, not better." Duane explained, "Yesterday, Jennifer suffered a great deal and we all saw it, but most of the time she suffers in silence. However, at the race this year we all witnessed a portion of her suffering." Duane cleared his throat and wiped the end of his nose. "I admire Jennifer a great deal because she endures her pain heroically."

"She doesn't deserve cancer and she doesn't deserve to be sick because she's the nicest person I've ever known." Justin allowed the release of tears to stream down his face.

Duane reached over and gripped his shoulders, "When the rain falls, it falls on everyone, and when the sun shines, it shines on everyone, both the righteous and the unrighteous."

The boys knew their dad was quoting scripture.

"Dad, are you and Mom going to keep helping Jennifer so she can get the treatment she needs and maybe someday have a regular life?" Jacob asked.

The tightness in Duane's throat kept him from answering, he simply nodded his head. Afterwards both boys went upstairs and Janis came into the kitchen with Angelina who was dressed in her pajamas. Janis watched the boys climb the stairs without racing and she could tell they were downhearted.

"Did the boys do something wrong?" she asked, while bringing a bottle out from inside the refrigerator.

Duane wiped his eyes and told her no, they hadn't done anything wrong, but as parents they could both be very proud of their sons. She agreed and placed Angelina in his arms. He walked into the living room and sat on the couch, with the baby on his lap. Janis joined them and handed Duane a warm bottle. She sat on the edge of the coffee table with her knees touching her husband's.

"I think Jennifer is doing too much, Duane." She tucked Angelina's damp curls behind her beautiful ears.

"I agree, but she doesn't want to waste any time resting because she wants to spend all her spare time with her children."

"I pray it comforts her to know that her children are loved by so many people." Janis tickled the tiny toes before her and admitted, "The boys are getting very attached to Angelina. Just last week when I dropped them off at school, they knew I was going to take her home and they didn't want to get out of the car."

"I know how they feel because I'm pretty attached to this little angel, myself." Duane bounced Angelina on his knees.

"Enjoying her company has been a blessing to our family," Janis said.

"Angelina is also a blessing to Bill and Rima," he said. "Perhaps she's filling in the gap while they wait for the blessing of a child to complete their marriage."

~ 31 ~

As they boarded the airplane from Michigan to Illinois, Jennifer told Mary she planned to sleep on the short flight and for her not to worry since they were unable to sit next to each other. Jennifer's appointment at CTCA was for two o'clock in the afternoon. Mary watched her board the plane ahead of her and she prayed Jennifer would not get airsick and need assistance. Six hours later, Mary was fast asleep in the hospital waiting room. The oncologist nurse, Sarah, gently tapped her knee and said, "Jennifer is through with her diagnostic testing and is ready for you to take her back to the hotel room."

Mary looked around, realized she had fallen asleep and then stood up to follow the nurse hypnotically down the hallway.

"Do you know that I enjoy being Jennifer's nurse because she makes my workday brighter with her positive attitude?" Sarah said, looking over at Mary. She waited a moment to make sure Mary was fully awake before she added, "It must be an honor for you to know Jennifer personally."

Mary's footsteps automatically slowed down, and once the cobwebs cleared her mind, she realized Sarah had summed things up with one simple word: honor. "Yes, it is an honor to know Jennifer," Mary replied.

Sarah opened one of the double doors and pointed in the direction of the scanning room. Ahead of her, Mary saw Jennifer talking with some other cancer patients. She was asking them about their health and how they were doing. As Mary approached Jennifer, she heard her giving encouragement to other women with breast cancer, promising she would pray for them.

They left the radiology department and rode the elevator down to the front lobby where the shuttle bus waited to take them to their hotel. On the ride back, Mary asked how the testing went, but Jennifer only shrugged her shoulders and made no comment.

Jennifer stayed inside the hotel room so she could rest before having dinner in the downstairs restaurant. Mary went outside to walk along the beach so she wouldn't disturb Jennifer's nap. The dry sand shifted beneath her footsteps and the seagulls circled noisily above her before landing on the shoreline to rest.

Lake Michigan was in all its glory. The strength and power that capped each breaking wave was beautiful to watch. It seemed the body of water was endless. Stretching out far to meet the horizon and eventually touching the sky. With barely one shade difference in the color, Mary strained to focus on the exact point where the water reached heaven. She slid her sunglasses back in place as Sarah's words echoed through her mind . . . *It must be an honor for you to know Jennifer personally.*

Mary took a few steps in the direction of the wind before she stopped and lifted her eyes to God just before the tears streamed down her face. She knew from Jennifer's silence during the ride back in the shuttle bus that the pending results from the PET scan was not going to be good news.

Jennifer understood diagnostic readings and equipment because of her education and experience as an electrical engineer. She could visually determine whether or not an object appearing on the monitor screen was normal or abnormal. As a result of her initial experience in being tragically misdiagnosed during the first eight months of her illness, Jennifer now studied every one of her medical reports and she had become extremely knowledgeable of the cancer treatment process.

Mary closed her eyes and prayed . . . *Almighty Father, I thank You for the honor of being part of Jennifer's life. I have learned so much of Your grace through her storm. Her unwavering faith brings me to my knees in deep humility. Through the power of the Holy Spirit, I will continue to serve You by demonstrating Christ-like characteristics to her. Thank You for this opportunity to discover more about Your love and to share in Jennifer's suffering. Amen.*

*   *   *

Later that evening, Sue, Mary's friend, drove out to Zion so she could meet her and Jennifer for dinner at the hotel. Sue was looking forward to seeing Mary and for the first time to meet Jennifer, who she had come to admire.

Their table in the restaurant gave them an open view of the lake and the dinner conversation rightfully centered on Jennifer's battle with breast cancer. As they ate, she openly talked about her disease and told Sue that Sue and her daughter, Nicole, should never forget their annual mammogram. Jennifer's soft lyrical voice took on a deeper tone when she explained that even though eight out of ten lumps are not cancerous, if you suspect something is wrong, push ahead and get another doctor's opinion. Thinking of her own experience Jennifer added, and if you think the second opinion is wrong, get a third opinion.

Jennifer stopped a moment to stir her flavor-rich coffee before saying, "You see, when breast cancer is found in the early stages, the survival rate is excellent and the good news is that over two million breast cancer survivors are alive today in America!"

Their waiter came to the table, took away their empty dishes, and brought them dessert. Jennifer thanked him and then blushed, "I'm sorry, I've monopolized our dinner conversation."

"Don't apologize Jennifer," Sue said, "I am struck by your ability to talk so candidly about your unfortunate experience." Sue folded her hands and marveled at Jennifer's beautiful appearance. "You're such a remarkable young woman," said Sue, her eyes pooling with tears.

"I'm not anyone special," Jennifer said.

"Oh, yeah, right!" Mary and Sue said in harmony.

"You two are funny!" Jennifer finished the last of her coffee and suggested, "Let's go for a walk while there's still some daylight left."

"Are you sure?" Together, the two friends asked Jennifer the same question.

"Yes, I'm absolutely sure." Jennifer smiled, and walked ahead of them toward the patio doors.

Mary raised her eyebrows and said to Sue, "Let's go for a walk with Jennifer!"

*   *   *

The wind had all but disappeared allowing the water's surface to be as smooth as a mirror. It now reflected the setting sun, perfectly. The shoreline was generous, letting the three of them walk side-by-side along its natural path. With no evening breeze, the freshwater smells surrounded the lake and filled their senses. They slowed their pace to enjoy the view before them.

"I love Lake Michigan." Sue broke the silence with an audible sigh.

"Did you grow up near the water, Sue?" Jennifer asked.

"Yes, and it brings to mind great childhood memories," Sue answered.

Jennifer turned and asked Mary, "What about you? Did you grow up near the water?"

"No, not me, I didn't have a carefree childhood like Sue," Mary teased. "As a matter of fact, I don't even know how to swim. I was raised on a farm, which was hard work, with little time for relaxing or summer vacations." Mary chuckled at her own somewhat mild exaggeration.

With a deep laugh, Sue exclaimed, "Poor, poor, Mary!" Sue kept laughing while watching Mary pry a rock from the sand. She turned to Jennifer and half-whispered, "You know every time Mary talks about her childhood it gets worse."

Mary chuckled at the way Sue loved to tease.

Jennifer laughed at their friendly banter and then happily clapped her hands to get their attention and said, "Mary, tell us a story about your childhood."

"Oh, Jennifer, she has some great stories!" Sue grinned at her life-long friend.

"Mary simply has a way with words, doesn't she?" Jennifer agreed with Sue.

"Yes, as a matter of fact I've been telling her for years that one day she'll write a book." Sue emphasized her words with a nod.

Mary was only half-listening to their conversation as she concentrated on unearthing a hidden rock buried deep within the layers of sand.

Jennifer thought Sue had a wonderful idea. She then said to Mary, "I agree with Sue – you should write a book!"

Mary looked from one enthused face to the other and openly laughed at the idea.

"For years I've encouraged her to set the pen into motion," Sue told Jennifer.

"Don't you want to write a book, Mary?" Jennifer's voice was special.

For a moment, everything seemed to stop as miles away the sun caressed the surface of the water. A quiet stillness surrounded them, and for the first time Mary didn't know what to say.

"I believe your gift is a blessing, and you should use it for His glory," Jennifer spoke, with wisdom beyond her years.

Mary was still crouched down on bent knees. She was surprised at Jennifer's remark and all she could think to say was, "As soon as I have something to write about, I will."

"Mary, you do have something to write about – " Sue's voice broke as she took Jennifer by the arm and drew her close to her side.

Mary watched the two of them, not knowing what to expect.

Sue gave a decisive nod at Mary and said, "You should write a book about Jennifer and tell everyone of her remarkable story."

The rock Mary was disturbing tumbled from its hiding place. It was no longer able to conceal the secret it had kept hidden for many years. The shifting sands where it rested had been shaken and its foundation gave way. The sparkling surface that was invisible before now shined in the light of the setting sun, for until now – only God knew what was underneath the surface.

"*Write a book, about me?*" Jennifer placed her hand over her heart and stared at Sue.

"Yes, Jennifer, Mary would write about your faith in God and your tremendous courage." Sue said, "The book would be centered on your battle with breast cancer, but more importantly the story would tell others about your unwavering faith and obedience to God, which I believe is extremely rare today and truly remarkable."

Mary stared at the two women standing before her as if they were strangers speaking in a foreign language, yet arm-in-arm they smiled and waited for her to say something. For a moment, she wondered if perhaps she had misunderstood their conversation.

"Well?" Sue asked.

Mary studied Jennifer's gleaming face and instantly knew there was no mistaking their words. For the past several months Mary had personally witnessed and understood the suffering Jennifer had gone through. She slowly stood to her full height and brushed off the sand from her hands. Mary needed a moment to collect her thoughts. She used a stall tactic and feeling somewhat like John Wayne in front of her shorter friends, she placed her hands on her hips and comically said, "So, little lady, you want me to write a book?"

The two cohorts roared with laughter at the horrible acting impersonation, but soon enough the joking stopped and the question hanging in mid-air required a response. Sue and Jennifer were still smiling with their arms locked, waiting in quiet anticipation.

Mary casually said, "Sure, I'll do it. After all, how hard can it be to write a book?" She laughed along with Sue and Jennifer before saying, "I mean half the battle is in knowing how to type, right?" But inwardly, Mary knew she didn't have a clue as to how difficult it would be to author any book – let alone the personal challenge of writing a book about Jennifer.

"You'll do it then?" Jennifer was like a child to her.

"Yes."

"As simple as that, Mary, you promise?" Jennifer's smile was overpowering.

"Yes, Jennifer, as simple as that, I promise." The joyful laughter from moments earlier quickly faded, and now Mary's heart cried out with compassion and respect for the young woman standing before her on the shore of Lake Michigan. Mary ignored her tears and said, "Jennifer, it would be an honor to write your story."

"Simply let your 'Yes' be 'Yes,' and your 'No,' 'No'."
Matthew 5:37

~ *32* ~

It was only mid-June, and much to Rima's surprise the full heat of Michigan's inescapable summer had arrived. The stretched white canvas was before her, waiting to soak up any color the brush offered, but Rima wasn't going to paint today. It was hotter than she ever dreamt possible this far north of Beauregard Parish, Louisiana.

She tied up her long black curls with several hair pins, but still felt no coolness in the heat of the early morning. She pulled the kitchen curtains to one side, hoping to allow a cool breeze free entry, but again there was none. Rima went to the sink for a cold glass of water, and over the sound of the running tap she heard the tread of footsteps behind her.

"Howdy, William!" she said without turning around.

But when she didn't hear a response, she turned and saw Bill stagger into the living room and slump against the back of the sofa, his strength was drained, and he could not take another step. Rima ran to his side forgetting to turn off the water faucet, and her first thought was . . . *he has suffered a stroke.*

She helped him into the chair and asked, "William, what's come over you?"

"I don't know," he could barely speak.

Rima's experience with providing home care for bed-ridden patients sent warning signals flashing through her mind. Her only thought was to call for help. She ran to the kitchen for the cordless telephone and turned off the running water. She rushed back to his side and started to dial 911.

"No," Bill stopped her.

She cried, "Why, you need help!"

"I'm fine; just let me rest for a minute," his speech was slurred.

Rima turned the telephone off before the emergency call was complete. She ran back into the kitchen and with trembling hands brought him a glass of cold water. "Here, drink this slowly." She knelt before him and lifted the glass to his mouth. It was then she noticed a deep rash covering the left side of his face. She felt his burning cheek and realized the corner of his left eye, matched the downward slope to the left side of his mouth. Again, the word stroke entered her mind.

"I'm going to call for an ambulance," she told him.

"I don't want an ambulance because you can drive me to the hospital."

"Y'all want me to drive?" Rima obtained her driver's license a few months earlier and was about to protest when she remembered . . . *I can do anything with God's help*.

*   *   *

Six hours later, Rima paced outside the hospital emergency room. Bill was seen by the physician on call and had been resting peacefully for almost two hours. They were told a stroke was a possibility, but while they waited, further tests were being performed to determine the cause of his sudden illness.

As Bill rested, his blood work and scanning results were evaluated. Rima prayed for his health and placed her trust in God. She went back to the examination room and stood by his bedside. She took his hand, and her loving touch woke him from a drowsy sleep.

Bill remembered where he was and why he was in the hospital.

"It's nice and cool in here," he said, but the left side of his face didn't reflect the smile he tried to show.

"I reckon so," Rima placed her hand, palm side up against his flushed cheek and felt the heat penetrate her flesh.

The door opened and the doctor stepped in saying, "We have your test results, Mr. Hardy, and you have Ramsay Hunt Syndrome." The physician wrote the words down on the medical chart as he spoke.

Rima and Bill exchanged glances. Neither of them had heard of this syndrome.

"It's more commonly known as shingles." The ER doctor said, "It's not fun, but much better than a stroke." He was writing several prescriptions for Bill.

Rima closed her eyes and said aloud, "Thank You, Jesus." She knew shingles could be painful, and the side effects were indeed uncomfortable, but in spite of everything else, she agreed with the doctor; it was much better than a stroke.

"Here you go." The doctor handed the prescriptions to Rima and said, "Get these filled on your way home. In the meantime, the nurse will provide you with additional information that will explain the symptoms and the recovery schedule your husband should experience within the next few weeks."

Rima thanked him.

The doctor told her, "Your husband will need plenty of rest." He clicked his fountain pen closed and clipped it inside his white lab coat pocket. "Carefully read the discharge instructions and follow up with your regular physician, and try not to worry because I've seen worse cases than this," he explained, nodding in Bill's direction.

*   *   *

Cathy was becoming overwhelmed in all areas of her life, and she was beginning to realize the emotional load she was carrying was simply too much. She had just returned to work after a week of family camping and she didn't feel refreshed or energized in the least. Her mother was living day-to-day with caution and fear, wondering when another seizure would take hold of her frail body. Since Cathy was an only child, she kept in close contact with her parents always making herself available to help them whenever they needed her.

She had visited with Jennifer yesterday and learned of Bill's trip to the emergency room over the past weekend. Everyone was thankful his prognosis was good and a favorable recovery was in the near future. Cathy asked Jennifer how she was doing, and Jennifer's response was a slight shrug of her right shoulder. She was feeling somewhat better, but she felt it was primarily due to the medication she was taking, and had very little to do with her gaining any strides in winning her battle against cancer.

As Cathy sat in the test lab, she reviewed in her mind the entire conversation she had with Jennifer, she began to wonder if perhaps Jennifer had misunderstood a few things. Jennifer told Cathy she had a wonderful time with Mary and Sue while in Illinois a few days ago, and Cathy was happy they enjoyed their time together. Apparently, Jennifer was well enough to visit at dinner and then go for a walk along the beach afterwards, but then Jennifer told Cathy about a promise Mary had made to her, and this was the portion of the conversation that Cathy was not sure had taken place.

"Hey, are you lost in space somewhere?" Duane tapped her on the shoulder.

"What?" Cathy turned too quickly, and the muscles in her neck reacted painfully, "Ouch!"

"Are you okay?" Duane dropped off the new modules for a customer in Australia on the work table next to her.

"Who knows – " Cathy rubbed her neck, and the pain subsided.

"How was your vacation?" he asked.

"Too short. The kids love to go camping, but it's such a let-down when we pull away with the trailer to come home." She retied her ponytail and asked Duane when he was leaving for his family vacation.

"We're going after my wife's birthday in a couple of weeks."

"Is this the 'Big-40' for Janis?" Cathy smiled.

"Yes, I received an e-mail from Jennifer this morning and she has offered to plan a surprise birthday party in two weeks. I hope Janis won't mind all the fuss."

"Janis will love a surprise birthday bash!"

Duane hoped so, but he didn't get a chance to say anything more once Kathy joined them at the technician's desk.

"I'm glad you're both here," Kathy said, "this is a get well card for Bill that I'd like you both to sign." She handed Duane the card and a pen.

"Why, what happened to Bill?" he asked.

Kathy repeated what she knew and then asked if Cathy had a more recent update.

"Yes, I spoke with Rima yesterday, and Bill is doing much better. The doctor gave him four weeks off work and he said Bill should recover nicely afterwards."

"Do they need any help?" Duane was always the first to volunteer.

"Rima said no, at least not right now anyway," Cathy told him.

While Duane signed the card, Cathy wanted to discuss the conversation she had with Jennifer and decided to run it by Duane and Kathy. "You guys, Jennifer mentioned something to me yesterday, and I was wondering if either of you know anything about it." Cathy signed Bill's get well card and then abruptly said, "This is about Mary."

"Oh no, what's happened to Mary?" Kathy asked because she felt there was a dark stream of unfortunate events happening to the Jen Possible Team members, all of which were distracting everyone and to some degree, preventing them from helping Jennifer.

"No, this isn't bad news," Cathy waved her hands in the air. "A few days ago, Mary went with Jen to Illinois, and Mary's friend, Sue, who lives in Chicago, met them for dinner at the hotel. Are you guys following me?"

They both nodded.

"Anywho," Cathy leaned in closer and lowered her voice. "Jennifer seems to think that Mary promised her she would – "

"Mary promised Jennifer what?" Duane leaned forward.

"Well, Jen is under the impression that Mary said she would write a book about Jennifer and her battle with breast cancer." Cathy blushed.

"Oh, that doesn't surprise me at all." Duane eased back into his chair.

"Good, then you can be the one to verify this Duane because I'm concerned that Jennifer has misunderstood Mary's promise." Cathy pushed the bangs away from her eyes and walked away, saying, "Write a book . . . *whew!*"

*   *   *

Although he wasn't surprised, Duane did want to check out the news. He rounded the corner and saw the overhead light shining into the hallway from Mary's workstation.

"Hi Mary, what are you doing?" He sat in the vacant chair next to her desk.

Mary slid her reading glasses down her nose and peered over the rim at him. "I'm busy working on the details of your shipment to Australia."

He laughed at her rough exterior knowing it was only a decoy.

Mary continued to sort through the international shipping documents on her desk and according to the sly look on her visitor's face; she could only assume the word had traveled fast about her writing a book. She could hardly believe the unexpected turn of events herself and it didn't surprise her that Duane would be curious.

"So what's new, Mary?" He tried to be casual.

"Nothing." She decided two could play this game.

"Hmm, I just heard something very interesting," he grinned.

"Really?" Her fingers typed away as she coolly replied to an e-mail.

He waited, but when Mary didn't bite on the line he was casting, he said, "I heard Jennifer had a nice visit with you and Sue."

"Yes, we all had a nice time, Duane." She hit the send button on the keyboard.

"Jennifer said that she really likes Sue," he said.

Mary smiled and turned slightly in his direction and said, "Everyone likes Sue, Duane."

He couldn't keep from smiling at her impatience. "Jennifer also told Cathy that you gals went for a walk along the beach." When Mary didn't flinch, he continued, "Apparently, Cathy talked with Jennifer, and Jennifer said something about you making her a promise." Duane knew, that Mary knew, what he was talking about and that did it.

Mary tossed her reading glasses onto the desk, she looked up at the ceiling and ran her fingers through her hair. She groaned and said, "You're bothering me, Duane, please go away."

"Not on your life!" He crossed his arms and waited.

"You're such a troublemaker." Mary debated and then told him what he came to hear. "Okay, yes, I made a promise to Jennifer," she blushed.

"I thought so, and for the record, I happen to think writing a book about Jennifer is an excellent idea."

"I'll bet you do, Duane." Mary faced him and crossed her arms, rocking in her chair.

"Yes, I do because Jennifer has said from the very beginning she would love to spread awareness about breast cancer." Duane was being honest when he said, "I also believe that writing a book about her experience would be a wonderful means of spreading the *Word* to others."

His spiritual emphasis struck a chord in Mary's heart because she knew Duane was right.

"Spreading the word about breast cancer awareness is necessary, but spreading the *Word* is a vital part of being a Christian," Duane said, remembering all that took place during the last year and a half. "We've seen God's glory at work in Jennifer's life and we've all been spiritually changed by witnessing His character in her."

"I won't argue with you Duane since I believe writing a book about Jennifer was part of God's design from the very beginning."

"You're right Mary, because both Christians and non-Christians need to hear about Jennifer's walk with Jesus." Duane reached over and tapped her arm with the paper he had rolled up in his hand and said, "I also believe that writing a book is part of God's plan for you."

Mary made no attempt to wipe away the single tear that spoke of her emotions. The seed planted that evening on the beach at Zion had taken root and was encompassing her heart. She recognized and understood the gentle whisper of . . . *The Shepherd's Voice.*

~ 33 ~

For Bill, the outward signs of Ramsay Hunt Syndrome were fading, and although he was still a little unsteady on his feet, he was feeling much better. It was a quiet morning and they were clearing the breakfast table when he noticed the tired look on Rima's face. He knew the strain of nursing him back to health had been an emotional event for her, and he thanked God for the joyful commitment she had demonstrated during the last month while he recovered.

"Honey, come sit down," he said.

Rima stopped to consider resting for a minute since her back was aching, and she felt constant cramping all morning in her lower abdomen.

"You've been working non-stop for weeks and you look especially tired this morning." Bill held out his hand, inviting her to sit on the couch next to him. "Is everything all right?"

Rima sat on the edge of the sofa, but she wasn't sure how much longer she could ignore the erratic spasms in her midsection. The sudden onset of what felt like muscle contractions were very real and the sensation persisted with increased intensity. Rima began to think of what she could have eaten that might have caused such a strong reaction.

It took a moment before she thought of when her last menstrual cycle was, and then she became intuitively aware that something was not right. It had been months, she thought, not weeks since her last cycle. She had lost track of time with helping Jennifer, babysitting Angelina and taking care of her husband. Immediately the room started to sway, and the overall sensation of labor contractions registered in her mind. She jumped from the sofa and raced down the hallway toward the bathroom.

"Rima?" Bill was quick to get to his feet, but the sudden movement jolted his equilibrium and he had to regain his balance before dashing after his wife.

The bathroom door was ajar and Bill tapped lightly before reaching for the door knob. He found her inside, holding tightly to her midriff, and with a rhythm only she could understand, she rocked back and forth mourning the loss of their unborn child.

"The Lord gave and the Lord has taken away;
may the name of the Lord be praised."
Job 1:21

*   *   *

It was the last Saturday of August and summer was ending. Mary was driving to Milford for a surprise birthday party and before getting into the heavy flow of traffic, she dialed Candice on her cell phone. It had been too long since they last spoke, and keeping in touch through e-mail was not the same as talking.

Mary knew Candice was busy most of the summer working in the church garden. The Garden Angels Club was preparing the grounds for a dedication service that would be held the following spring. Happily, Candice was at home working in her yard and when her cell phone rang she reached into her pocket to answer the call. They always had much to talk about: their families, friends, neighbors and of course, their faith. After catching up on most things, Candice asked, "Tell me about Jennifer, how is she doing?"

Mary stopped at a red light and said, "Her next decision is serious Candice, because she is considering a bone marrow transplant."

"Oh, that is very serious." Candice swept the dirt away from the potting shed onto the grassy lawn.

"Yes it is, and Jennifer will have to leave the country for the special type of procedure her doctors are recommending."

Candice stopped to lean on the broom handle and watched the woodpeckers fly through the pine trees while listening to Mary.

"Unfortunately, her last scan showed new activity near her left lung which means the available treatment here in the United States is not combating her rare form of breast cancer."

"I'm so sorry. When does Jennifer need to make a decision?"

"She has to make her decision within the next few months," Mary told her.

Candice went toward the front of the house and asked, "How are Keith and the children doing?" The tufts of Elijah Blue grass surrounded her footsteps as she walked.

"I think Jennifer's children are too young to comprehend what is happening, although they do know their mother is very ill."

Candice pulled dead leaves from the ivy that grew unchecked along the side of the house and asked, "What about Keith, how is he handling everything?" She came around the corner and watched her husband, Walt, mowing the front yard.

Mary stopped at another traffic light and said, "Candice, it's hard to tell how Keith is doing because he's very private, the opposite of Jennifer."

"I pray he has someone to confide in," Candice said.

"I'm not sure if he does or not; he seems so isolated."

"It's hard to determine where the invisible lines of privacy are drawn for some people, but I believe Keith knows that Jennifer's friends are there for him, too." Candice was momentarily distracted by Walt's uncharacteristic behavior. He was wiping his brow and sweating more than normal from simply cutting the grass. He had stopped the lawnmower and was sitting on the porch steps. She looked his way, and he waved at her, indicating he was tired.

On the road ahead, Mary saw the ramp for I-696 West, and said, "I'd better hang up now before I merge onto the Motor City's Indy-500."

"Oh, be careful driving Mary, we'll talk again soon." With concern, Candice walked over to join her husband on the front steps.

*   *   *

Keith and Jennifer parked their car in the Lanyon's driveway. Secretly, Jennifer had planned with Duane a surprise party for Janis and she was excited as Keith helped her by carrying the birthday cake. Jennifer's hands were full of birthday plates, napkins, and of course a party tiara with sequin numbers of 40.

"This is thoughtful!" Janis said, watching Jennifer set the items on the picnic table.

Nicholas ran to the goldfish pond in the backyard, but Natalie stayed close to her mom, hugging the right leg of Jennifer's black jeans. Keith stood on the deck opening a can of pop and nodded hello to Duane.

Janis helped unpack the bag of party decorations and gave Natalie one saying, "Gee, you would think a lot of people were coming over. Look at how many party decorations your mommy brought!"

"Surprise!" Cathy and Jim shouted with their children; Rebecca, Ryan, and Emily.

"Happy Birthday, Janis!" Mary, Al, and Sheila called out from behind the Britton family.

"What is going on?" Janis smiled and adjusted her party hat.

"We're celebrating your special birthday!" Jennifer laughed and clapped her hands.

"You shouldn't have – " Janis said, as she was indeed surprised.

Kathy and Bob along with their children; Rose, Jacob, and Lydia, had parked their car in the driveway next to the Abraham family.

"Hello, Susan." Kathy was happy that Susan came to celebrate with her co-workers.

"How is beautiful Lydia?" Susan kissed the toddler's fingertips. Her husband, Abe, smiled at the baby while their teenagers, Michelle and Michael, got out of the car.

"Lydia is doing very well, thank you for asking, Susan." Kathy introduced her family to the Abraham's.

Abe shook Bob's hand, then they went to join the others in the backyard and the birthday party started. The children all played outdoor games while the adults sat comfortably in the shade. Everyone was happy, and the conversations started to overlap as the noise level grew. Jennifer was delighted by seeing everyone she had worked with. She loved her job and truly missed the working connection in her life.

"Al Partington, you look great!" Jennifer complimented her boss.

"Thank you." Al smiled putting his arm around Sheila, his wife.

"Mary!" Jennifer held her tightly, letting their embrace linger for a moment before she asked, "Where are your children, Christopher and Jessica?"

326

"They're working today, but they told me to say hello." Mary held her at arm's length and exclaimed, "Jennifer, you look terrific!"

"Thank you." Jennifer tugged self-consciously at her wig, making sure it was securely in place.

Duane walked over to them and asked, "We're ready to order the pizza. Are Bill and Rima coming?"

"No, they won't be here because Rima isn't feeling well." Jennifer's smile seemed to disappear as she took Duane by the arm and walked over to the picnic table with him.

Cathy was scooping salsa onto a plate and asked, "Where are your children, Mary?"

"Working." Mary took a handful of grapes.

"Man, I never get to see them anymore," she said.

"That's funny, neither do I. Where is your husband, Cathy?"

She nodded toward the badminton net and said, "Jimbo has already divided the kids into teams, and the first game is almost over."

Mary watched the commotion in the backyard and could tell by his personality that he was a teacher, a good teacher. Jim had things organized and the children occupied in no time. She turned back to Cathy and commented, "Jennifer looks great today, doesn't she?"

"Yes, she does." Cathy wiped a salsa stain from the front of her t-shirt and laughed, "Oops, I tell my kids not to get dirty, but look at me." Ignoring the stain, she gave Mary an update and said, "Jennifer told me the doctors are scheduling her for another PET scan in two months to determine the effectiveness of the most recent round of chemotherapy, and if the results show no progress, she'll go forward with her plans on leaving the country for alternative treatment. She plans to have a fairly new procedure called a donor lymphocyte infusion."

"Did Jennifer say which country she would go to for this procedure?"

"No, she doesn't want to say anything until she and Keith have agreed on the location, but I believe they're looking at two different countries." Cathy couldn't imagine being in Jennifer's position and having to make such a life-changing decision. She wondered if she could leave her children and travel to another country, all in an effort to save her life.

"Cathy, please don't worry because God will be with Jennifer no matter where she goes," Mary said.

Just then Emily ran onto the deck, wanting her mother to play badminton. Cathy left and raced the three-year-old across the grassy lawn. Mary strolled over to sit with Al and Sheila, who were listening to Susan. She was discussing how cancer has forced her family to make necessary adjustments in their lifestyle. Kathy was helping Janis with the ice cooler. Eventually the group of engineers, who were co-workers and friends with much in common, settled into a relaxing afternoon of conversation and fellowship.

Jennifer walked through the noisy crowd following Janis into the house, and when Jennifer passed Mary, she paused and lovingly squeezed Mary's shoulders. Mary felt something extraordinary was stirring from within Jennifer, and she had a feeling Jennifer knew more about her current medical condition than what she chose to reveal at this time.

There was an air of melancholy surrounding Jennifer, and Mary could sense it. Across the yard Mary saw Keith leaning against the picnic table and decided to go over to talk with him. Keith saw her coming and he nervously cleared his throat. It wasn't as though he was intimidated by her, but he was uncomfortable in her presence because Keith knew Jennifer confided a great deal in Mary.

"Hello, Keith, how are you doing?" she asked him.

He looked away and calmly asked, "Do you really want to know?"

Mary gave him an exasperated huff that quickly turned into a slight grin when she saw a faint smile appear on his face. Keith didn't say anything, but his eyes sparkled with a rare humor.

"Keith, when I leave you a voice message or send you an e-mail asking how you're doing, I want you to know that I don't mean to be intrusive." Mary's tone was gentle. "I just want you to know that I care about you."

"I know that." He swirled the cup of pop in his hand before taking a swallow.

"Everyone here cares about you, Keith," she told him.

"I know that." He took another swallow.

"Is there anything in particular that you'd like us to do for you?"

"Nope." He finished the last sip.

Duane brought out the pizza and placed it on a folding table outside in the shade. He noticed Mary and Keith talking and after weighing the situation over in his mind, he decided to join them. "Keith, would you like some pizza?" Duane's invitation was kind and friendly.

"Sure, we never have pizza at home," Keith mumbled.

Duane and Mary glanced at each other, trying to decipher his humor; was he serious or joking they wondered.

"Where is Jennifer?" Keith asked Duane.

"She's inside the house with Janis, getting Angelina up from her nap. Would you like me to see what is taking them so long?" Duane offered.

"No." Out of nowhere the volleyball dropped at Keith's feet. He tossed it back to the players and then walked over to the goldfish pond to be with his son, Nicholas.

Duane and Mary hopelessly watched him walk away.

*   *   *

Inside the house, Janis finished changing Angelina's diaper and started to dress her in a little pink sundress with a matching hat, when she asked Jennifer, "Do you want me to put her shoes on?"

"Not today, Janis, let her feel the grass with her toes." Jennifer tickled her daughter's bare feet and asked, "Is she trying to walk yet?"

"She's trying, but I don't encourage it." Janis buttoned the front of the baby's sundress and said, "Rima and I have talked and we want you to be the first one to see Angelina walk."

Jennifer sighed and said, "That's very kind of you, but I don't think you should hold her back on account of me." She smoothed her baby daughter's fine hair over to one side and said, "I'm gone so much of the time that if you wait for me, she might be three-years-old before she walks." Jennifer leaned over the bed and kissed her daughter on the cheek.

Unexpectedly, the coarse strands of hair from her wig poked Angelina's face making her cry. Jennifer tucked the strands of blended synthetic fiber behind her ears as she tried to soothe the baby, but Angelina was being too fussy and wanted no part of the stranger who was imitating her mother's voice.

"Oh, what's wrong, baby girl?" Jennifer cooed.

"I think she's hungry, let me get her a bottle."

But, when Janis got up to leave, Angelina turned from her mother, and held out her tiny arms in mid-air toward Janis. In her infant mind, she didn't want to be alone with someone who sounded like, but didn't look like, her mother.

"She doesn't know who I am." Tears welled in Jennifer's eyes.

"No, Jennifer, she's just teething and not feeling well today." Janis tried to conceal the child's innocent behavior.

"No, that's not it at all," Jennifer wept. "She doesn't know who I am."

Janis was dumbfounded and didn't know who to comfort first: the baby or her mother. She brought Angelina back over to Jennifer, but the baby squirmed in her arms and wanted no part of the exchange. Janis stepped away and carried Angelina into the bathroom to get a box of tissues. She then handed them to Jennifer saying, "All babies go through this stage." She bounced Angelina in her arms and suggested, "Let's try it again – "

It was no use, Jennifer stood at the dresser and cried, "All I've gone through and my child doesn't even know me." Jennifer opened her eyes and looked at the stranger in the mirror. She instantly understood why Angelina didn't know her, because truthfully – she hardly recognized her own reflection anymore. In truth, Angelina only knew Jennifer during her battle with breast cancer. Her daughter didn't know the Jennifer from the past, the Jennifer that now seemed to be gone forever.

Jennifer slid the auburn wig off her scalp and dabbed at the streaks of mascara that darkened the corners of her eyes. She knew what must be done in order to calm her daughter. Jennifer remembered her Grandmother Catherine's wisdom about remaining happy even under sad circumstances. She could hear her grandmother's voice echoing in her mind . . . *Rejoice and be glad for this is the day the Lord has made. (Psalm 118:24)*

*   *   *

Janis waited and prayed the squirming toddler would recall and identify with the woman in the mirror as being her loving mother. Jennifer cooed softly, reminding Janis of the morning dove that nested outside on the branches of the old Noble Firs that stood so tall and formed their property line. Angelina kept crying, but Jennifer wouldn't give up. She kept the soft rhythmic sound of her voice alive and waited patiently for her daughter's response.

Soon, Angelina peeked around the side of Janis' neck with the dawning of recognition shining in her gleaming eyes. Jennifer held out her arms and welcomed a hug. Janis placed Angelina in her mother's right arm and then without saying a word, Janis left the room and closed the door.

Jennifer spoke softly while Angelina played with the familiar piece of jewelry around her neck; she knew it could only belong to her mother. Jennifer dangled the mustard seeds in front of the baby's tear-stained hands. She lowered herself to the edge of the bed and held the child next to her heart. Jennifer pointed to each seed in the glass vile and individually recited the names of everyone outside at the birthday party.

~ *34* ~

The next morning, Nicholas was playing in the kitchen and asked Jennifer, "Mom, how come Aunt Rima and Uncle Bill didn't go to the birthday party yesterday?" He finished breakfast before she had a chance to wipe the grape jelly from his hands. She could see he had transferred the sticky mess to his Star Trek toy.

Jennifer folded the kitchen towel while thinking of the right response to her son's question. She had spent the last few weeks comforting Rima over the telephone since she also knew the sorrow of losing an unborn child. Although Rima's mother, Mrs. Holland, had offered to make the trip to Michigan from Louisiana in order to be with her daughter, Rima declined the heartfelt offer. For now, Rima was slowly coming to understand what Jennifer learned through personal experience; only the Father could comfort a mother who had lost a child.

Nicholas spun his toy around in circles, and Jennifer wondered if he was too young to comprehend their tragedy. Up and down he flew the Starship, making sputtering noises imitating a galactic engine failure. Jennifer's thoughts also spiraled into a future orbit and she wondered if someday she would be there to answer the questions her son would surely have during his adolescence.

"Nicholas, do you know where babies come from?" she asked.

"Uh-huh." His imaginary galaxy exploded as he fell to the floor and glided his ship to a safe landing.

"Okay, tell Mommy where you think babies come from." Her son was five-years-old.

"All babies come from God, but how come Aunt Rima and Uncle Bill weren't at the party?"

Jennifer gazed at him and made the wise decision that he was too young to understand God's perfect design. "Aunt Rima isn't feeling well, and Uncle Bill is helping her get better."

Nicholas fixed the broken wing of the aircraft and innocently asked, "Does Aunt Rima have cancer?"

"Honey, no, she doesn't have cancer!" Jennifer held him to her side and reassured him, "Aunt Rima only has a tummy ache, but she'll be here in a few days to help us, you'll see." Jennifer wondered if he had overheard the adult conversations yesterday surrounding Lydia and Susan's cancer and probably her own. She was sure this was all too much for him to understand.

Nicholas snapped the landing gear up and down several times.

"Do you believe me?" Jennifer lifted his chin to meet her gaze.

He grinned when he discovered he couldn't nod his head because she held his chin so tightly. She bent over and kissed the tip of his upturned nose and asked, "Any more questions?" She wanted desperately to be with him in the future to answer all his questions, but she knew the choice was not hers to make.

Nicholas answered her with a quick no and then ran into the living room just as her cell phone chirped from inside her backpack.

"Hello?" she answered.

"I'm in your driveway, Jennifer, do you need anything?" Shari asked since she was on her way to the store before going into her beauty salon.

"You're a life saver Shari, because Angelina is wearing her last diaper."

After asking Shari to pickup a few more items, Jennifer walked over and stepped down into the family room. She had gone to the store recently and knew she had brought home a box of diapers, but she couldn't find them anywhere. It was frustrating because everything was scattered about, making it all but impossible to find things anymore.

"Mommy, look at me!" Natalie twirled in her Cinderella dress.

"What are you wearing?" Jennifer asked in disbelief.

"Your hair!" The little girl spread her arms and joyfully laughed.

"Along with Mommy's lipstick and make-up," Jennifer sighed.

"And look, your shoes too!" Natalie pointed a toe at her mother and happily said, "I look like you Mommy; I look beautiful!"

"Natalie, whoever said your Mommy was beautiful?" Jennifer was on her knees, looking in the storage bins for a diaper of any size.

"Everybody says you're beautiful!" Natalie held her magic wand over Jennifer's head, she tapped her mother's shoulder three times and whispered softly, "There's no place like home. There's no place like home." Natalie magically clicked the back of the oversize shoes together and repeated once more, "There's no place like home." She quickly stepped out of Jennifer's shoes and ran back up the stairs.

Jennifer picked up the silver slippers and remembered the last time she had worn them. She carefully strapped the loose band closed on the one slipper as loving memories took her back in time . . . *there's no place like home.*

She thought back to when she and Keith were at Disneyland and even though it was late in January, they decided to celebrate their eleventh wedding anniversary earlier that year, 2004. She recalled playfully bouncing her silver-strapped toe under the table, gently nudging Keith's leg while waiting for the right moment to tell him she was pregnant.

Jennifer was happily married, a mother of two, and a successful engineer working in the Motor City. Her life was perfect, or so it seemed, until she found a small lump. Somehow, try as she may, she simply couldn't keep herself from wondering how the surgeon, and the consulting radiologist tragically misdiagnosed her cancer.

Often times she pictured herself sitting in the waiting room of Dr. Zachariah Jordan's medical practice, and how the artistic photographs of the Holy Land had given her such peace. Did she fail to see God's direction at the time? Looking back, she now wondered if her feelings of peace were veiled in deception. Jennifer wasn't certain, but for now her only comfort was in the knowledge that one day all things would be revealed.

Each night she prayed for unsuspecting women in her position. She prayed they would seek a second opinion in the early stages of their discovery, and this is where Jennifer struggled with her circumstances because she *did* seek a second opinion.

She held the silver slipper against her heart and prayed . . . *Dear God, empty me of any unforgiving thoughts I may still have because I only want to be filled with Your love and kindness. Please give me abundant wisdom to remember that You are a sovereign God and judgment is in Your hands only. Forgive me of any bitterness I harbor and free me from clinging to feelings of resentment. Amen.*

*   *   *

"Knock, knock!" Shari stood at the door with a few groceries and two bags of diapers.

"Come on in." Jennifer had lost track of time as she walked into the foyer carrying her shoes.

"Those are pretty shoes. Are you going out tonight?" Shari placed the bag of diapers on the foyer table.

"No." Jennifer tossed her shoes on the floor and followed Shari into the kitchen. "Thank you for always helping me out, Shari."

"You're welcome, but I can't visit today because I have a million things to do before Jeff and I leave on our vacation."

"I completely forgot about your Mediterranean cruise." Jennifer clapped her hands and said, "Is there something I can help you with before you leave, Shari?"

"Well, I would love to find some romantic evening shawls for when Jeff and I stroll along the ship's deck in the moonlight." Shari danced about in the confines of the small kitchen, holding a box of cereal as her partner.

"Wait right here." Jennifer left before Shari could protest.

She soon returned and handed Shari two elegantly beaded shawls. One was made of a sheer black crepe with inlaid beads and it shimmered when held up to the light. The other was a soft woven fabric of sparkling gold yarn. Both wraps were special, and Jennifer wanted Shari to enjoy them.

"These are exactly what I would have picked out." Shari wrapped them around her shoulders and twirled in circles asking Jennifer how she looked.

"You look spectacular!" Jennifer leaned against the kitchen counter and laughed with her friend. "Take them with you, Shari, and enjoy your second honeymoon."

"Thank you, Jennifer, and when I wear them it'll make me feel as if you are there with me, which will make the cruise even more special." Shari folded the wraps and walked to the door, saying she and Jeff would stop by on Wednesday night to drive her to the mid-week service at church. "You will be able to come, won't you?"

Jennifer kept her eyes focused on Shari's smile and said, "Yes, I have it marked on my calendar."

"Wonderful; our pastor will be releasing caged butterflies at the service to signify that, as believers in Christ, we have surrendered our lives to Him and we are free – free indeed!" Shari struggled with the tightness in her throat and said, "Jeff and I would love to have you there with us to share in our Christian freedom."

Star of Bethlehem
Autumn of 2005

~ 35 ~
❦

S eptember 8th was Angelina's first birthday and the family chose to spend the day quietly at home. Nicholas played on the computer while Natalie watched the Disney channel on television, and Angelina was fast asleep after being showered with attention on her special day.

"Would you like more birthday cake?" Jennifer asked Keith.

"No, thanks." He put the ice cream back into the freezer.

Jennifer returned home the night before from the Cancer Treatment Center of America in Zion after receiving another round of chemotherapy, and Keith was anxious to learn of her progress. They needed to talk, but neither one knew where to begin. Until recently, the possibility of cancer treatment outside the United States was a bridge to cross somewhere in the future. But now, only a short distance away, the bridge loomed on the horizon, and crossing over was no longer a matter of choice.

"It's time for us to make a decision regarding your treatment, isn't it?" Keith asked.

"Yes," Jennifer replied.

"How much time do we have?" His stomach began its familiar churning.

"We have five, maybe six, weeks to decide." Jennifer walked to the couch and he followed, sitting next to her. "Keith, my case study was turned down at Bethesda," she told him.

His stomach tightened, and his shoulders slumped. "Why?"

"In my particular case, the doctors need a clean scan with no metastasis." Jennifer nervously fiddled with the corner of the pillow and said, "So, my current doctors will continue with my treatment in Zion until you and I make a decision on where I should go next."

He clasped his hands behind his head and stared at the ceiling.

"Keith, the only choices I have for treatment are not covered by our health insurance – I'm sorry," she whispered.

"I don't want you to be sorry Jennifer, because none of this is your fault," he sighed. "Tell me what medical choices we have at this point."

Jennifer took a deep breath and said, "We have two options: either Mexico or Israel."

Keith had heard about treatment in Mexico, but with surprise he asked, "Where in Israel?"

"Jerusalem." With her lyrical voice she sang the word.

He leaned forward with his elbows on his knees and turned to face her. He knew she had already made her decision. "We're going to Jerusalem, aren't we?"

"Yes." Although she was smiling, she couldn't keep her tears from falling.

Keith embraced her as his stomach increased its tightening grip. He kissed the tip of her nose and said, "Who would have known, less than two years ago, we would be traveling halfway around the world in search of a cancer treatment?"

"We didn't know Keith, but God has known all along."
Keith whispered in her ear, "Jennifer in Jerusalem."

*   *   *

Bill and Rima drove along in silence, listening only to the Corvette's horsepower pulsating from underneath the hood of the sports car. It was mid-September and time heals all wounds. Through prayer and with God's love they were both well and smiling again.

Bill returned to work several weeks ago, which helped in making their lives more of a routine, but today he thought a long drive in the country might be good for them. He drove along admiring the beauty of nature and noticed the trees were already turning orange and yellow. He knew God was working in Rima's heart to heal the sorrow of their lost child, but something else was wrong. He shifted gears at the four-way stop and felt the vibration of the powerful engine.

"Rima, how was your visit with Jennifer yesterday?" Bill eased off the clutch.

"It was very sad." Rima looked through the passenger side window.

"Yes, I know the results of her recent scans were not good."

"No the results were not good, and yesterday it was difficult listening to her say, that after all this time and suffering, her treatment has ultimately failed." Rima was tired of crying.

Bill shifted smoothly into first, then second gear.

"Do you think she'll go to Hadassah University Hospital in Israel for treatment?"

Rima recalled her conversation with Jennifer and said, "Yes, and I pray she'll experience God's peace while she's in the Holy Land."

"Jerusalem means: The City of Peace," Bill said. "And even though God is everywhere, it'll be an added comfort to Jennifer that she'll undergo her last chance for survival in the Holy Land."

In silence, they drove a bit further down the country road before Rima said, "William, I feel as though God is providing this opportunity for Jennifer to experience first hand, His remarkable love."

"I'm thinking the same thing, Rima," he agreed.

On the road in front of them, two pheasants, a female and her mate with a vibrant white ring at the base of his neck, took flight from the side of the road where they were feeding. The sun was a perfect circle, setting across the fading cornfield. It dipped lower, and black shadows of dry corn husks danced in front of the blazing orange fireball.

*　　　*　　　*

It had been a fruitful morning and Sue was done weeding through an array of Shasta daises. She took off her work gloves and stood to get a better look at her progress; her backyard garden was beautiful and the upkeep was a labor of love. She bent to pull a stray weed from the undergrowth when her cell phone chirped. Sue quickly discarded the pulled weed and rummaged through her garden apron for the tiny electrical device.

"Hi, Mary." She walked toward the patio and said, "I called your house earlier this morning, did you get my message?"

"Yes, I did," Mary said, while unpacking groceries. "It looks like you and Bill will have perfect weather for a bike trip to Saugatuck today. Who are you riding with?"

"We're riding out with my sister, Shawn, in an hour. Then we'll meet up with Pam and John later this afternoon. It's funny, but after all these years we still love riding motorcycles."

Sue dusted off her work gloves before resting in the lounge chair, and after several minutes of small talk, she asked how Jennifer was doing. She listened to Mary explain the two options that Jennifer has for treatment; either she will go to Mexico or Israel, but Mary sensed Jennifer was praying about Israel.

"It will be a spiritual pilgrimage for her to travel to Jerusalem," Mary added.

"Yes, it will be, and God will enable her to endure the trip," Sue said.

"Jennifer has come so far and she sees no reason to stop now, and besides, it's her desire to continue running the race which God has placed before her."

"Mary, this is such a remarkable story."

"Yes, it is truly a remarkable story, and what an extraordinary blessing it's been for all of us to witness."

The sound of motorcycle engines echoed through the garage and filtered into the backyard. Bill and Sue's sister, Shawn, came out to the patio dressed in riding gear; they wanted to leave. Sue got up from the lounge chair, nodded in their direction indicating she would be ready in a minute.

The love of riding motorcycles was the common thread that held the three sisters together; Sue, Pam, and Shawn – yet individually they were as different as night and day. Hearing the commotion on the other end of the line, Mary said good-bye and told her friend to be safe. Sue raced upstairs to pack her leather bag for the road trip, only to find it sitting on the floor ready to go. Her husband, Bill, had packed for her while she was talking on the telephone.

The roar of the Harley's twin mufflers filled her thoughts, drawing Sue to the freedom of the ride. Bill waited in the kitchen with her leather jacket, helmet, riding gloves, and a smile. Shawn was waiting at the end of the driveway, ready to follow his lead. Bill straddled the running engine, balancing the bike while Sue curled in behind him. He shifted into gear and nodded at Shawn, who pulled out after him . . . *they were ready to ride.*

*   *   *

September 29 was Jennifer's thirty-fourth birthday and a few of her friends gathered at Cathy's home for a quiet celebration. The men sat around the television with appetizers and snacks as the season was underway for college football. The children were scattered throughout the house and the women busied themselves with preparing the table for dessert. There was a church-like stillness in the air; a strong apprehension that everyone could sense.

Janis was occupied with clearing off the counter and Kathy sat at the table with Lydia who was fast asleep in her arms. Sheila brought out the cake with extra plates and napkins, and Cathy was brewing a second pot of coffee when Mary came into the kitchen through the living room.

"How is Jennifer doing?" Cathy asked, knowing Mary had been talking privately with Jennifer.

"She's made a decision regarding her treatment and she plans to tell everyone shortly." Mary washed her hands at the sink.

Cathy lit the birthday candles, the men stood around the kitchen table, and the children stopped playing long enough to harmonize as best they could, singing happy birthday to Jennifer.

The glow from the flickering candles reflected in Jennifer's eyes as she focused on the flames and held Natalie safely by her side. Jennifer thoughtfully ran the vile of mustard seeds along the gold chain she wore every day, but today she wasn't wearing the smile that everyone loved.

Janis held Angelina while she finished her bottle, and Nicholas knelt on the chair next to his mother. With an obvious trace of uncertainty, Keith leaned against the door frame and watched his wife blow out her birthday candles. His hand automatically rubbed his stomach when Cathy offered him a piece of birthday cake and he politely declined. Unnoticed, he quietly slipped back into the family room.

Rima scooped ice cream for everyone while Sheila helped cut the cake, and Mary poured the last of the coffee. Jennifer sat at the table and being careful not to use her left hand, she blended hazelnut cream and raw brown sugar into her coffee, and finishing it off by sprinkling cinnamon on top. She took one sip and added a touch more cream.

"Mary?" Jennifer asked.

"Hmm?" She was sitting next to her at the table.

"Have you always enjoyed your coffee plain with nothing else in it?" she wondered.

"Yes." Mary wasn't exactly sure what Jennifer meant by the unusual question.

"I admire that about you." Jennifer blew lightly over the rim of her mug.

Mary frowned at the sadness in Jennifer's voice and said, "I don't understand what you mean, Jennifer."

The children were scattered back into the living room, and the men were watching the football game. Only the women sat at the kitchen table listening to the peculiar conversation.

"What I mean is this; you like coffee because its coffee and you don't change it by adding flavoring, sugar, spices, or whipped cream." Emotional tears moistened Jennifer's eyes. "In other words, you don't try to make it into something it's not – you simply enjoy coffee for what it is." Jennifer took a deep breath and sighed, "It brings to mind that I'm guilty of wasting too much time doing unnecessary and often mean-ingless things throughout my life. There have been many times when I've changed things to be more of what I wanted, when in fact, I should have looked deeper and appreciated the beauty of pure simplicity, like drinking black coffee."

Rima handed Jennifer a tissue.

"Jen, you have always appreciated things." Cathy comforted her.

"We all have the same thoughts," Sheila said, "because no matter how old you are, you will always regret wasting time."

"And time is no longer on my side." Jennifer straightened her back and lifted her shoulders. Her friends patiently waited for her to tell them the news they feared and did not want to hear. "I've been scheduled for my final round of cancer treatment at CTCA."

Even though Jennifer placed little emphasis on it, the word *final* echoed loudly around the table. Everyone waited anxiously for her to continue.

"It would be wrong of me to mislead all of you by trying to sugarcoat this news, but I'm sorry to say that my chemotherapy and radiation have failed." A nervous laugh escaped before she said, "The doctors have advised me that continuing with the same type of treatment available in the United States is unwise and counterproductive."

Rima and Cathy were forewarned of the news, but still they couldn't stop their tears from falling. Mary reached out and covered Jennifer's hand, touching her with encouragement because there was more to be said.

"Keith and I have discussed my options, and with prayerful consideration, I have made the decision to travel to Israel for cancer treatment." Jennifer loved every tear-stained face she saw before her. "I'll be leaving in six weeks for the Holy Land." She gave a decisive nod with a radiant smile. In the air she gave a thumbs-up signal and declared, "I'm going to Jerusalem!"

~ 36 ~

It was mid-October and oddly enough it was hot outside. Candice pulled into the parking lot and quickly went into the restaurant to enjoy the coolness of air conditioning. She joined Mary in the corner booth for breakfast.

"Can you believe how warm it is?" Mary greeted her.

"Yes, it is unseasonably warm for this time of year." Candice asked the waitress for ice water.

"How was your weekend get-away trip to Oscoda?"

"It was wonderful, but I packed all the wrong clothes," Candice laughed.

"You needed shorts with t-shirts, but you packed sweaters and long pants, right?" Mary smiled.

"Exactly, but we still had a wonderful time." She sipped her ice water and said, "We love four-wheeling through the woods and along the shores of Lake Huron, but toward the end Mary, Walt was getting tired and it concerned me." Candice tucked her short blonde hair behind her ears.

"It concerned you that he was tired?"

"No, it's not just being tired; he was short of breath and pale." Candice opened the menu and said, "I'm going to talk him into seeing the doctor very soon."

"What do you think the problem is, Candice?"

"I don't know, but I would feel better if he saw his cardiologist."

The waitress took their orders, and while waiting for breakfast, they enjoyed visiting and catching up on the details of one another's life. A short time later Candice said, "Tell me how things are going with Jennifer."

Mary spun the coffee cup in her hands several times before she told Candice about Jennifer's plans for Israel. This was the first Candice had heard about the decision and she was surprised.

"Jerusalem?" Candice could only mouth the word. She dared not say it aloud because she was so astonished.

Mary nodded.

"Israel?" Candice whispered, wanting to make sure she understood.

"Yes, she and Keith are leaving in six weeks."

"In six weeks?" Her shoulders slumped at the reality of the journey and she stated, "This is so sudden."

"Jennifer doesn't have a lot of time," Mary sighed.

"Oh, Mary, I'm sorry." Candice wanted to absorb the news before asking, "What about their children, who'll take care of them while they're gone?"

Mary explained that Nicholas and Natalie would stay at home, and their teacher from Red Bell Day Care would temporarily move into the house so she could care for them while Keith and Jennifer are in the Middle East. Angelina would stay at Bill and Rima's during the week, but on weekends they would have all three children together. Then, Duane and Janis would watch them whenever Bill and Rima had plans and could not.

After finishing, Mary concentrated on her words before saying, "Candice, I want to tell you something special that Jennifer shared with me recently."

"Yes, I'm listening," Candice leaned forward.

"Jennifer told me – " Mary stopped to compose herself and she tried again. "Jennifer told me that she was grateful for her illness because it has served as a mechanism to bring her closer to Jesus Christ."

Candice gave Mary a startled look from across the table.

Mary explained, "Yes, that's exactly what Jennifer told me. She believes that her breast cancer has magnified her personal relationship with our Lord, and she's thankful for that blessing. Jennifer said that she sees beyond her circumstances and views her suffering as a blessing that has resulted in an opportunity for her to know Our Lord and Savior on a more intimate and much deeper level."

Their breakfast plates remained untouched.

Candice gathered her thoughts and asked, "Mary, does Jennifer feel that because she's known pain and suffering, as Christ knew suffering, that she has a clearer understanding of His love for her?"

Mary nodded, and after the waitress cleared away their unwanted meal, it was Candice who spoke first, "Are you thinking what I'm thinking?"

Mary leaned forward and rested her elbows on the table. "I'm not sure, Candice, tell me what you would do in her situation?"

Candice carefully thought her words over and then said, "If I were Jennifer, I would go to Jerusalem."

"I would go, too." Mary cried.

"Nothing would stop me," Candice said with a strong spiritual conviction.

Two cups of plain black coffee sat between them as they discussed the details of the trip. Candice naturally offered to help with the arrangements, but Mary assured her that the Jen Possible Team members had already set things into motion. Everyone was eagerly waiting to be assigned a task to help Jennifer and Keith.

"So in everything, do to others what you
would have them do to you."
Matthew 7:12.

*　　　*　　　*

Shari was home unpacking her luggage when she came
across the black beaded shawl Jennifer loaned her for the
romantic Mediterranean cruise. One last time Shari draped
the fabric across her shoulders and swayed as memories of
the past four weeks danced in her thoughts.

While on vacation, Shari prayed daily for increased spiritual strength and wisdom for Jennifer, and that she would
not falter in seeking God's plan for her life and His purpose
for her illness. Shari looked for the other shawl and found it
in another suitcase.

During their vacation, she and Jeff met other couples,
all of whom told stories of years spent together in marriage
and while listening to them, her thoughts traveled across the
ocean to the young married couple in Plymouth, Michigan.

She stopped to gather the delicate fabrics in her hands
and then hurried into the kitchen. She took her car keys and
left the house as a sudden urgency to visit Jennifer filled
her thoughts. On her way into town, Shari stopped for gas
and after filling her tank, she turned to leave when she was
stopped by a young woman at the pump next to hers.

"Hello, my name is Heidi Livingston." She extended her
hand in greeting and explained, "I believe we know each
other through Jennifer Hayse?"

"Yes, I know Jennifer." Shari caught the way the woman's voice trembled when she spoke Jennifer's name.

"I'd like to do something special for Jennifer and since
you know her personally, I thought you might know what
needs to be done in the next couple of weeks. If so, I'd like
to offer my help in making it happen."

"What sort of special help would Jennifer need?" Shari didn't understand.

"I thought since Jennifer recently found out – " Heidi stopped in mid-sentence realizing from the look on Shari's face that she was not aware of the news.

"Since Jennifer recently found out what?" Shari was engulfed with a sickening feeling. She shook her head to clear her thoughts before saying, "My husband and I just got back in town from an extended vacation, and I haven't talked with Jennifer in several weeks. So, I'm a little confused, what news are you talking about?"

"I'm terribly sorry," Heidi felt awful, "I didn't realize you were out of town and didn't know."

Shari felt her knees give way; she leaned against her vehicle.

Heidi turned to walk away.

"Wait!" Shari reached out to stop her.

"I shouldn't have said anything." Heidi was embarrassed. "I just wanted to do something more significant to help out."

Shari told Heidi there was no need to apologize and then asked her to explain what had taken place while she was gone.

"We've been asked, that is, the women in her neighborhood who have been helping Jennifer, were asked to offer additional help with preparing meals and doing laundry." Heidi began to cry and found it difficult to continue. "We've increased our prayers for Jennifer because she's been told – she has little time left."

Shari left Heidi standing alone as she moved quickly and got into her car. She fumbled with her keys before starting the vehicle and pulling out of the gas station. She prayed frantically during the four mile drive to Jennifer's home . . . *Dear God, please don't let this be true!*

The black Ford Explorer was parked in the driveway, indicating that Jennifer was home. Shari's left hand guided her vehicle into the drive as her right hand searched her purse for her cell phone; blindly she flipped it open and pressed the speed dial to Jennifer's home.

"Hello?" Jennifer was groggy from her morning dose of medication.

"I'm in your driveway," Shari briskly said.

"Shari, welcome home." The voice on the telephone didn't sound like Jennifer's.

"Would you like some company?" Shari wiped her tears.

"Yes, I'll be at the front door in a minute." Jennifer sat up and rubbed her eyes as she slowly moved her legs to the side of the bed and then reached for her bathrobe. She found her glasses and shoved her feet into her slippers. She tied the front of her robe and purposely did not glance at the mirror before leaving the bedroom because she knew this morning she looked as awful as she felt.

Shari watched through her car windshield as the welcome wreath on Jennifer's front door moved inward toward the foyer. The morning sun was covered over by gray clouds and thunder rumbled as the rain began to fall, just as Shari stepped onto the front porch. A brisk wind along with fallen autumn leaves followed her footsteps into the house. Shari was startled by Jennifer's appearance because when she left on vacation several weeks ago, Jennifer was bright and cheerful, but now the drastic change in her appearance was shocking. In a flash, Shari knew and didn't need to confirm the possibility of any false rumors. Tears filled her eyes and Jennifer led her to the bottom of the stairs so they could sit and talk.

"When did you find out?" Jennifer asked, holding Shari's hand.

"Just now." Shari dabbed her nose with a tissue.

"I'm sorry you came home from your lovely vacation and this is the first bit of news you heard." Jennifer wrapped her arm around her mentor.

"Oh, Jennifer," Shari held her breath, trying to contain her sorrow, "please tell me what happened."

Jennifer didn't want to repeat the unfortunate news, but Shari was special. "My last scan indicated small sightings in the pelvic area and the spots discovered on the side of my neck last month have grown in size."

"The cancer treatment isn't working then," Shari said, as she clearly understood.

"No, it's not. My type of cancer is very rare and aggressive. It is also resistant to chemotherapy." Jennifer sighed, "My doctor's have tried several types of treatment, but so far all have failed, including two separate series of weekly radiation."

"Then what's the next step?"

"I've been accepted as a candidate for a bone marrow transplant."

A small ray of hope lifted Shari's spirit.

"Actually, it's more complicated than a BMT," Jennifer stated, covering her mouth while suppressing a nagging cough. "The procedure is called a donor lymphocyte infusion and Professor Shimon Slavin from Hadassah University Medical Center will be taking over my case study. I'll be leaving in five weeks for experimental treatment in Jerusalem, Israel." Jennifer waited as Shari adjusted to the news and then said, "I truly have no choice in the matter because my cancer continues to grow despite conventional treatment here in the United States."

"What can I do to help you, Jennifer?"

"Everything is being accomplished that needs to be done, all I can ask is that you increase your prayers for me." Jennifer tried to hide her tears, but it was useless. "God gave me a special blessing when He directed me to you, Shari, and

I want you to know how much I've appreciated all you've done for me."

On the stair steps in the foyer, they clung tightly to each other knowing they had experienced the same terrible disease, but with much different outcomes. Time passed, and with nothing more to say, Shari gave back to Jennifer the two borrowed shawls from her vacation. Jennifer held them lovingly against her cheek. She closed her eyes and thought about past occasions when she had worn them, and then gently gave them back to her friend and said, "Here, I want you to have them."

Shari couldn't possibly take them and shook her head in protest.

"Please, I want you to have them," Jennifer smiled.

Outside the rain continued to fall, the sky grew dark, the thunder crashed, lightning blazed across the afternoon sky, and they both knew – a terrible storm was coming.

"For I know that through your prayers and the help given
by the Spirit of Jesus Christ, what has happened to
me will turn out for my deliverance."
Philippians 1:19

~ 37 ~

Under the cover of morning darkness and through a rain storm, Duane made his way into work. Traffic was heavy and the ride was tiring. There was still a lot of work to be done on the prototype modules in preparation for his upcoming trip to Melbourne, Australia, which was only three months from now. He felt uneasy that he would be in Australia while Jennifer was in Israel, and what if something happened to her while he was out of the country?

The timing for the model launch in Australia was conflicting with his commitment to support Jennifer and her cause, but Duane knew God was in control and all things would be done according to His will and for His glory.

Lately he was constantly thinking about Keith, and Susan's husband, Abe. He could not imagine what they were enduring. He thought of how hard it would be to cope with the possibility of losing your wife.

Duane knew Jennifer and Susan were remarkable women with tremendous faith in God. He also knew they were loving wives, devoted mothers, and automotive engineers who were intelligent, resourceful, and hard working. Jennifer and Susan were very similar in many ways. However, the contrast between their husbands was much more complex. Primarily, the main difference between Keith and Abe was the foundation their lives were built upon.

The two men where set apart in their trust and belief, and that alone made a huge distinction in their lives. It was Abe's faith that served as a strong foundation for him during times of trouble. Abe was not fearful because he lived in a safe harbor and could take refuge in God, but for Keith it appeared his life was built on shifting sand giving him no foothold during turbulent storms.

Duane prayed the journey to the Holy Land would awaken Keith's heart, open his eyes to set the stage for complete surrender to Jesus. What a miraculous gift it would be for Jennifer to witness her husband's salvation in Jerusalem.

The next few weeks were going to be busy. He and Kathy had scheduled several meetings to be held during their lunch breaks so they could arrange fundraisers and charitable events organized by the Jen Possible Team. They were hoping to offset travel and other expenses Keith and Jennifer would soon be facing. Several events were already underway, including a Christmas Gala Dance, return pop can drives, family night at local restaurants, bake sales, coin harvest competitions at work, raffle drawings for sporting events, creating a website, silent auctions, and even a golf outing that was planned for later in the spring, 2006.

Everyone was getting involved and there was a tremendous amount of work to be done, including things Jennifer would like to have finished around the house. Duane knew with the help of others, everything would be accomplished and completed before Jennifer left in five short weeks. Things were moving fast and very soon . . . *she would be gone.*

*   *   *

Two weeks later, just before Halloween, Mary came home from work and parked her car in the driveway since she wouldn't have the use of her garage for the next couple of days while Christopher and Jessica turned it into a haunted house. Mary walked into the garage and started to rummage through bags of purchased items from the discount store and satisfied at what she saw, she reminded them to keep the haunted house theme rated-G.

"No problem, Mom." Christopher laughed and said, "It will be ghostly and gory!"

"Very funny." Mary knew he was joking.

"And, it will ghastly and ghoulish!" Jessica added.

Mary didn't hear much of their conversation, but her children knew her thoughts were distant and surmised what was on her mind.

Awhile later, Christopher asked, "Mom, when does Jennifer leave for Jerusalem?"

"She leaves in three weeks on November 11."

"Wow, so soon?" Jessica hung black crepe paper from the ceiling.

"The time has gone by fast, hasn't it?" Mary plugged in the orange lights to see if they worked.

"Are you going with her to Zion for her last cancer treatment after Halloween?" Christopher asked.

"No, I won't be going because Sue has offered to meet Jennifer at CTCA to keep her company." Mary explained.

Jessica rested on the bottom rung of the ladder and said, "God has placed many Christians into Jennifer's life who have helped during her illness."

Christopher agreed, and said, "That's why Jennifer always says, '*I am so blessed*'!"

Mary felt her children were old enough to realize the seriousness of Jennifer's circumstances, but she wanted to be sure, so she asked them, "Do you both understand that Jennifer may not survive the medical procedure in Jerusalem?"

Christopher glanced at his sister. He understood, but before saying anything he wanted to make sure Jessica understood and he could tell by the misty tears veiling her hazel eyes that she was aware of the possibility.

"Yes, we understand," he answered.

Tears fell from her eyes as Jessica stepped down from the ladder and said, "You know Mom, I feel blessed to know Jennifer because not many people get to meet someone like her."

"You can tell Jennifer is special," Christopher said, moving the ladder, "because God is taking her to His special place, and she gets to walk where Jesus walked."

"That's how I feel too, Chris," Jessica said, "because it's almost like going to Jerusalem is part of her reward – her reward for keeping her faith and being obedient to God's will."

"And if something happens to her while she's in Jerusalem, she'll be at peace." Christopher swallowed the lump in his throat and said, "It does seem like going to the Holy Land is a gift from God."

Mary was filled with love for them as her children clearly voiced her own spiritual thoughts.

*   *   *

Keith came home from work early and when he pulled into his driveway, he wondered who had decorated the outside of their home. Rima and Cathy were standing on the front lawn admiring the nicely set up Halloween display.

"Is Jennifer home yet?" he asked.

"No." Rima replied.

"By the way, where is she?" Cathy asked Rima.

"She's with Shari picking up copies of her medical records to take with her to Israel." Rima bent to pick up Angelina.

Keith said, "I thought maybe she would be home by now." He stared at the bale of straw angled in the corner of their yard with a scarecrow sitting on top of it, along with three pumpkins and a stalk of dried corn. He knew Jennifer would like the arrangement and asked, "Who put up these Halloween decorations?"

"A local Girl Scout troop came by after school with their moms and asked if they could place the decorations on the lawn," Cathy explained while helping Natalie get off her bicycle.

"Here comes your mommy!" Rima said to the girls.

They stepped off the driveway and Cathy directed everyone to stand behind the bale of straw because she wanted Jennifer to see how festive the yard looked. Shari smiled and waved as she turned off the car. Jennifer got out and was surprised to see her husband home so early.

"Hi, Keith." She greeted him first with a kiss before she said hello to the others, and then she asked, "What is everyone celebrating?" Jennifer reached over to smooth the top of Angelina's hair.

Cathy pretended she was speaking for Angelina, and said, "How-wha-ween!"

Everyone laughed, including Angelina, and Jennifer kissed her daughter on the cheek and said, "You're so pretty!"

Rima sat Angelina down on the lawn so she could help Shari unload the medical records and take them into the house. Jennifer turned to Cathy and asked how her mother was doing.

"It's hard to say Jen, because one day she's fine, and the next day she isn't," Cathy answered in dismay.

"I wish there was something I could do to help," Jennifer sighed.

"Thanks, but for now all we can do is pray the medication will work and the seizures will stop." Cathy called out for her children to come with her since it was time to go home. "I'll be going over to visit with my mother later on tonight."

Jennifer told Cathy, "Please say hello for me."

"Okay, I will." Cathy and her three children cut across the backyard to their home.

Rima and Shari came out of the house and said goodbye because they too had to get home. Jennifer stood on the sidewalk waving to them as their cars pulled away. She then turned to Keith and asked who had decorated the house.

He told her about the Girls Scouts stopping by and said, "It looks nice, doesn't it?"

"Mmm-hmm." Jennifer looked at every detail on the display and was pleased to see it was exactly how she would have decorated. "That was very kind of the Girl Scouts. But Keith, why do you suppose they did it?" She lovingly tucked the fallen pieces of straw back under the scarecrows checkered hat.

"I suppose they read the article about you in the Observer and Eccentric newspapers." He watched Angelina play in the grass.

"There are so many people who are being kind and thoughtful to us." She took Angelina by the hand and began to walk her up the front stairs, but Angelina protested and wanted to stay outside with the other children. Keith lifted her in his arms and held the front door open for Jennifer.

She stepped inside and kicked off her shoes leaving them next to his in the foyer. She asked him, "Are you hungry?"

"Not really," Keith said, since he had no appetite lately. He placed Angelina in the high chair and put some dry Cheerios on her tray. "It's Friday night Jennifer, and since there's no school tomorrow, why don't we let the kids play outside awhile longer and we can eat later. I think I'll change my clothes and go outside to mow the lawn." He took a handful of grapes from the sink and looked out the kitchen window and said, "This will probably be the last chance I get to cut the lawn this year."

Jennifer wasn't listening because she was drawn into the dining room where on the table stacks of medical records were piled. The late afternoon sun was shining through the window by the corner hutch. She opened the oversized manila folder containing the films of her first mammogram. The colored label for Ridgeway Medical Center for Women was adhered to the outside of the envelope. Underneath it was the date, July 30, 2003, along with her name stamped in black ink.

Jennifer held the x-ray film to the window and studied the white, shadowy image, wondering how the experts could have missed the blurred cloudy mass – she could clearly see it. With her fingertips she traced the outlines of what used to be her breasts. It was an odd and peculiar feeling, seeing the image of what was the distinct shape that outlined her feminine figure.

She was grateful the phantom dreams no longer haunted her sleep because they were frightening and always left her feeling empty inside. She inhaled deeply, held her breath for a moment, and then gradually let it escape. She returned the x-ray film to the protective envelope and she tried to step away.

Jennifer fought against the compelling urge to open the sealed wrapper and read the transcripts from Dr. Zechariah Jordan's office. She turned the large white envelope over, and with her fingernail began to break the seal, when she stopped and questioned her own actions . . . *Why am I doing this?*

She closed her eyes and rubbed her temples in a circular motion when from deep within her, she was aware of a gentle whisper – a still soft voice. Her hands stopped their rotation at the temples, and she listened again, carefully. It was more of a feeling than the actual sound of a voice whispering to her words of compassion, love, and forgiveness. The Holy Spirit filled her with words of comfort reminding her to . . . *Trust in Me*.

She recalled that Christ forgave those who crucified Him, and as a believer, then she also was expected to do the same thing. She called upon the name of the Lord and following her Savior's example; Jennifer turned from the medical records and walked away in His footsteps of forgiveness.

~ 38 ~

Just before daybreak in Chicago, on Saturday, October 29, Sue's telephone rang. It was her sister, Shawn, calling with life-shattering news. The night before, their sister, Pam and brother-in-law John, were coming home on their motorcycle. They had spent an evening riding and having dinner with friends. Pam and John were less than one mile from their home when the fatal accident occurred.

The ambulances rushed them to Mount Clemens General Hospital where the emergency room staff immediately responded. The hospital was well equipped with the latest in medical technology to handle accident trauma victims, but at times such as this, there was little anyone could do.

An hour after learning of the tragedy, Sue's husband, Bill, drove steadily along I-94 East. The drive home to Michigan would take them just under five hours. He knew the way to Pam and John's home by heart, yet he couldn't believe the reason for this unexpected trip. Countless times he and Sue had driven the same stretch of highway during the past nine years, but it had always been for happy occasions – not this time.

Over the years, Sue came home on several occasions to be with her family for special events. Then, there were other times when she would come home for no reason at all. She would simply come home to visit with those she loved. This was her first trip home for a funeral and never could she have imagined it would be for Pam and John, together. But life was immeasurable and the length of days, along with the number of years allocated to us, was beyond our control. Our lives, which are uniquely planned and chiseled into time according to a universal and sovereign design, are in God's hands, not ours.

Sue fought a wave of nausea as she watched the sunrise through the car windshield while Bill continued to drive along in silence. Her thoughts turned to her nephews, Eric and Adam, and she could clearly see them as toddlers through the lens of her camera, as if it were just yesterday. They were swimming in the pool in her backyard, playing baseball, or chasing her dog, Scooter, around the house. Sue's mind kept playing tricks on her as she saw visions of Pam and John; they were dream-like images in slow motion, running along side their sons.

With both hands on the steering wheel Bill glanced her way. He knew how distraught Sue was over this monumental tragedy. This was going to be devastating to their entire family. Bill's heart was breaking as he listened to her cries of pain. The mournful sound of pure agony filled the interior of their vehicle and his eyes blurred as he concentrated on driving, but he found it impossible to absorb this horrific loss. It was just a few weeks ago when they were together riding through Saugatuck and enjoying a carefree weekend. How many times Bill wondered had John told everyone – this would be their last bike ride of the season.

Outside the window the leaves still clung miraculously on the branches of the trees. How odd for Indian Summer to have lingered so long this year, extending the motorcycle season further into the year. Had the weather been colder, more characteristic for this time of year, Pam and John would have driven their car to meet their friends for dinner. They would have left their Anniversary Ultra Classic Harley covered over with a tarp and stored away in the far corner of their garage.

Bill shook his head, wondering what could possibly be God's purpose in this catastrophe. He glanced at the clock on the instrument panel. Another two hours before they would be in Michigan with their family and friends. Bill reached over and held Sue's hand, not letting go of it until they turned onto Woodlake Drive in Macomb County.

*   *   *

It was Halloween, and all three of her children hurried around the side of the garage and through the connecting yard to Jennifer's home. Cathy called out and told them to wait on the front porch for her to catch up. She walked along leisurely guessing Jennifer wouldn't be ready. She tugged on the hem of her husband's Red Wing hockey jersey; it was all she could think of for her costume this year.

Keith was struggling to fasten the wings on Natalie's little outfit. He still wasn't certain if she was a princess or the tooth fairy. Nicholas, who was dressed in a Star Wars uniform, waited on the porch for Ryan. Angelina walked around inside the house, carrying the empty box to her sister's Disney dress. She would be staying home tonight with her daddy.

Upstairs and alone in her bedroom, Jennifer smoothed out the front of her gown. She was surprised to discover the organza fabric held its color and still looked fresh after all this time. She recalled years ago ordering the dress from the catalog in her favorite color – Paradise Pink.

She turned around in the mirror, and looking over her shoulder she viewed the back of the dress, and then swinging forward she faced herself full-length and placed both hands on her hips. The dress was tight but not uncomfortable, after all she was only eighteen years old when she last wore the gown to her high school senior prom.

Jennifer applied another stroke of pink blush to her cheeks and retouched her lipstick before adjusting her wig. Next, she opened the faded box sitting on the end of her bedroom dresser. She was delighted when Keith found the storage container of glamorous stage clothing in the basement. Jennifer smiled when she saw the winning tiara from her brief moment of fame years ago in a beauty competition. The rhinestones were faded, and some of the teeth from the plastic comb were broken. She positioned the crown carefully over her head and placed it firmly into the weave of someone else's hair. She dropped her hands in front of her and laced her fingers together. She thoughtfully gazed into the mirror, and for the very last time, she studied the reflection of someone – she used to know.

"Mommy!" Natalie impatiently called up the stairs.

"I'm coming." She took a pair of sparkling dangle earrings and clipped them on while walking down the stairs. To Jennifer, Halloween was an evening of play-acting pretending you were someone else, and tonight she would play perhaps what she always wanted to be . . . *a royal princess.*

Cathy remembered Jennifer saying she had planned on wearing her prom dress if the weather cooperated. Once Cathy saw her, she smiled and tugged on Jim's hockey jersey thinking of how opposite she and Jennifer really were. Together, they gathered their children and set out down the street for an evening of trick-or-treating.

Cathy retied her ponytail and teased Jennifer by asking, "I suppose, back-in-the-day, you were the prom queen, huh?"

"No, I didn't qualify," Jennifer said with an exaggerated pout.

"*You* didn't qualify Jen, how could that be?" Cathy was astonished.

Jennifer clapped and joyfully remembered, "I didn't qualify because I was crowned homecoming queen earlier that year!"

"I should have guessed." Cathy laughed and a few streets later she asked, "When do you go back to Zion?"

"Tomorrow." Jennifer stepped aside for a dad pulling a red wagon with a set of twins dressed as white bunnies.

"How long will you be gone?" Cathy waved to their neighbor who was placing extra candy in Nicholas and Natalie's treat bags.

"I will be gone for two days and then home again on Wednesday night." She stopped to admire a Mickey Mouse and Donald Duck duo across the street, skipping along hand-in-hand.

"Is Mary going with you?" Cathy asked.

"Not this time. Instead her friend, Sue, plans on coming to the Center in the morning to spend the day with me. It's always nice to have company during treatment because it helps to keep my mind occupied with other things, if you know what I mean."

Yes, Cathy did know what she meant and she waited for Jennifer to continue, but when she didn't, Cathy knew it was a sign that she would rather not talk about her illness. Like any true friend Cathy clearly understood Jennifer's unspoken signal.

It was just yesterday when she and Jennifer visited over morning coffee that Jennifer had asked Cathy to tell the other members of the Jen Possible Team that when the time came for her to leave for Jerusalem, Jennifer didn't want any tearful good-byes. She'd like everyone to remain upbeat and positive, but most importantly she wants them to smile. It would break Jennifer's heart to see everyone crying and to be sad, and besides, her children would be at home from now on, and she didn't want them to worry or be upset, surrounded by sad and tearful adults.

*   *   *

On Wednesday, November 2, the sky was a deep shade of blue with no clouds in sight. The sun cast an early shadow on the endless formation of Harley motorcycles. The bikers waited silently, lining the parking lot of St. Blase Catholic Church while sixteen pallbearers rolled the two caskets to the hearses, parked side by side.

Next to her father, Sue waited outside with her hand in the crook of his arm. She understood the distant look in his eyes and knew he was remembering Pamela from a much brighter day. It was twenty-seven years ago when Pam and John walked through the same church doors, and came out into the parking lot as newlyweds. Sue's heart broke as she carefully watched her father's footsteps. Mr. Hotton seemed frail and elderly today. Bill took her elbow, helping Sue assist her father and respectfully he walked with them to the waiting limousine.

In the shadows of disbelief, Mary, Christopher, and Jessica, stood amongst those who knew and loved the Cardamone and Hotton families. Christopher's arm was around his mother, thinking of what an awful tragedy the accident was for everyone involved. Jessica's beautiful heart ached as she had watched Eric and Adam over the last few days.

Near their cars, Mary said good-bye to her children and she watched as brother and sister crossed the busy parking lot, holding hands. Mary listened as the rumble of more than one-hundred-forty big twins filled the air with the motorcycles roar and then the funeral procession began. Several members from the Wolverine Chapter of the Harley Owner's Group paid their last respects by leading the motorcade to Clinton Grove Cemetery. Mary held her breath as the uniformed bikers rode off, two at a time.

A half an hour later, the iron gates to the century-old resting place were opened wide. The paved lane through the cemetery was lined with huge trees, indicating they had been there a very long time and because of the season, their branches were dressed in magnificent color. The green grass was carpeted with their fallen leaves, blanketed over in a harvest collection of red, orange, and yellow. The wind blew strong with the sound of old creaking timber filling the air as no other noise was heard. The Harley engines were hushed while the crowd of silent mourners continued to grow.

Mary stepped closer so she could respond to the final prayers at the burial sites. Through the crowd she caught an occasional glimpse of Sue, who sat in the front row between her nephews, Eric and Adam, while Bill and Shawn were seated on either side of each young man. Sue's daughter, Nicole, sat with her future husband, Chris, and they were surrounded by her family of cousins and grandparents, along with John's family.

As the service came to a close, Mary watched Eric and Adam. They were tall and handsomely dressed in black suits. The brothers were a unique and separate image of their parents. One at a time, the crowd dispersed and the sound of fading Harley bikes drifted through the peaceful cemetery. Time stood still for the Cardamone and Hotton families, but life continued for everyone else.

Mary was filled with respectful love for Sue. Over the years they had indeed been through a lot together, both good times and bad, but never before had they encountered a hardship such as this. Mary no longer wiped her tears. She let them fall and placed her hands inside the pockets of her gray wool jacket and the sun continued to shine, no matter how sorrowful the circumstances.

Across the unearthed ground, Mary's eyes were fixed on Sue and she heard her sorrowful cries above the sound of the heavy moving equipment. Bill placed his arm around Sue and she hugged him dearly. Then he took her by the elbow and led her over to Mary and with open arms the two women held onto each other and wept.

After everyone else left, there they stood alone by the covered gravesites, thinking this was all impossible, yet it was true; undoubtedly the hand of God works in mysterious ways. Although Mary would have stood there long into the evening, it was Sue who stepped away from the rich black soil and onto the single lane of the asphalt drive.

Allowing her to lead, Mary walked along with Sue as she held tightly to her arm. She had prayed endlessly for her friend during the last five days and tried to spend as much time with Sue as could be allowed under the circumstances.

"This is a beautiful cemetery, isn't it, Mary?" Sue stopped to appreciate the wonders of God's changing seasons and comfort rested upon her soul as she recalled the third chapter of Ecclesiastes . . . *There is a time and a season for everything.*

"Yes, it is beautiful," Mary agreed with her.

The wind swirled a mound of dry leaves around their feet and they walked amongst a circle of colors in silence. Moments passed before Sue spoke with misty eyes and said, "You know, Mary, I'm grateful that my sister and her husband went to heaven together because there could never be a Pam without John, or a John without Pam, they were just meant to be together, forever."

"Sue, one day in God's perfect timing, He will shed light on this tragedy. I believe He will allow glimpses of understanding that will surface and help you to adjust and comprehend His way." Mary paused, listening to the sound of rustling leaves. "With all you've endured so far in life, Sue, I'm certain this tragedy will stand out as being an extraordinary test of your faith and trust in God."

Sue cried, "My heart is aching Mary. Tell me what to do."

"As a Christian, you need to trust in God because His way is perfect in all circumstances and no matter what – you must trust in Him."

"I trust God with all my heart, Mary. I know He gives and He takes away, all according to His plan, and right now the choice is mine to continue praising Him." As Sue opened the passenger car door the gentle winds of autumn engulfed her and surrounded her with spiritual warmth.

Before leaving the century-old resting place, Mary and Sue glanced up at the sky and followed the sound of many geese flying as one unbroken body. Each bird was fulfilling its purpose and soaring on the wind beneath its wings. Together they were inspired by watching God's perfect plan demonstrated to them through the glory of nature.

The feathered creatures understood that during their journey, they were required to support each other and never leave their formation, because alone, and singlehandedly, they were unable to arrive at their destination. It's only together by helping one another that they can achieve their purpose and by the power of His love they will soar to even greater heights.

*   *   *

Several times Jennifer had called and left messages for Mary and Sue until she came to the realization they must have been involved in an unfortunate situation because it was highly unusual that neither of them had returned her telephone calls. Jennifer prayed for God's protection over them as the chemotherapy medicine slowly dripped from the IV bag into her bloodstream. She had just closed her eyes to rest when her cell phone rang. She answered without looking at the caller ID, hoping it was Mary. "Hello?"

"Hello, Jennifer, this is Susan Abraham, how are you?"

"I'm doing fine Susan, how nice of you to call." Jennifer was glad to have someone to talk with and when asked, she told Susan she was at CTCA going through her final treatment. They talked for a long time, and during their conversation Jennifer learned Susan's latest test results continued to be favorable.

"I am in complete remission," Susan said.

"Oh, thank God, you are a breast cancer survivor, Susan!" Jennifer clapped her hands in celebration.

Susan was filled with mixed emotions and found it difficult to restrain herself as her sobbing filled the invisible telephone line.

"Susan, please don't cry," Jennifer said.

"Jennifer, I wish you were rejoicing as a survivor with me," Susan cried.

Jennifer didn't respond with any comment about herself. Instead she talked positively for several minutes about baby Lydia. "I have talked with Kathy and I know she and her husband, Bob, are very grateful for Lydia's clear scans."

"Yes, they are grateful and we continue to pray for the same good news for you and Keith."

"Thank you, Susan, because it encourages me and gives me hope when I hear of stories such as yours and Lydia's. It means there are cancer survivors and your stories help to shine a light on this dark disease."

Susan asked Jennifer to update her regarding the final plans for her journey to Israel and then she asked, "How long will you be gone?"

A slight change in Jennifer's spirit took place. Try as she may, there were times when the statistical facts surrounding her health were difficult to ignore. But in this instance Jennifer kept the knowledge to herself and cheerfully said, "If all goes as planned, Susan, I'll be home Christmas Eve!"

"How wonderful and I'll pray continuously for you while you're gone." Susan knew of the medical procedure Jennifer was about to undergo, along with the associated risks to the patient. She respected Jennifer's courage and faith.

"Susan, you know what I've been through because you've endured suffering in the same way." Jennifer wiped away her silent tears and said, "I thank God for all the times you listened and helped me along my journey. You took the same path as I and walked with me one step at a time."

"I'll continue to spiritually walk with you, Jennifer, no matter how far away you are."

~ *39* ~

After school, Jacob and Justin played on adjacent soccer fields while Janis walked along the sidelines between their two games, alternating a watchful eye from one son to the other. She kept her distance from the other parents because she wanted time alone in prayer. Last night, Duane showed her the newspaper article and explained how closely connected Mary was to the motorcycle accident victims. Today, her prayers were for everyone involved in the Jen Possible Team as she paced back and forth.

Duane telephoned her earlier in the day from work saying Jennifer had finally gotten through to Mary while waiting at the Chicago O'Hare Airport. He explained that Mary felt telling Jennifer about the accident would only add to her burden of sorrow, but Mary also couldn't find any other way to explain her absence along with Sue's for the past five days.

Duane felt the Jen Possible Team was surrounded with heartache and it seemed as though the people trying the most to help Jennifer were now bound in some level of their own private grief. The accumulation of tragic events could only be seen as a dark effort to prevent Jennifer's journey to Jerusalem. Janis prayed for heavenly protection over her family and the others who were linked by obedience in this Kingdom effort.

Janis and her family were dealing with the emotions of disconnecting from Angelina because she had grown to be part of them, and they missed her joyful laughter. With the days narrowing down and the time for her parents to leave getting closer, Bill and Rima were now doing the majority of caring for the little angel. Everyone agreed it was the best arrangement for Angelina.

So many things were unsettled, and life around Janis was beginning to shift in a whole new direction. Even the small everyday routines that she had become accustomed to were evolving into something different. Janis did not resist change; she adjusted quickly, but inwardly there was something about Jennifer leaving for Israel that she felt would ultimately change all of their lives.

Duane pulled into the parking lot and scanned the playing fields for his family when he noticed his wife standing off by herself. He pulled on his jacket and walked toward her, knowing the reason for her solitude was because of thoughtful prayer. She saw him walking over and when he approached he asked what the score was.

"We're winning on both fields," she answered. "You look tired Duane, how was your day?" She was pleased that over the past two years Duane had kept his promise and was sharing more details of his work life.

"You're right, I am tired and my day was very long." He adjusted his ball cap and said, "Mary came into the office today, and for the first time ever, she looked tired."

"Did you get a chance to talk with her?"

"No." He kicked at the ground.

With only a few minutes left in the first half they continued to walk in silence until Duane solemnly pointed out, "We always have to be spiritually prepared, Janis."

"Yes, because we'll never know our time of death." She took his hand and together they walked toward the crowded sidelines.

*   *   *

Traffic inched its way along I-94 East as Kathy drove away from Metro Detroit Airport toward Plymouth. She listened to Jennifer explain how difficult it was to say good-bye to the medical staff at the Cancer Treatment Center of America in Zion because during the past eleven months, she had come to know some of the staff members on a personal level.

"We exchanged e-mail addresses, and I hope to keep in touch with a few of them while I'm in Israel." Jennifer made sure her pink notebook was inside her backpack because it contained precious information.

"I understand how you feel because I felt the same way when we brought Lydia home from the hospital." Kathy said, "The people who cared for my daughter will always have a special place in my heart."

"It would have been a wonderful profession to work in the field of medicine, don't you think?" Jennifer asked her.

"Yes, it would be rewarding," Kathy agreed.

Jennifer sighed and smiled at the woman stuck in traffic next to them, but the woman chose to ignore Jennifer, even though the natural inclination is to return a stranger's smile. Jennifer gazed out at the string of cars four lanes wide and asked, "Kathy, do you ever wonder what sort of difficulties the person right next to you is facing in his or her daily life?"

"I do more now, Jennifer, than I used to," Kathy said, being honest.

"How do you suppose those who don't have Christ in their lives, and don't know Him as their personal Lord and Savior, make it through their times of trouble?"

"I don't know how they do it, Jennifer." Kathy's throat was tightening with sadness.

"Although," Jennifer stopped to smile, "being a Christian doesn't mean you will sail through life without hitting turbulent waters."

"No, it doesn't, but being a Christian means that when the storm waters rise, we have a Rock to cling to, a place of safety and refuge."

"Yes, we have a secure harbor to drop anchor and rest in the shelter of God's embrace."

An opening in traffic appeared, and Kathy squeezed in so she could take the next exit and before long they were parked in Jennifer's driveway. Kathy didn't want to say good-bye, but she knew her schedule would not allow time for her to visit with Jennifer again before she left in the next few days. Tears blurred Kathy's vision, and Jennifer handed her a tissue.

"I don't want to say good-bye," Kathy cried.

"Then we won't." Jennifer hugged her from across the front seat.

"I will pray for you each day," Kathy whispered.

*   *   *

It was only five days before Jennifer would be leaving and she wasn't making any progress with packing. She answered the telephone and was touched to hear Al and Sheila's voices on the other end. Although they were enjoying their first year of retirement and were traveling throughout the states in their RV, they had faithfully kept in touch with Jennifer through telephone calls such as this one.

"How nice of you to call," Jennifer said. "I received your beautiful card the other day and want to thank you for your thoughtfulness."

"You're welcome Jennifer. How are you feeling about your trip?" Sheila asked.

"I'm feeling all right, well, maybe just a little bit nervous."

"That is understandable. How are Keith and the children?" Al asked.

"Keith is doing fine, and the children know we are leaving together for a trip to see a doctor in another country." Simba came and sat on Jennifer's lap. "I feel they're much too young to understand the details, but they know the cancer is growing and that's a bad thing."

"Jeez, Jennifer, is there anything we can do for you?" Al asked.

"Not really, I just need to get motivated and start to pack because there is nothing else left to do." She calmly stroked the cat and said, "Before I leave Al, I want to thank you for allowing everyone at work to help me. I know that unexpected and urgent requests for vacation crossed your desk at inopportune times, throwing the department into a tailspin, but everyone followed your example of humble leadership and pitched in to help out."

"You give me far too much credit, Jennifer, because when those tailspin moments happened, we worked matters out together, like any first-rate team of engineers would do." Al's eyes stung with tears, recalling the past events.

"Jennifer, I think you know that you hold a special place within Al's heart," Sheila said.

"Thank you, because that means a lot to me." Jennifer dabbed a tissue to her nose.

"I know you have much to do and we only wanted to call and say we'll be praying for you and we'll be informed of your progress through Duane and Kathy while you're gone," Sheila told her.

"Oh, I just remembered, do you know about the Christmas Gala being held at Grace Lutheran Church in Redford that Duane has organized with his church council?" Jennifer wanted Al and Sheila to be included.

"Yes, Duane placed us on the list to help with decorations and the bake sale. Don't worry, Jennifer, we'll be there." Sheila could tell that Al was too emotional to finish their conversation.

"Well, good-bye, Jennifer, we love you." Sheila said.

~ *40* ~

The morning of November 9, Mary sat in Jennifer's driveway, praying for the courage to step out of the car. Today she needed a strong hold on her emotions for Jennifer's sake. Over the past two years she had been there to support Jennifer, both physically and emotionally, and Mary didn't want to fail Jennifer – especially now.

Jennifer stood in her foyer waiting for Mary, and they greeted each other with a warm embrace before sitting down on the stairs as they did so many times before. It seemed there was so much to be said before Jennifer left for Jerusalem in only three days.

"Mary, I can't tell you how sorry I am for Sue and her family. It breaks my heart when I think about their sorrow and what they've been through."

"This has been very hard on their entire family. I talk with Sue every day, and she's staying with her nephews for the time being, helping them to settle matters."

"How is her faith?" Jennifer asked.

"Sue's faith is strong because God has equipped her for this trial," Mary sighed. "Sue is a Christian; therefore she lives by faith and not by sight."

"It all comes down to that, doesn't it, Mary?"

Mary nodded and said, "Faith is the cornerstone of Christianity and our faith has to go beyond what we can see because our sight is limited, but our faith is not; our faith, which is the measuring rod of our belief in God must be unlimited."

"And it's our faith that can move mountains," Jennifer sighed, while twirling her mustard seed necklace.

Mary forced back the tears burning to be released and said, "When we struggle with our faith, we need to study chapter eleven in the book of Hebrews."

"Yes, I know," said Jennifer, wishing she could be of some help to Mary. "Please tell Sue that I'm praying for her."

"She knows you're praying for her Jennifer – " Mary began to cry.

"Miss Mary, is there something you haven't told me?"

"Oh, Jennifer, so much tragedy is happening all at once."

"What else has happened Mary, tell me?" Jennifer implored.

Mary gazed at Jennifer and was amazed at how, under her dire circumstances, she could be genuinely concerned about others. Jennifer's behavior was something Mary found hard to explain, apart from the indwelling of the Holy Spirit and the divine grace of God, both of which were clearly present in Jennifer's life. For it is impossible to walk through storms such as Jennifer's and still demonstrate Christ-like behavior without the Holy Spirit living in us.

The flood gates holding back Mary's emotions broke loose. She then told Jennifer that last night Candice had telephoned her from St. John's Hospital. Candice explained that yesterday afternoon Walt suddenly asked her to drive him to the cardiologist office. Up until then, he had ignored the mild chest pain he was experiencing for the last two days, but yesterday the pain escalated to an unbearable level.

Mary told Jennifer that as soon as they arrived, the cardiologist sent Walt to the hospital for evaluation. Immediately the physician on duty in the emergency room admitted Walt to the cardiac care unit and within hours he was scheduled for lifesaving open heart surgery.

"Oh, Mary, praise God. Walt is so blessed that he didn't delay any longer."

Mary nodded and dried her tears, saying, "It is a miracle because the operation consisted of three major artery bypasses. There is no doubt that Walt was near death."

"How awful to experience such a close call. Tell me, how long have Candice and Walt been married?"

"They have been married almost thirty-seven years." Mary began to smile and said, "Candice believes God will strengthen Walt's heart which will enable him to serve at their church and be married to her for many years to come."

Mary took in a deep breath and decided not to allow herself any more time for crying. Enough was enough, and she placed everything in God's hands. She knew the words of the prophet, Jeremiah, who in the Old Testament promised a time of blessing, restoration, and a day when God would turn our mourning into gladness . . . *Our Lord will end our sorrow and restore joy.*

Mary then noticed the house was unusually quiet, she asked, "Where are your children?"

"Cathy's watching them this morning so I could have special time alone with you – to give you this." She reached between the staircase spindles for the small package on the foyer table and handed it to Mary.

In turn, Mary gave her a pink gift bag and said, "Open your gift first."

"No, you go first," Jennifer clapped her hands and waited.

"Absolutely not; you go first!" Mary insisted.

"Okay." Jennifer peeked inside the stellar pink gift package and brought out a loaf of oven-warm banana bread. She held it under her nose, enjoying the fleeting aroma and said, "I sure will miss your homemade banana bread, Miss Mary!"

"And I will miss watching you enjoy it."

Jennifer reached back into the bag and brought out a wrapped present, but before opening it, she rested the gift on her lap and said, "Mary, do you know how special you've been to me during the last two years?" Jennifer wanted to express her appreciation and love.

Mary nodded, of course she knew.

Jennifer then opened the gift, and her smile widened when she saw the words written across the cover of a pink journal – *I Am Blessed*. Jennifer opened the first page and read the personal inscription. "Mary, I treasure your words because they're beautiful and they mean so much to me."

"Oh, my words are nothing more than pure Blarney – it's the Irish in me." Mary laughed and gently rubbed Jennifer's back.

"It's not Blarney, Mary, it's the Holy Spirit!" Jennifer started to laugh and Mary joined her in the unexpected outburst of humor. It was a release of emotional tension allowing them to laugh and cry at the same time. After catching her breath, Jennifer said, "I'm going to miss you very much, Mary."

"Yes, and I'm going to miss you too, but we'll talk on the telephone often while you're in Jerusalem."

"Do you promise?" Jennifer wiped her nose.

Although still in good humor Mary hesitated, she recalled the last time she promised Jennifer something and her fading smile returned to full laughter.

"What's so funny?" Jennifer laughed along with her.

Through tears of joy, Mary said, "Young lady, I remember the last time you cornered me into making you a promise!"

"Hmm, I have no idea what you're talking about," Jennifer said in a voice seeped with innocence. She nonchalantly thumbed through the empty pages of the journal, with a smile illuminating her face.

"*Jennifer?*" Mary continued to laugh.

"Okay, I seem to recall a teeny weenie promise." Jennifer giggled.

"You call writing a book – a teeny weenie promise?" Mary caught her breath and after wiping away joyful tears, she said, "Isn't our God wonderful to bring us laughter at a time like this?"

Jennifer agreed and then cheerfully pointed at her present for Mary and coaxed Mary into opening it.

"You didn't have to get me anything, Jennifer," she smiled.

"But, I wanted to," she said, closely watching Mary's expression as Mary unwrapped the package.

"Why Jennifer, this is beautiful!" Mary carefully held the gift in her hand and admired the ornate brass key. Hanging from it by a single gold thread, as if it were a locket, was a tiny crystal heart. "I will hang this in a special place among my collection of keys, thank you."

They hugged each other for a long time, remembering all they had been through and how important they had become to one another during this storm. Jennifer closed her eyes, kissed Mary on the cheek, and told her she loved her and Mary did the same.

*   *   *

Fifteen minutes later, Duane parked his truck in front of Jennifer's house. As he got out, he looked directly across the street to the white birch tree now filled with empty branches that were reaching toward heaven. He knocked at the door, and Mary let him inside. Jennifer was standing next to her sealing a plastic bag filled with medication and she smiled at the sound of Duane's voice.

"Hello, Sunshine," he said to Jennifer. Today he would say good-bye to a dear friend and a sister-in-Christ. Jennifer closed her eyes and held onto his embrace. She often described to others that her relationship with Duane was one of an older brother, and she wished there was a way to refrain from saying good-bye.

Mary left them in the foyer and walked into the kitchen. As she gazed through the kitchen window, it was hard for her to imagine how much had taken place since she first met Jennifer and the group of engineers from Visteon. It saddened her that she couldn't place her arms around the span of time and hold everyone securely in place where she could keep them far away from pain and suffering. But, she knew God was capable of placing His outstretched arms around them and within His embrace, they would find comfort and rest.

Across the backyard Mary saw Cathy at her window talking on the telephone. Cathy noticed Mary and was reminded that she too was expected at Jennifer's home soon. Cathy waved through the window to Mary and realized it was time to end her telephone conversation. She knew today would be a stressful day for everyone.

Duane was with Jennifer in the living room securely fastening the pieces of luggage that were finally packed. While completing the task he thoughtfully told her, "When I was growing up, Jennifer, I was a sports nut, and my heroes were those who could hit a ball or score more goals than anyone else."

Jennifer leaned against the computer cabinet in the living room, listening to him talk as he wrestled with the heavy baggage.

He finished, stood tall and told her, "But now, I have a new definition of a hero – and it's you, Sunshine." He filled his lungs, placed his hands on hips, and said, "Sharing your experience with the Jen Possible Team has been nothing short of inspirational to all of us, Jennifer. And personally,

I admire you greatly, and I'm honored to be someone you chose to include in your life." His throat instantly tightened with emotion.

Jennifer smiled and reminded him, "It was God who crisscrossed our lives, Duane, so we could learn more about Him from one another."

"Yes, and what a blessing sharing in your storm has been to me and my family." He took off his ball cap and ran his fingers through his curly hair. Ignoring his blurry vision and before replacing his baseball hat, he humbly said, "Thank you, Jennifer."

"Duane, I don't want to make saying good-bye hard on anyone." She smiled and took him by the hand and said, "Let's go into the kitchen and have a slice of Mary's banana bread."

Duane sat down at the table and asked, "Where's Cathy?"

"She should be over shortly, I think," Jennifer answered, as Mary refilled their coffee mugs and joined them.

"Janis will be here Friday morning to help you with any last minute things." Duane told her.

"I'm glad because I want a lot of people over on Friday to keep me company." Jennifer gave a high-pitched, nervous laugh.

"What time will the television crew be here tomorrow, Jennifer?" Mary asked.

"Oh my goodness, I almost forgot!" She got up and wrote a huge note, and then taped it to the kitchen cupboard before saying, "I hope Keith remembers to leave work early tomorrow. I know he's under a lot of stress, but he needs to concentrate on us leaving because there's still a lot to do," she sighed.

"Don't worry, Jennifer, we're here to help you," Duane said, pointing to himself and Mary.

During the next couple of hours, Jennifer reviewed detailed instructions about what she would like to have accomplished in the house while she was gone. She explained to Duane and Mary that the neighborhood moms would continue to prepare meals and do the children's laundry. She handed them a list of the volunteers' names and phone numbers.

"These women are special to me because their kindness has been a tremendous help, and I pray for them daily that God would continue to provide for them, so in turn they can provide for my family."

Next, they went upstairs so Jennifer could show them how she wanted the new furniture she had recently ordered to be arranged for the children's rooms. Nicholas' furniture would be a tight fit, and after checking the room dimensions, she decided to change the angle of the bed. On paper, Jennifer drew the bed directly under the window and Duane took additional notes on everything she wanted done for her son.

The girls' room was next. It had more square footage and her layout worked perfectly. Jennifer said the shade of pink, once the room was painted, would match the bedspreads and curtains she had on order. Duane and Mary understood that Jennifer was doing what the Lord commanded King Hezekiah to do . . . *she was putting her house in order*.

It was a heart rendering moment as they watched Jennifer hold the baby doll that rested in Angelina's empty crib. She smoothed the doll's curly locks to one side of its painted porcelain face and said, "I love babies, and when we got married, Keith and I wanted to fill our home with children." She lovingly laid the doll in the crib and left the bedroom. She led them down the hallway toward the stairs when Mary asked about the corner bedroom and whether she wanted any rearranging or painting done to that room. Jennifer said no because she'd gone over the details of that particular room with Cathy personally, and if need be, Cathy would know what to do.

Jennifer opened the spare room to show them her crafts and inside she had numerous drawers filled with crystal beads for jewelry. Mary's watchful eye noticed enough scrapbooking material to keep five moms busy. A family photograph was pinned to a corkboard frame that hung above her covered sewing machine, which she had not plugged into the wall since they moved away from their home on Pond View Drive.

One of the photographs was a candid snapshot of she and Natalie. They were dressed alike, sitting in the grass on a hillside near an outdoor garden. Duane asked where the photograph was taken and Jennifer told him it was from Bill and Rima's wedding in Louisiana. She smiled, remembering she had sewn the matching outfits herself.

Next to it was a picture of she and Cathy. They were in mid-air, playing on the swing set and dressed in their Sunday clothes. Jennifer was happy and carefree as a child. She explained this photograph was also taken at the Hardy's wedding.

Jennifer went to her bead table and placed a set of unfinished earrings into a small bag. She then counted out the extra beads necessary to complete the work and added them loosely inside with the earrings. While she concentrated on selecting the perfect shades of pink, Mary and Duane watched her in the crowded room with intense respect and feelings of humility.

The amount of faith Jennifer possessed was beyond their explanation and her degree of composure mixed with dignity was forever engraved upon their hearts. What a beautiful experience to witness God's grace before their very eyes as Jennifer's ability to go forward with a smile proved her trust in Him was . . . *Supernatural.*

Mary was overwhelmed and couldn't stay in the tiny room any longer. She discretely left and went back down the stairs because she wanted to honor Jennifer's request and not become an inconsolable burden. She found Cathy sitting at the kitchen table, wiping her tears and when she saw Mary she whispered, "Where's Jen?"

"She's upstairs with Duane." Mary asked, "Why, what's wrong Cathy?"

"I've been on the telephone with my step-dad all morning." She pulled a fresh tissue from the box. "My mom has been admitted into the hospital, and I have to leave."

"Oh, Cathy – " Mary sat in the chair next to her and asked, "What can we do for you?"

"You and Duane have enough to do already." Cathy leaned back and closed her eyes and said, "Mary, I don't want Jennifer to know about my mom because it will only add to her worries. I can't believe the amount of adversity that's happening to all of us, it seems unreal." She sighed and pushed the bangs out of her eyes. "I need to leave for the hospital now and spend time with my mother so that I can be with Jennifer during the next two days. I can't disappoint Jennifer. She's depending on me to be with her."

Mary agreed with Cathy and understood the feeling of darkness surrounding everyone.

Cathy blinked away her tears and said, "I want to be here on Friday because I can't let Jen go without being by her side and telling her, good-bye."

"Cathy, please don't worry about things. I want you to leave and take care of your parents." As Mary walked her to the patio door, Cathy told her that Jim was home from school and he would continue to watch all the children. Cathy then dashed across the backyard just as Duane and Jennifer walked into the kitchen.

"Was that Cathy?" Jennifer asked.

"Yes, it was." Mary latched the sliding glass door. "She forgot about a meeting at school for Ryan and said she'd be back in the morning, but Jim will watch Nicholas and Natalie until Keith gets home," said Mary, chafing at the white lie.

"Keith will be home in half an hour." Jennifer looked at the kitchen clock; time was sweeping its hands quickly through her life.

"Yikes, the soccer game starts in thirty minutes!" As always, Duane was helping the coach and he needed to leave.

The time had come for them to say good-bye.

With heavy hearts they walked to the front door. Jennifer reached for the door handle, and Duane was the first to step outside, followed by Mary and Jennifer. The Holy Spirit moved within them and as they joined hands, Duane prayed aloud, "Father God, we stand before You not knowing what the future may bring for Jennifer. We humbly ask You to provide her and Keith with a safe pilgrimage to Your Holy City. We pray that Jennifer will be abundantly filled with Your strength and the courage needed to see her through this last hope for winning the battle against breast cancer. May her faith be strong and her trust in You be securely anchored. In the name of Jesus, we pray. Amen."

Together they prayed aloud the Lord's Prayer and when finished, Mary looked across at Duane who was looking up at the sky. Jennifer's eyes were closed tightly and tears were streaming down her face. Mary released Duane's hand and took Jennifer in her arms.

"Oh, Jennifer, I would trade places with you if I could." Mary rocked Jennifer in her arms and felt how thin and frail she had become. "Sweetheart, God is with you. He will comfort you and hold you in His arms. Please don't be afraid because you are not alone."

"I want you to know that I can feel God's incredibly strong presence daily in my life." Jennifer assured them.

"Amen." Duane replaced his ball cap.

Jennifer took both their hands and said, "I can't thank you enough for all you've done for me." She held tightly to their hands and said to Duane, "Your family has shown me love and warmth and may God abundantly bless and protect those you love." Jennifer then turned to Mary and said, "Write my story Mary, because I don't want anyone else to needlessly go through what I've gone through."

"I promise you, Jennifer, I'll write your story."

"I'll see you again, Sunshine," Duane softly spoke to her.

Jennifer nodded, for she truly believed someday they would indeed see each other again. She then reached into her pocket and turning to Mary, she carefully placed in her friend's open palm a small trinket and then closed Mary's fingers around it.

"Mary, I don't want to chance losing this, so I want you to care for it while I'm gone." Jennifer firmly grasped Mary's closed hand and held her attention with her eyes. "And if I don't come home, you'll know what to do with it."

Jennifer let go and walked away. She climbed the steps to her front porch and without looking back closed the door behind her. Slowly, one at a time, Mary's fingers unfolded, and laying in the palm of her right hand was . . . *Jennifer's mustard seed pendant.*

~ 41 ~

The next day, November 10, Jennifer poured coffee and blended in her usual mixture of flavoring. She was leaving tomorrow, and today was the last day she had to prepare for her journey.

The telephone rang and she stopped to pick up the call. It was WDIV Detroit Channel 4 News, confirming their midday appointment. She told the news team to come over at any time and then went back into the kitchen to take her daily medication. She concentrated while organizing which pills to take and how many of each one; lately this task required her full attention. She finished and sat down on the couch with Simba to spend a few moments in peace.

Last night, after Keith came home and got the children from Jim, they all sat down to a quiet family dinner. They needed an opportunity to explain more clearly to their children the reason for their parent's far away trip. Simba purred in her lap as she closed her eyes and recalled the meaningful conversation with her children.

Keith began by reassuring them they would be safe and loved by others while he and their mommy were gone. Uncle Bill and Aunt Rima would take good care of them, along with many others and as soon as mommy was feeling better they would come home. It was all Keith could say before his voice cracked and his eyes clouded over. Then it was Jennifer's calm voice and loving touch that brought the moment back to a level the children could better understand.

"You know Mommy has cancer?" she asked Nicholas and Natalie. They both nodded their heads. They didn't fully grasp the meaning of the word, but they knew their mommy was sick – very sick.

"And that Mommy's cancer has gotten bigger instead of smaller?" Again they knew this. "And you know that's a bad thing, right?" Nicholas stared at his food while Natalie drank her milk. Traces of infant wisdom directed Angelina to be still as she sensed the stirring of emotions in her mother's controlled voice.

Jennifer gave a strained smile to her children and told them how proud she was to be their mother. She picked up her fork and knife and sliced a piece of chicken on her plate. She wanted them to see her as being calm, in control, and most importantly – not afraid.

Keith had stopped eating and he was rotating his pop can in slow circles. He didn't trust himself to look at the innocent faces of his children or the beautiful face of his loving wife. Instead, he watched the pop can label come and go as Jennifer began to explain heaven to his children.

"You know about the story of Christmas?" They smiled and told her yes. "And you know the baby born in the manger grew to be a man, and we call Him Jesus Christ?" Nicholas watched his mom without blinking while Natalie rested her chin in her hands. Jennifer's children were listening carefully to her every word.

Jennifer moved her dinner plate away and folded her arms on the edge of the table. She was trying to keep their little minds focused as she explained, "Jesus was a kind and loving man. He obeyed His Father, who is God, and Jesus did everything God asked of Him." She filled her lungs before saying, "And after Jesus did everything God asked Him to do, Jesus went to heaven so He could be with His Father."

Natalie sighed loudly, and Nicholas blinked repeatedly. Keith got up and took their dirty plates from the table to the kitchen counter.

"Why did Jesus go to heaven, Mommy?" Little Natalie's eyes widened as she asked the important question.

"Because He finished the work God planned for Him, and it was time for Jesus to be with God."

"Oh." Natalie gave Jennifer a sad frown.

"God has a plan for all of us, and when we complete His plan, we leave and go to heaven to be with Him." Jennifer smiled.

"Are you going to heaven, Mommy?" Nicholas wanted to know.

Keith walked away since he no longer trusted his ability to remain in control. He couldn't stay and listen to his wife explain to his six-year-old son that she may not be coming home. Keith closed off the painful memory from his own childhood of when he was six-years-old, and his mother suddenly left one day and she never came home again.

"If I don't come home from Jerusalem with Daddy, then yes, Nicholas, I will be in heaven." But, Jennifer quickly reminded them that in her heart she planned to be home on Christmas Eve to open gifts.

Jennifer's reflection of last night soon faded as her thoughts returned to the time at hand. Simba jumped down from her lap at the sound of Cathy tapping at the back door. At the same time, Keith walked in the front door and Nicholas came running into the family room shouting that the news van was parked outside, and the television crew was walking up the driveway. Jennifer tightened her navy blue scarf and rubbed her cheeks to bring out a trace of color. She asked Cathy, "How do I look?"

"Beautiful," Cathy said with a smile.

Jennifer moistened her lips, placed her hand over her heart, and closed her eyes to pray . . . *Holy Spirit, fill me with courage and wisdom. Fill me with Your light so Your love shines from within me to others. Allow me to portray Your comfort to those who are watching and let me fulfill Your desire for my life – help me to finish the race You have designed for me. Amen.*

*   *   *

The filming had gone remarkably well, and the people from the news station knew exactly what questions to ask. They captured Jennifer, her family, and her story perfectly. She was confident and hoped her message would be seen and heard by many women of all ages. Jennifer prayed her words would echo in their minds throughout their lives, reminding them to trust their instincts and, when in doubt, to seek other medical opinions.

When the reporter asked, she explained she had run out of treatment options in the United States. However, she was fortunate to learn of Hadassah University Hospital in Jerusalem and Professor Shimon Slavin, who heads the Department of Bone Marrow Transplantation and Cancer Immunotherapy. Jennifer briefly outlined her medical process, beginning with high doses of chemotherapy, a bone marrow transplant, and a procedure called donor lymphocyte infusion.

She smiled into the camera lens and solemnly added that there was a risk her body may not withstand the treatment, but it was a risk she was willing to take. She finished the interview by saying she wasn't fighting breast cancer just for herself; she was fighting the disease for everyone – even for those she didn't know.

In what seemed to be no time at all, the news van pulled away from the curb, taking with them an emotional sliver of her personal life recorded on film, forever. Jennifer did this in an effort to spread awareness and educate others regarding the importance of early detection.

"You did remarkably well, Jen." Cathy congratulated her for the courage to face the television camera with such strong character and dignity, especially on the day before leaving for Israel.

She smiled and confessed, "It wasn't as easy as it may have looked, Cathy." She was folding the Jen Possible banner she had shown the news reporter.

"No, I'm sure it wasn't." Cathy's stomach was in knots because she couldn't deny the strong mixture of emotions she felt surrounding Jennifer's departure. "How do you feel about leaving, Jennifer?"

"I'm a little scared." Jennifer laid the banner over the kitchen chair.

"I would be, too." Cathy tried to imagine what it would be like to walk in Jennifer's place.

Jennifer studied Cathy and noticed her drained and weary look as if she hadn't been sleeping well lately. "You look tired Cathy, is everything all right?"

"Mmm-hmm." She waved nonchalantly with a dismissive hand and quickly said, "I have some errands to run in a few minutes. Do you need anything?"

Jennifer looked around at the disarray of her home and said, "I have no idea what I need."

"Well, if you think of something, give me a call," Cathy smiled.

"Thank you, but Shari will be here tonight to give the children haircuts, and if I need something I'll let her know."

"Okeydokey."

*   *   *

Later that night, Shari finished cutting Nicholas' hair. Next was Natalie and then Angelina. She combed Natalie's endless waves of soft brown curls to one side and remembered that Jennifer had asked her to only trim Natalie's hair

396

an inch, all the way around. Shari carefully snipped the first ringlet and then the next.

Shari watched Jennifer as she continued to cut Natalie's hair. She was surprised at how calm and at-ease Jennifer was, knowing tomorrow Jeff would be at their door, ready to drive her and Keith to the airport.

"You're awfully calm, Jennifer." Shari tilted Natalie's chin down.

"I'm a little scared, but I'm not having second thoughts because going to Jerusalem is the right thing to do." She sat on the family room carpet with her back toward them. She found what she was looking for and began to finish what she'd started months earlier.

Shari combed Natalie's hair at a right angle and again clipped off exactly one inch and wondered what Jennifer was doing. "Can I help you find something?" she asked.

"No, thank you." Jennifer placed two pink crystal beads on the wire mesh and firmly pushed them into place.

"Here, take a look at Natalie," Shari said, "is this length okay?"

"Oh, she looks so pretty and the length is perfect." Jennifer's sing-song voice made her daughter smile.

Once done, Shari helped Natalie down from the chair and lifted Angelina into the booster seat so she could trim her bangs. Jennifer continued her beadwork while Shari concentrated on Angelina's bangs. Little pieces of clippings fell onto the characters of the book Angelina was studying. She laughed, and with little fingers she dusted the tiny pieces of hair away.

"There you go, Angelina, you're all done." Shari set her on the floor, and off she ran to the living room to be with her siblings. Shari folded the plastic cape and took it outdoors to shake off the clippings. The feather-like strands of hair drifted away on the late evening breeze. She had visited longer than intended, and it was time to leave. One more snap of the plastic cape and she was done. She prayed for spiritual strength before stepping back inside.

"Well, Jennifer, it's time for me to leave."

"Oh no, don't go yet!" Jennifer angled her shoulder to conceal the bead work. "Please stay a little while longer."

"Jennifer, what are you doing?" Shari knelt down beside her.

"Oh, I wanted to finish these for you, but I ran out of time." Jennifer held up a partially finished earring in the air. "They were supposed to be your birthday present, but honestly I don't know where the time has gone and I still have so much to do." Her voice quivered as she slid her glasses upward on her nose and reached for another pink crystal bead.

"Here, let me see what you've done so far." Shari carefully took the beadwork from Jennifer's trembling hand. She placed the one completed chandelier earring against her earlobe, making it dance and said, "This is beautiful."

"It is pretty Shari, please let me finish the other one for you." Jennifer smiled.

"No." Shari placed both pieces inside the zip-lock bag and said she would take them home and finish them later. "It's nine o'clock at night, and you're leaving for Israel tomorrow, Jennifer, you have a million things to do and you want to make earrings for me?" Shari's eyes flooded with tears.

"Yes, to show my appreciation for all you've done," she explained.

"Jennifer, it was a joy helping you." She tucked the plastic bag inside her blue jean pocket.

"But, I wanted you to have the earrings for your vacation in Florida."

"Okay, I'll finish them tonight when I get home and I'll take them with me to Florida." She gathered the hair cutting supplies into her travel bag and put on her jacket. "Jeff will be here tomorrow at four o'clock to take you and Keith to the airport." Shari kept her eyes focused on her car keys.

Jennifer reached out and hugged a very special friend that came into her life unexpectedly and wonderfully.

"It's hard to imagine that tomorrow night you'll be sleeping in the Holy Land."

"Yes, and this takes me full circle Shari, because my journey with breast cancer began with a connection to Israel and now it will end with treatment in Israel."

Shari understood how the lines of destiny came together from the very beginning until now, between Dr. Zechariah Jordan and Professor Shimon Slavin. The physician, who tragically misdiagnosed Jennifer, in July 2003, was from Israel and now the professor who would try and save her life was also from Israel.

They stood in the foyer, holding hands at the foot of the stairs and in the flickering shadows from the living room television set, they said good-bye. They whispered their sisterly love for one another, as the connection between them was more than their battle with breast cancer; they were sisters-in-Christ.

Shari's hand was shaking as she opened the door and stepped outside into the cover of darkness. She no longer fought to restrain her tears as she pulled out of the driveway – wondering if she would ever come back again to Mayflower Drive.

~ 42 ~

Jennifer was leaving for Tel Aviv in three hours, and she would not allow Satan to bind her in fear, for she was dressed in the Armor of God. She was anxious about going and fought the unsettling feeling with continuous prayer. She stayed within God's will and gained peace through the Holy Spirit.

Keith was at the store with Nicholas getting last-minute computer gadgets. Janis came by earlier with Cathy and they just left, taking the girls over to Cathy's house to give them lunch and a bath. Jennifer was upstairs alone, and she wondered if after leaving today if she would ever come back home.

Jennifer had spent countless hours in prayer during the last several weeks, and now the time had come for her to leave. She walked into Nicholas' room first and sat on his unmade bed holding his pillow against her cheek. Scattered around his room were all his toys, clothes, and books for school. She closed her eyes and prayed for her son . . . *Dear Father, only You can understand the depth of love I have for my son. I leave him in Your hands for You to guide and protect him all the days of his life. Help Nicholas to remember me always and to understand Your love for him. I pray to You in the name of Your son, Jesus Christ. Amen.*

In the girls' bedroom there were dolls and dollhouses along with Cinderella clothes everywhere. The white lace curtains were drawn fully across the windows now that the colder weather was settling back into Michigan. She adjusted the draw length of the shades, making both windows symmetrical.

Jennifer straightened the covers on Natalie's bed and tucked the pillow neatly under the spread. She smoothed out the corners and placed the discarded coloring book and crayons on the night stand. She knelt by the bedside while holding Natalie's tiny pink nightgown next to her heart. She breathed in the essence of her little girl and then prayed for Natalie . . .*Dear God, how grateful I am to have my little Natalie. She is so much like me, and I love her dearly. Please send Your angels to watch over her steps, and with Your love, guard her mind and protect her heart. Help her to grow strong and show Your love to others. I pray Natalie will always remember the loving examples I have taught her all in Jesus' name. Amen.*

Jennifer walked over to the baby crib where a teddy bear's sad brown eyes stared back at her while she adjusted the red checkered bowtie around its neck. It was Angelina's favorite snuggle toy and everywhere she went she kept the teddy bear close to her side.

Baby Angelina was fourteen months old, and Jennifer was given the blessing of motherly knowledge in knowing that her personality was deeply rooted within this child's heart. She kissed the teddy bear and cuddled it while she prayed for her youngest child . . . *Dear God, keep Angelina close to Your side for she is Your miracle. With all my heart, I thank You for the precious gift of her life and the courage You gave me to bring forth the seed You allowed to be planted within me. May her brother and sister love her dearly and understand what a blessing she is to our family. I pray her heart will be filled with love, her mind will be filled with Your ways, and her life will always be blessed. I pray for Your hand on Angelina now and always. Amen.*

From downstairs, she heard the commotion of familiar voices. She went to join her friends and she carried with her Angelina's teddy bear. Cathy and Janis were surrounded by little girls; Rebecca, Emily, Natalie, and Angelina, all wanting equal attention.

"Mommy!" Natalie called from Cathy's arms. Jennifer walked over, and placed butterfly kisses on her clean rosy cheeks. Natalie laughed and hugged her mommy's neck. Cathy could hardly keep from crying as she eased Natalie to the floor.

"Look at how pretty you are!" Jennifer then turned to Angelina. Janis was barely able to hold on to her as she grabbed the teddy bear from her mother's hand. Jennifer kissed Angelina's hair and whispered lightly in her ear. Janis watched the little girl's face beam with love.

One at a time, the girls ran off to the living room to spend the next few minutes playing before Aunt Rima and Uncle Bill arrived. Janis looked at the clock and knew it was time to leave. Her eyes filled with tears that she tried to conceal.

She said to Jennifer, "It's time for me to leave."

Jennifer embraced her, "Yes, it is time to say good-bye."

Cathy went into the living room to keep the girls occupied.

"Stay close to God, Jennifer," Janis softly prayed.

"I will." Holding Janis' hands, Jennifer thanked her for the love and kindness she had shown to Angelina. "Tell Jacob and Justin thank you for sharing their parents with my daughter, your sons are fine young men – please tell them, I love them."

"I will and thank you, Jennifer, it was an honor that you trusted me with your baby," Janis wiped her tears. "Angelina brought joy to my family and we miss her a great deal. It was our pleasure; rather, it was our privilege to help you." Janis turned to leave.

"Wait, I have something for you." Jennifer stepped over to the sink and took the little silver angel from the window-sill and handed it to Janis.

"Oh, it's your little angel." Janis closed her hand around the small figure.

"Do you remember how many times you asked me to move it and warned me – *'Someday that little angel is going to fall down the sink'!"* Jennifer laughed and said, "Now the angel is yours, and I know she'll be in safe hands."

"Thank you." Janis gave her one last hug and quickly left.

*   *   *

Cathy rinsed out the coffee pot while Jennifer made one last telephone call to Karmanos. Cathy listened as Jennifer thanked them for their kindness, but especially for the knowledge they gave her in making educated decisions regarding her health.

Cathy set the empty coffee pot back on the burner and sighed, thinking of how many times she and Jennifer had shared hours of conversation over cups of hot coffee. She thought back to the day she stood alone with her in the doctor's office, the day she was correctly diagnosed with breast cancer. At that time, they compared statistical charts and data, and from that day forward Cathy knew what Jennifer's chances of survival were.

All during the last twenty months, almost two years now, Cathy had never once witnessed Jennifer being angry with God or asking – why me? Even though she felt Jennifer must have had bad days, Cathy above anyone else, knew that was not the tenor with Jennifer, as it would have been with many other women. Since she was there, Cathy knew from the very beginning that Jennifer without fail, trusted completely in God Almighty.

"Jen – " She started to say something, but stopped because her daughters came running through the kitchen asking if they could go home. Cathy told them yes and the sound of the girls slamming the front door filled the kitchen.

Once it was quiet, Jennifer said, "Cathy, I want you to know how much I'm going to miss you." Jennifer dabbed her nose and wiped away her tears, "You mean so much to me."

"Jen, I can't say good-bye." Cathy softly cried.

"Then we won't because we did agree not to say good-bye, remember?" Jennifer straightened her shoulders and said, "Cathy, I want you to know that I left something very special in Mary's care, and she'll know what to do – " The constraining lump in Jennifer's throat hurt so badly she found it difficult to speak. "Cathy, if anything happens to me, talk with Mary because she knows my final wishes."

Jennifer's hug lingered, and Cathy searched for the right words to say, but none could be found. They had talked for hours last week, and Cathy knew all the things Jennifer wanted to have set aside for her children – one day in the future.

"I have to go home for a short while, Jen, but I'll be back again before you leave," Cathy broke their embrace.

Jennifer faced her and said, "Cathy, you don't have to come back because I know how hard this is for you. I want to tell you before I leave for Jerusalem, that I love you and saying thank you is just not enough for all you've done for me."

"I love you, too." Cathy wiped her tears and said, "I'll be back in an hour."

As she turned to leave, Jennifer stopped her and in her soft angelic voice, she told her, "Cathy, you're my best friend."

*   *   *

Keith pulled into the driveway just as Cathy walked through the backyard. He turned off the engine and stepped out of the car when Bill and Rima pulled in behind him. Nicholas ran to give his aunt and uncle a quick hug and then raced back inside the house.

"Hello, Keith." Bill shook his hand.

Keith nodded, and Rima gave him a hug. She asked how Jennifer was doing and he said she was doing remarkably well. They were finally packed and Jeff would be there soon.

Rima gently asked him, "Keith, are y'all prepared for what's ahead?"

Keith bent to take the purchased computer gadgets from his car and not being certain if he was prepared or not, he said, "I'm not sure Rima, but making this trip is Jennifer's only chance of surviving."

"Aunt Rima," Natalie shouted and ran to her.

"Howdy, Natalie." She returned the hug and gave her a kiss. "Are you ready to come and stay with me and Uncle Bill?"

"Uh-huh." Natalie took Rima by the hand and led her upstairs. She wanted her aunt to see her new Cinderella suitcase and to help her bring it downstairs.

"Jennifer?" Bill called out from the foyer.

"Yes?" She was in the kitchen.

"Come here and show me which suitcases are ready so I can place them on the porch for Jeff." Bill studied the stack of luggage in the living room and wasn't sure which ones should be loaded first.

"Hello, Bill." She stood on her tiptoes and gave him a kiss on the cheek. "The suitcases over there are packed and you can take them outside."

He gladly started the chore, wanting something to do with his hands. He was having difficulty with the emotional heaviness surrounding his heart.

"Keith, are you finished packing?" Jennifer called to him.

"I don't know, Jennifer." Suddenly his mind was spinning at the reality and the responsibility of taking his cancer stricken wife to the Middle East in search of a cure.

"I'm sure you're finished." She surveyed the luggage and told Bill, "Please take everything outside except for the two overnight bags on the kitchen table."

"Where is your medication, Jennifer?" Rima asked while coming down the stairs.

"It's in my overnight bag," Jennifer assured her.

"All right then." Rima hoisted the girls' backpacks over her shoulder and then she called out to Nicholas, asking where his things were.

Everyone was moving about hurriedly because it was almost four o'clock and time to leave. Shari had called ten minutes ago, letting them know Jeff was on his way.

*   *   *

Cathy was crying and it broke her son Ryan's heart to see his mom so terribly upset. Ryan listened to his dad urging his mom to go back to Jennifer's one last time to say good-bye.

"I can't go back, Jimbo," Cathy sobbed, "Jennifer made all of us promise not to make a tearful scene." Cathy muffled her cries in the dishtowel and gazed through her kitchen window at Jennifer's backyard.

Ryan, along with his two sisters, Rebecca and Emily, sat at the kitchen table and listened to their parents softly speak to one another.

"Cathy, I think you should go back," Jim told her once again.

"Mom?" Ryan spoke up.

Cathy tossed her bangs away from her eyes and stared at her three children through her tears. They sat quietly at the kitchen table with bewildered stares and Cathy wondered . . . *Could I ever have such faith as Jennifer – to leave my children?*

"Mom, just go!" Ryan's voice cracked, and from behind his glasses tears flooded his eyes.

*   *   *

Rima loaded the children's belongings into the van while she talked cheerfully with Nicholas about going to the park tomorrow to play because it was still beautiful weather for November 11.

Time was escaping Jennifer's grasp. She watched Bill and Keith prepare to load Jeff's car. She inhaled deeply and slowly released the air from her lungs. She placed her Bible inside her overnight bag, zipped it closed, and rolled it to the foyer. She grabbed her backpack and the overcoat she had borrowed from Shari. Jeff met her halfway, smiled, and took her things.

Without glancing back inside, and before closing the door, out of sheer habit Jennifer reached over and turned on the front porch light because she disliked coming home to a dark house. She stepped out into the evening sunset and smiled as her three children ran to meet her on the porch steps.

"Do you know how much I love you?" she asked Nicholas. He nodded his head while he watched her hands holding his. "Give me a kiss good-bye," she whispered to him. Nicholas kissed her softly and held tightly to her neck. Jennifer closed her eyes and took in the feel of her son, so wonderful, his heart next to hers, and it was then she noticed how tall he had grown.

She held back her tears and sat down on the steps as Natalie hugged and kissed her a dozen times, six times on each cheek and Jennifer said she loved her with each loving embrace. She tucked the strands of fly-away hair behind Natalie's beautiful ears and looking into her child's eyes, she saw her own reflection.

Angelina wiggled her way onto her mommy's lap and her youngest gave her a quick hug and then ran off to be with the others. Jennifer gazed across the yard to the magnificent white birch tree, its branches reaching to the sky as it swayed in the early evening breeze. She wondered if she would ever see the tree blossom with green leaves again and whether she would be able to witness its natural cycle into another season of life.

Just before leaving, Rima was asked to take a family photograph of Jennifer, Keith, and their children. Bill helped by calling the children together and posing them in front of their parents as best he could. Rima found it difficult to focus through her veil of tears as she adjusted the camera. She steadied her hands and concentrated on the beautiful family of five that she saw through the lens of her camera. Keith placed Angelina in the arms of her mother and everyone was asked to smile.

Moments later, Bill took the children by the hand and led them to his car. Rima buckled Angelina into the car seat, and Natalie strapped herself in next to her sister. Nicholas squeezed in through the open door and scrambled across the seat to the opposite side of the vehicle.

Jeff sat patiently behind the driver's seat trying not to look at the clock on the dashboard while he waited for the adults to say good-bye. Bill shook Keith's hand and assured him everything would be all right with his family while they were gone. Bill told him there were many people who loved his children and they would all be looking after them and their home.

Rima held tightly to Jennifer and softly said prayers of praise and worship with her on the front lawn and afterwards she told Jennifer, "Y'all know I love the children and will watch over them as if they were my own while you're gone."

"Yes, I know and I am blessed to leave my family in your care." Jennifer smiled and said, "God is filling your arms with my babies, and to simply say thank you is not enough because you are like a sister to me, Rima."

"We are sisters, Jennifer," Rima cried.

Bill tapped Jennifer on the shoulder. Keith was in the car, and Jeff had shifted the vehicle into reverse. "Jennifer, you're going to miss your plane." He teased and held her gently.

"Bill, I couldn't have made this trip without knowing you and Rima were here for me." She kissed his cheek and said, "God bless you, William Hardy."

"God be with you, Jennifer." He lifted his glasses to wipe his eyes.

*   *   *

Cathy stood at the kitchen window surrounded by her family. All of them were crying. Her children knew Miss Jennifer was going far away to see a doctor and this was the reason for their sadness and their mother's tears. They continued to listen as their dad spoke tenderly and held their mom's hand.

"Cathy, go back over there to say good-bye," Jim encouraged.

"Jen would be disappointed in me running over there crying, just to say good-bye one last time." Cathy twisted the damp tissue in her hand.

"Nevertheless, I think you should go." He gently coaxed her away from the window.

"Yeah, Mom, just go." Ryan agreed with his dad.

Cathy's moist eyes went from her husband to her children and back again.

"Go!" they told her.

Cathy opened the patio door and dashed across her backyard while franticly calling out Jennifer's name. She came around the garage into the front yard and saw the Hardy's van with Rima sitting in the front seat and the Hayse children securely buckled in the back, ready to leave. The garage door was closing, and Bill bent low, ducking out of its way.

"*Jennifer!*" Cathy cried aloud as she watched the taillights to Jeff's vehicle round the corner from Mayflower Drive onto Baywood Drive.

"She's gone, Cathy." Bill placed his hands on her shoulder.

"No, I didn't get to say good-bye." Cathy clasped her hand over her mouth and cried into Bill's arms.

"Shush." He soothed her, but Bill felt the same way because he too, really didn't get to say a proper good-bye either, but it was Jennifer's wish. All he could say to comfort his friend was, "She knows we love her."

*   *   *

Inside the dimly lit airplane, while everyone slept, Jennifer gazed out at the starlit sky and the Mediterranean Sea below. She felt the plane making its descent and through the darkness she could vaguely see the horizon come into focus over Tel Aviv.

This would be her final battle, her last fight in conquering breast cancer. During the overseas flight, she recalled stories of countless battles in the Old Testament of how the Israelites, God's chosen people, were victorious in gaining entry into the Promised Land.

The thought gave Jennifer peace of mind and the spiritual dwelling within her soul magnified itself. She adjusted the pink scarf that was tied around her scalp and through the window she glanced at her silhouette. She smiled at her beautiful reflection – this was the Jennifer that she had finally learned to accept. In the dark sky, a lone star caught her attention. She moved closer to the tiny window and beckoning her to come to Jerusalem was . . . *The Star of Bethlehem.*

Stairway to Heaven
Winter of 2005

~ *43* ~

The Park Plaza Hotel in Jerusalem was located on Vilnay Street, and room number 228 would be their home for the next several weeks, perhaps even months. After settling in and adjusting to the time change, Jennifer contacted Hadassah Hospital. She confirmed her first set of appointments and marked the dates on her calendar. She felt somewhat unsettled, knowing many of the appointments were scheduled for Sunday mornings, but she was now in Israel amid Jews, and Saturday was their customary day of Sabbath.

For the next two weeks, she would visit the clinic as an outpatient while the team of doctors and professors evaluated her medical condition. This was necessary in order to determine which steps she would undergo once admitted to the hospital and during her evaluation period, Jennifer was well enough to visit some of the nearby sites of the Holy Land. She saw Israel as a distinct mixture of ancient times blended with modern buildings, shopping, transportation, and village markets.

To her, Jerusalem was a place of beauty, none like she had ever seen before. Across the vast desert which surrounded the city were the mountain ranges and endless valleys of the Promised Land. Soon after they arrived, Keith hired a tour guide whose name was Shmuel, and he understood Jennifer's physical limitations. Shmuel was willing to assist them with seeing the Old and New Jerusalem, but Jennifer wanted her first visit to be in the town of Bethlehem, the birthplace of Jesus. So Keith asked Shmuel to take them to the Church of the Nativity.

Sitting in the front seat of his taxicab, Jennifer was captivated by the desert landscape and she felt as if her heart, at any time, could burst forth with praise and worship. As they drove along, she envisioned what the landscape was like when, over two thousand years ago, Jesus traveled the same short distance between Jerusalem and Bethlehem.

After parking his cab, Shmuel told Jennifer and Keith about the western entrance to the Church, known as the "Door of Humility." This was traditionally where most Christian visitors entered. Shmuel walked with them in the direction of the sandstone cloisters leading to the tiny door where directly above her, Jennifer could clearly see the outline of the original 6th century medieval archway. They stood next to the entrance which now measured no more than five feet high, and listened to their tour guide explain the surrounding history.

It was during the time of the Crusaders, when the original arched doorway was reduced in size to prevent villagers from entering on horseback. However, it makes today's entry an appropriate, humbling experience as you must, in sheer reverence, bend low and stoop before descending the ancient stairs.

Inside the dimly lit grotto, the smell of incense and burning candles saturated the air. Jennifer carefully felt along the cool stone wall as she placed her trembling feet on the smooth surface and with each step she took, it brought her deeper into the cave of the Nativity. Once through the stairwell, she entered the grotto, which is said to be the birthplace of Jesus, the Incarnation – the mystery of God becoming man. The enclosed area was not more than eight feet high and thirteen feet across. Jennifer knelt on the inlaid marble floor and touched the fourteen-pointed star. Tears fell without effort as she recalled her favorite Christmas hymn . . . *O come, let us adore Him, Christ the Lord!*

Shmuel pointed to the overhead pillars, showing her what remained of the mosaic tiles that told of the ancestry of Jesus. On the northern wall was written the ancestry as recorded in the Gospels by Luke, and the southern wall shows the ancestors of Jesus chronicled by Matthew. How wonderful to be standing here, centuries later, in the traditional spot of where the Savior was born. Jennifer was in awe of the undeniable feeling she was experiencing.

Keith, with hands in his pockets, stood by her side and waited before leading her down three short steps to the Chapel of the Manger. This was the spot where it is said Mary placed her newborn baby. Jennifer bent low and placed her left hand on the marble footsteps in front of the glass-enclosed manger. It, too, was very small. She felt the cold, underground stones beneath her hands, she bowed her head and recalled . . . *for unto us a Savior is born.*

Keith went to her side, but several minutes passed before she took his hand to stand next to him. She didn't want to leave, and she made sure Keith had taken a number of photographs before they climbed the stairs and departed. All at once, childhood memories of Christmas filled her mind, and Jennifer realized how much she missed her Grandmother Catherine. She prayed Nicholas, Natalie, and Angelina would carry with them into adulthood the true meaning of Christmas, the birth of the Messiah.

Shmuel took them to the opposite side of the original entrance and once outside he explained to Jennifer the crowded construction of many churches in the immediate area of Bethlehem. Jennifer turned in a slow semi-circle as

Shmuel pointed out that she was standing in the courtyard to the . . . *Church of St. Catherine.*

*   *   *

Early the next morning, Keith and Jennifer went to Hadassah Hospital. Her first meeting was scheduled with Dr. Benny Gezunheit and on her next visit she would see Professor Shimon Slavin. The professional atmosphere in Hadassah was much different than what she was accustomed to. She listened to Dr. Gezunheit telephone the laboratory himself for her medical records that were on file from the United States.

Dr. Gezunheit sat comfortably on a metal stool next to the file cabinet while he jotted down the findings in her medical chart. For now, his handwritten notes would suffice until her files were through the digital scanning process. With the telephone in the crook of his neck, he poured black coffee into a mug and lifted the pot to Jennifer asking if she would like some. She smiled and said yes, as he poured her a cup of plain black coffee. Jennifer looked around and noticed there was no raw sugar, cinnamon or flavored cream to enhance the beverage. She sipped the rich dark coffee and for the first time she thoroughly enjoyed its authentic flavor.

By mid-afternoon, the next two weeks were carefully planned. Jennifer was scheduled every two days for scanning, blood work, and other testing. Her medical team would evaluate her condition, and when the decision was made as to which course of action they would recommend, she would be admitted to the hospital.

Keith and Jennifer were grateful and very impressed with the professionalism at Hadassah Hospital and before leaving, the doctors gave her renewals on her prescriptions along with new medications. Jennifer was happy to note on her next visit she was to have a blood transfusion which would increase her energy level.

Not being familiar with where to go, they had dinner at the hospital cafeteria and then went directly back to their hotel room. Keith spent the evening downloading special software to his laptop so they could use the wireless capability offered in Jerusalem.

Jennifer telephoned home and talked with her children. Nicholas questioned why she didn't sound far away and said he was disappointed because there was no echo on the telephone line. Jennifer smiled over the 6,000 miles that covered the expanse between them and told him it was because he was so close to her heart that her voice would never carry an echo.

Looking over her appointment schedule she noticed there were days between each hospital visit. She thumbed through the tourist brochures to make travel plans and although there was so much to see, she wanted to make sure she could visit the places that were dearest to her heart first.

On the nightstand was her Bible. She opened it to the back pages where she had noted her favorite scriptures and her eyes were drawn to Luke, Chapter 19, and the story of Zacchaeus in the town of Jericho. She located Jericho on the map and discovered it was only ten miles northwest of where the Jordan River enters the Dead Sea. Cheerfully, she turned to Keith and told him about their travel plans for the next day and before kissing him good night, she told him that nothing would keep her from seeing the sites of the Holy Land.

*   *   *

The following morning, Shmuel held the passenger door of his taxicab open for Jennifer while Keith climbed into the backseat. Lately, sitting in the front seat of any vehicle helped her to avoid motion sickness. She had never experienced this before and wondered if it was partly due to her medication. Shmuel knew their plans for the day and suggested they travel first to Jericho; second they would visit the Dead Sea and later in the day come back to Jerusalem. Then he told them if time permitted, they could walk in the evening through the New City close to their hotel.

Along the way, the two men talked casually about local customs and places of interest outside the religious realm. Keith learned which restaurants to visit and what spices to avoid when ordering his meals because his stomach was increasingly sensitive to certain foods. Shmuel gave him additional maps of downtown sites that were close to the Park Plaza Hotel and Hadassah Hospital.

Jennifer rode along in silence. She was thinking of the Bible stories associated with Jericho and she recalled falling asleep last night after reading the parable of the Good Samaritan. Looking out the window at people passing by, she believed that everyone, no matter where they lived, were her neighbors and that God's love has no boundaries.

She praised God for sending numerous people into her life over the past two years. They were people who did not pass her by without showing their kindness and offering their help. They were modern-day Good Samaritans who gave of their time and resources to care for her, and some of those who did help were strangers to her. Jennifer recalled Matthew 22:39 . . . *"Love your neighbor as yourself."*

Jennifer stepped out of the taxicab and onto the paved sidewalk which led to the ancient, gated sycamore tree. Keith walked next to her with his camera ready while she ran her fingers across the individual rods to the iron gate. Like a harpist playing music that only she could hear, Jennifer listened to the inner symphony of her heart strings, and she knew the orchestrator was God.

Stepping closer to the Tree of Jericho, she read the large copper plaque that described the story of Zacchaeus, who was a Roman tax collector. The sycamore was estimated to be two thousand years old, which dated the tree to the time of Christ's visit to the city. Jennifer loved the story, as Jesus selected among all those surrounding Him to have supper with this small man in his home.

At the time, tax collectors were known for their thievery, but Jesus wanted Zacchaeus to repent for his evil ways and Jesus took the time to gently lead this man to salvation. After their brief time together, Zacchaeus surrendered his life to Christ, gave half his possessions to the poor, and returned to anyone he had cheated – four times the stolen amount. More than that, everyone who witnessed the remarkable change in Zacchaeus understood the change in his character came from knowing who Jesus was – Zacchaeus understood that Jesus was indeed the Son of God.

They left Jericho, and during their short ride in the cab, Jennifer talked to Keith and Shmuel of how Joshua marched around the city of Jericho. The priest carried before Joshua and his army, the Ark of the Covenant, which in the Old Testament signified the presence and power of God. Jennifer recalled her grandmother, rocking in her wicker chair and singing the old spiritual hymn she loved at Mountain Hope Baptist Church . . . *and the walls of Jericho come a-tumblin' down.*

*   *   *

Next, they stopped for lunch at an outdoor cafe along the shoreline of the Dead Sea and when they had finished, Jennifer ventured into the murky water because she didn't want to miss out on this precious opportunity. The water's temperature was surprisingly warm and she giggled at Keith, whose nose wrinkled at the pungent smell of the high mineral content. Jennifer grazed her hand over the water's surface and gently splashed its medicinal values onto her legs and his, and within moments they were lathered in the sea's black mud.

The Dead Sea is the lowest point on earth, meaning the water in the lake does not drain anywhere; it must evaporate. They learned from another tourist who was floating effortlessly nearby, that seven million tons of water has evaporated from the Sea, but the minerals remain and it contains over ten times the amount of salt that is present in the oceans.

Jennifer stayed in the water long after Keith rinsed off at the fresh water spas. He walked the shoreline among the pillars of salt, looking across at the sweeping mountains and the dramatic rocky desert. Suddenly, it struck Keith where he was and how far away from home they actually were. The seriousness of the trip and the outcome of the weeks ahead weighed heavily on his mind.

Keith knew the frail state of Jennifer's physical condition, yet she continued to be cheerful and constantly smiled. He watched from a distance as she defied gravity and drifted on the gentle ripples of salt water. She visited with the others floating next to her, talking with them as if she hadn't a care . . . *in this earthly world.*

Keith took out the camera and snapped several photographs of how beautiful she looked through the lens of his camera. He stepped toward the edge of the shore and she smiled directly at him. Water cascaded from her cupped hand as she wiped the black mud from her shoulder.

Over her swimsuit, she wore a pink tank top and a sheer, pink scarf reaching to her calves. It was tied at her waist and floated next to her on the surface of the heavy sea. Under her wide-rimmed, natural straw hat, she wore a pink bandana. Jennifer was covered in mud, but her smile was radiant. It was a picture of poised perfection, and it was at this moment Keith became fully aware of her inner peace. He held out his hand, and she rose to take it.

Later that day on the beach, Jennifer rested on a wooden chaise lounge under the shade of an umbrella. She called for Keith and told him that suddenly she was feeling queasy and very weak. He handed her the last of his soft drink and some crackers from inside her backpack, and then he silently scolded himself for allowing her to do too much in one day.

Shmuel watched them from his table inside the restaurant and stopped one of the waiters to ask for a cold bottle of water, some fresh fruit, and a package of saltine crackers. He took the carry-out box for Jennifer over to where Keith was standing. He explained that at times the heat of the desert often drained unaware visitors of their strength.

Jennifer sat in the shade and replenished her system with the carry-out food while Keith and Shmuel carried their bags to the taxi. Keith returned to help Jennifer step over the quarry rocks and into the air-conditioned vehicle. Shmuel assisted Jennifer as she slid into the front seat and on the ride back to the hotel, Jennifer slept.

~ 44 ~

Two days later, after examining Jennifer in the morning, Professor Slavin ordered a blood transfusion. She knew from past experience that soon after the procedure she would regain lost energy, if only for a short while. Keith waited by her side in the clinic at Hadassah Hospital and helped her fill out what seemed to be an endless amount of paperwork.

By six o'clock in the evening they were back at the hotel and exhausted from the day. Keith surmised this would be the way of things for the next couple of months and getting used to the *new-normal* would take time. At this point, he wondered if Jennifer realized that going home on Christmas Eve seemed highly unlikely.

The medicinal program she was on certainly helped to relieve the pain associated with cancer, but Keith could see in her eyes that she was not completely free from discomfort. Several times he noticed her stopping to catch her breath while holding tightly to the lower portion of her back.

He asked the doctor what could be done for her back discomfort, and for the time being it was recommended that she try an adjustable support brace. Within hours he was fastening it around her waist. He admired Jennifer greatly for her determination and courage because she still wanted to tour the ancient structures of the city.

Jennifer tried not to think of why she was experiencing the sudden pain in her lower back because the only reason was obvious; the cancer was spreading. She knew the possibility of it invading the lymph nodes in her pelvic area was the most likely explanation for her pain.

*   *   *

Shmuel waited at Hadassah Hospital to take Keith and Jennifer on a short afternoon excursion and an hour later they were outside the main entrance to the Church of the Holy Sepulchre. In the parking lot, Jennifer stayed inside the taxi while Shmuel talked privately with Keith. She watched through the rearview side door mirror as the tour guide spoke with passion, using his hands freely. She wondered what was happening when she saw Keith consent and nod in agreement as Shmuel opened the trunk to his taxicab.

On her own, Jennifer stepped out of the vehicle and watched Shmuel unfold a gently used wheelchair. The men turned at the sound of her lyrical voice. Keith was apprehensive and Shmuel was uncertain as to how she might react to the assisted chair, but without a word Jennifer sat down in the worn leather seat.

Keith watched as the cab driver, their tour guide, without hesitation bent down to adjust the foot rests and locked them in place for her comfort. Shmuel walked behind her while he compassionately rolled the chair in front of him and then proceeded to tell them about the history of the church they were about to visit.

Keith walked beside them into the huge courtyard filled with other tourists, and he instantly understood Shmuel's thoughtfulness. The area before them was spread-out and immense, which would require a great deal of walking. Jennifer reached over her shoulder to the handle of the wheelchair and patted Shmuel's hand showing him her unspoken appreciation.

Once through the crowded doors to the sanctuary, her eyes were drawn to the massive columns and the great rotunda with its high ceiling – this was indeed a church of remarkable proportions. Keith took a brochure showing the interior layout along with the history of each chapel within the great church. After Jennifer stood, Shmuel folded the chair and waited outside for them in the Plaza Square. He was confident they would find their way back to him.

In the center of the great shrine, on the floor for everyone to touch, was a large slab of natural limestone. It commemorated the place where the body of Jesus may have been laid before His burial. It was called the Stone of Anointing.

While others kneeled and prayed nearby, Jennifer held fast to sound, Biblical teachings and the knowledge that the presence of Jesus is everywhere. Although beckoned to come, she knew God's miraculous healing power was equally available in Plymouth, Michigan, as it was in Jerusalem. The empty tomb, the Resurrection of Jesus, and the indwelling of the Holy Spirit were all valid historical proof that yes, our Redeemer lives . . . *everywhere.*

Jennifer was drawn to the beautiful memorial and knelt with Keith by her side. The tears cascaded down her cheeks as she bowed her head and placed her left hand over the stone. Keith, too, was moved by the atmosphere of hushed prayers and the chanting of worship surrounding him. Jennifer was at a loss for words because the humble act of kneeling in Jerusalem was extremely profound. She spoke to God with her heart, knowing He heard and understood her petition . . . *Dear God, whatever happens to me, may it be Your will, not mine.*

Next, they visited the Chapel of Mary Magdalene and inside the chapel a marble lid covered the tomb where perhaps the crucified Lord was taken. Jennifer also prayed at the

Chapel of Derision, believed to hold a section of the stone column where Jesus was mocked and treated with contempt. Keith stayed by her side as they walked down the stairs to the Chapel of St. Helena and along the stairway still able to be seen, were many crosses carved into the ancient stone walls by the pilgrims centuries ago. Next they visited the Rock of Calvary, the Chapel of the Nailing of the Cross, and the Agony of the Virgins.

It was an emotional day. Soon Jennifer's steps faltered and when Keith helped her, she was barely able to make her way outside to the Christian corridor. Waiting for them under a tiny patch of afternoon shade, Shmuel waved to them and wasted no time in getting the wheelchair to her side. Keith eased her into the seat and Jennifer asked to be taken back to the hotel where she could rest.

*   *   *

The next morning, Jennifer woke refreshed and Keith was taken by surprise with her renewed stamina. Although he hesitated, he didn't resist when she told him of her plans for the day. He knew the depth of her desire to visit the holy places and since he was not sure how much time she had before being admitted to Hadassah – he could not refuse her request. After today, she was scheduled at the clinic for more testing and scans. He knew Jennifer would be too tired and unable to tour the city after the medical procedures and perhaps today would be her last chance.

By mid-morning they stood on the east bank of the Kidron Valley in the foothills of the Mount of Olives outside the Church of all Nations. It was a Catholic Franciscan church, built by donations from many countries and because of its location next to the Garden of Gethsemane, it is also known as the Basilica of the Agony. The Mount of Olives is the highest peak surrounding Jerusalem and it is many times referred to as . . . *Mt. Zion.*

Above the front entrance of the church, they stopped to admire the mosaic tiles illustrating Christ as the link between God and humanity. The artwork also depicted Jesus holding two Greek letters, the Alpha and the Omega, the beginning and the end. Before entering the church, Jennifer turned to capture the breathtaking view from the Mount of Olives down the slopes toward the walls of Jerusalem.

She was filled with the presence of the Holy Spirit and she was blessed with the understanding that she was humbly walking in the footsteps of her Savior. Regardless of the noted geographic uncertainties to the places she was visiting, there was no uncertainty in her heart. Jennifer felt the presence of Jesus, and even though her circumstances may appear unfavorable to many others, she was filled with great joy.

Once inside the church, Jennifer was drawn to the domed ceiling where on each of the twelve separate domes, inlaid in blue, were the coat-of-arms for the twelve contributing nations. A glorious painting of Jesus praying in the Garden surrounded by olive trees spanned the entire width of the interior.

Keith stayed by her side, while one at a time the other visitors stepped away and at last, a clear path was given for Jennifer to approach the foot of the altar. On the floor, in the center of the Nave was a large stone, depicting the Gethsemane stone. The stone was encircled with wrought iron, designed to represent the crown of thorns given to our King. This is where archeologists believe Jesus prayed on the night he was betrayed. Jennifer removed her straw hat, sank to her knees, and bowed face down. She was filled with an overpowering sense of spiritual wisdom as her trembling hand reached for the Rock of Agony.

The open shrine with its massive pillars of support was reverently still and everyone moved about in hushed whispers. Her tears fell on her folded hands. She couldn't keep from crying, yet she was not sad because she was filled with the . . . *sureness of eternity.*

Her heart spoke to Jesus as her tear-drenched eyes studied the spectacular painting. Jesus was in the depths of sorrow as he prayed in the Garden to His Father to take the cup of agony from Him. Jesus knew the grim reality and the necessity of the Cross; it was the burden He must carry for mankind's sin. His feelings of despair on that dark night could not be comprehended by man, for we are unable to imagine the weight of our sins on the shoulders of the One who knew no sin. Jennifer prayed, being fully aware that during the next few weeks she would be scheduled for intense chemotherapy plus full body radiation. She knew the suffering she was about to endure and the reality if the treatment failed.

Keith held out his hand and whispered softly to her. He then gave her a fresh tissue and helped her to stand. He wrapped his arm around her waist and led her through the open doors to the outside garden where the bright sun was temporarily blinding. Jennifer shielded her eyes to block the brilliant rays and then she replaced her straw hat.

Shmuel was visiting with a group of his friends who were also in the tourist industry. Jennifer heard them across the small olive grove talking with one another in Hebrew; she smiled and politely waited. One of the men bowed slightly in her direction, and Shmuel quickly left the group, pushing the wheelchair ahead of him.

Jennifer sat comfortably as Shmuel casually wheeled the chair down the paved bricks alongside the large ancient olive trees. He told Keith and Jennifer the trees could very likely be descendants from the original olive trees in the times of Jesus, but it was difficult to tell how old any of the trees were because their roots were all ancient.

While the two men discussed the afternoon agenda, Jennifer brought out her camera and focused on a single pink rose growing amongst the desert rocks. She recalled the Blushing Knockout roses planted on Pond View Drive when she and Keith first moved into their home in New Boston. It seemed like such a long time ago, and how different their lives were now as compared to what they had planned back then. At the time, they dreamed of a perfect life together, a strong marriage, and a thriving family.

Jennifer concentrated as she blocked all other greenery from the lens of the camera and snapped the single rose against the desert rocks. She took one more photograph, wanting to make sure she had captured the isolated flower. She studied the delicacy of the rose and contemplated the hardship it endured while struggling to blossom in the desert wilderness.

The rose is a thing of beauty, she thought to herself, and should be displayed in an atrium where others can admire it and those who love the rose can easily care for it. How could one survive in the desert? She left the wheelchair and bent down to appreciate the flower; its fragrance was strong, and the petals were like silk against her fingertips.

Jennifer dusted away the dry, scorched rocks from the base of the stem and again she wondered how the flower could bloom under such parched conditions. Yet it did. It was magnificent, and even in the worst of circumstances the rose rejoiced and blossomed. The rose came to accept its role in life and the desert in which it was planted. The rose trusted in God to provide for its daily needs and as the prophet Isaiah recorded in chapter 35 – this is the Excellency of our God.

On their way back to the taxicab, Shmuel wheeled Jennifer through the side doors of the church and greeting other visitors near the entrance was Father Fergus Clarke, a Franciscan monk. Often times, Father Clarke would visit the Church of all Nations even though his home church was St. John the Baptist, located just four miles west of Jerusalem.

Shmuel was Jewish, but he was personally acquainted with the Catholic priest and respected Father Clarke's steadfast devotion to Christ Jesus.

Shmuel hoped Jennifer would take kindly to his offer of being introduced to Father Clarke and when she thanked him for the caring gesture, he caught the Franciscan's attention with a wave of his hand. Father Clarke walked over to them and when Jennifer explained her medical condition he offered to pray for her. Jennifer removed her straw hat and bowed her head, and the monk placed one hand over his heart and the other on the pink scarf that covered her scalp. Father Clarke prayed over Jennifer on the steps of the Church of all Nations that overlooked the city of Jerusalem. After he finished praying, Keith shook his hand and Jennifer smiled with gratitude, and while Keith wheeled Jennifer into the parking lot, Fergus patted Shmuel on the back and inquired about his job and how his family was doing, because the two men were friends.

*   *   *

Later that afternoon, they finished their lunch in the Market Square and relaxed while they watched the diverse people of Jerusalem. Today the streets were filled with nuns, priests, rabbis, and imams, representing three religions: Christianity, Judaism, and Islam. A great mixture of beliefs hurried past one another to fulfill God's work in his or her own way.

Jennifer basked in the fading warmth of the sun, enjoying the busyness of the streets. People passed by them on their way to afternoon prayer, work, or shopping, before going home for the evening to their families.

Keith stood and finished the last of his herbal tea and Jennifer stood next to him. Keith carried her shopping bags containing the keepsakes she purchased for loved ones back home. He appreciated her loyalty by thinking of others during this time and because she needed cheering up – he smiled and took her hand.

Together they walked to the Temple Mount so Jennifer could visit the Western Wall before the day was through. During their lunch Keith read the regulations concerning respectful visitation to both sites and when they approached the public entrance to the Temple, he was amazed at its size, for it covered over thirty-five acres in the middle of the city.

A short distance away, they watched Jewish men pray in the Wall Plaza, an open-air synagogue, and in keeping with Orthodox Jewish tradition, the women prayed behind a divided screen. The Wailing Wall is believed to be the sole remnant of the Holy Temple where untouched greenery can be seen flourishing between the ancient crevices.

Jennifer was overcome by the magnificent structure and since she had only seen the Wall from a distance, she was amazed at the enormous stones holding the foundation securely in place. Keith pointed to the northern section near the Wilson's Arch where a single extraordinary stone alone weighed approximately 570 tons.

Keith told Jennifer that over one million prayers a year were written and inserted into the crevices of the Wall. He told her the prayer requests were collected twice a year and buried on the Mount of Olives. They walked quietly past the men praying and began the long climb up the stairs to the Temple entrance.

Jennifer remembered stories her grandmother told her as a child, how Mary and Joseph, after Jesus' birth, brought Him to the Temple for dedication. Then, at the age of twelve, how Jesus impressed the Jewish teachers with His knowledge of the Old Testament.

She took the steps slowly, not because she was overly tired, but because she wanted to savor the spiritual moment. As she ascended the stairs, her heart wanted to burst open with praise because she was overcome with the knowledge that Jesus walked the same steps they were treading. Her heart raced as her mind tried to absorb the sacredness of the Temple. This was God's holy place, and she was beckoned into the Courts of the King. Humbly she praised Him for the blessing of this spiritual experience and with each movement she felt the steps beneath her feet were indeed the . . . *Stairway to Heaven.*

*   *   *

Approximately five days later, after the results of her scans and tests were studied, Jennifer was admitted to Hadassah Hospital. Professor Slavin planned to perform two procedures: the bone marrow transplant plus the donor lymphocyte infusion. The estimated length of time for this course of action was about three months.

After going through several days of chemotherapy and full body radiation, in two weeks she would be transferred to the isolation ward. There, she would be under strict observation because her immune system would be almost non-existent and nearly destroyed. Jennifer's particular combative treatment attacked and destroyed her blood cells. On account of this, she was extremely tired, at risk for infection, and in serious danger if she came upon any bruises or cuts. Even a minor paper cut could prove fatal at this point because her white blood cells, red blood cells, and platelets were at dangerously low levels. In medical terms, she would be taken to the threshold of death.

She spent her time getting to know the hospital staff, talking on the telephone, e-mailing loved ones back home, and playing cards with Keith. But mostly, she spent long hours reading her Bible and praying while waiting for the chemotherapy and radiation to kill the abnormal cancer cells.

Since her back pain was under control she felt well enough to walk down the isolated hospital corridor and one afternoon with the help of an aide, she was going back to her room after a short walk. Jennifer rounded the corner, and saw hanging over her bed the Jen Possible Team banner from the 2004 Susan G. Komen Detroit Race for the Cure.

While she was out of her room the hospital staff wanted to surprise her and with Keith's help, they hung the banner that was mailed to them from her friends at Visteon. Jennifer was extremely touched and the act of kindness brought tears to her eyes. Her mind was flooded with memories of everyone she missed, especially Nicholas, Natalie, and Angelina.

From inside her room, Davina, who was her bedside nurse, was there to help her back into bed. Jennifer reserved a special place within her heart for Davina, whom she later discovered was Shmuel's younger sister.

Often times during her late-night rounds, Davina would find Jennifer reading the Bible. She would stand politely in the doorway and respectfully wait for Jennifer to acknowledge her presence before entering the hospital room. Davina did not want to interrupt Jennifer's prayer time with the Christian King, the prophet Davina simply knew as Jesus.

"But you will receive power when the
Holy Spirit comes to you;
and you will be my witnesses in Jerusalem . . ."
Acts 1:8

~ 45 ~

Shortly after Christmas, although a battle was raging as her system was still fighting the cancer, Jennifer was well enough to be discharged from the hospital, but not well enough to return to Michigan. During the next four to five weeks, she would stay at the hotel and go back to the clinic several times a week for close monitoring.

Following the transplants, her DNA testing showed the new bone marrow in her system to reflect that of the donor; Jennifer no longer exhibited her own DNA. However, the time to celebrate was far off, as she was experiencing an uncomfortable rash and severe gastro-intestinal trouble. These were anticipated side-effects, indicating the success of the procedure was somewhat promising.

Jennifer remained hopeful even though the doctors told her the recent test results confirmed their suspicion – the cancer was now throughout her body. The original left aux-iliary tumor under her arm was still evident along with mul-tiple other tumors, all adding up to an increased amount of active cancer for the new immune system to conquer.

The doctors were careful to instruct her to get plenty of rest and not overdo things during her outpatient status. Keith took her to their hotel, focusing on a positive outcome. He was confident Jennifer would finally win the battle with breast cancer, and they would be leaving Israel shortly.

*   *   *

Years before when Jennifer surrendered her life to Christ, she gave her destiny to Him, and from that moment on she willingly understood her life was no longer hers. Early one morning, several weeks after her hospital discharge, Jennifer sat at the tiny desk in their hotel room. She had spent the last few hours praying continuously for those she loved and for those whose medical care she was under in Jerusalem. She carefully tore a page from her journal where she had listed the names of several people.

She folded the paper and placed it inside her coat pocket, then woke Keith and asked him to telephone Shmuel. Jennifer urgently wanted to return to Bethlehem, the birthplace of Jesus, to visit the Church of the Nativity. The short drive from Jerusalem to Bethlehem was only a matter of six miles, however today the congested morning traffic and stops along the way made the drive seem endless. Jennifer closed her eyes and rested until the murmur of the taxicab's motor ceased.

Shmuel tried to hide his concern for Jennifer as he helped Keith maneuver the wheelchair out of the trunk. He rolled it to the front passenger seat and gently nudged Jennifer awake. Keith's stomach was in knots and the familiar ache was intensified as he watched his wife gingerly step from the taxicab into the assisted chair.

Jennifer held her husband's hand while Shmuel guided them past the customary entrance way because Shmuel knew that in the back of the church, overlooking the Shepherd's Field, was a special access ramp. The dedicated and hardworking palms of Shmuel's hands begin to perspire as he gripped the handles to Jennifer's wheelchair.

Within her spirit, scripture spoke softly to Jennifer as she looked across the barren field where the shepherds lay sleeping the night Jesus was born. The shepherds were terrified when the angel of the Lord appeared, but Jennifer closed her eyes and searched her memory for the words the angel first spoke to them . . . *Do not be afraid.*

Inside the Chapel of the Manger, Jennifer rested in the last pew and close to the entrance, Keith stood off to the side underneath the archway. It was still very early in the morning, and no one else was present in the tiny enclosure. Jennifer was grateful for the solitude and delighted in the perfection of God's timing. She meditated on the love that was bestowed upon her by the Maker of heaven and earth.

Soon, Jennifer turned to Keith, and he quickly came to her side. She unfolded the paper from inside her coat pocket and told him she wanted to light a prayer candle for each family on the list. Keith did what she requested and lit more than a dozen of the distinctive, Ethiopian prayer sticks. He had seen many of these candlesticks since they arrived in Jerusalem. He lit the candles while Jennifer prayed for the families who went out of their way to help her along this journey. She explained to Keith that the burning flame symbolized the resurrection of . . . *Jesus, the Living Savior.*

Moments later they were in the taxicab with Shmuel driving back into the city. The traffic had somewhat dissipated which helped to make their trip faster, and for this they were grateful. But, as they approached the vicinity of Vilnay Street, Jennifer placed her hand on Shmuel's arm and told him to drive past their hotel and take her directly to Hadassah Hospital.

Shmuel was filled with compassion and through blurred vision he looked in the rearview mirror, trying to catch a glimpse of Keith. When his profile came into view there was no need to confirm Jennifer's request because Shmuel could clearly see the tears racing down Keith's sorrowful face.

*   *   *

It was the third week into the New Year when Jennifer was immediately admitted to Hadassah Hospital because she was experiencing severe gastro-intestinal pain along with complicated side effects from the steroid medication. Although heartbroken to re-admit his wife, Keith was relieved in knowing Jennifer would be under the supervision of the medical team.

He sat in the chair next to her bed, listening to the constant rhythm of the medical equipment that was monitoring Jennifer's vital signs. Out the corner of his eye, Keith noticed one of the nurses on duty standing in the doorway, hesitating. She appeared to be waiting for permission to enter the hospital room.

Keith waved to her, and when she stepped into the dim light of the room, he recognized the familiar character of the nurse, a character that was filled with meekness and humility. Although Jennifer was no longer in the isolation ward, Keith knew the nurse standing in front of him was Davina. She explained to Keith that the first of the year she was transferred to the second floor of the hospital where she was randomly, by chance, assigned to Jennifer's bedside.

Davina entered the room and ignored the tears moistening her cheeks as she walked over to check the diagnostic reading on the medical equipment. Jennifer stirred as Davina held a moist cool cloth to her forehead and she smiled with gratitude at the affectionate touch, because Jennifer knew it was Shmuel's wonderful sister, Davina.

The next morning, Keith was awakened in the hospital chair when he heard Jennifer's soft lyrical voice calling out his name. She smiled as he sat down next to her on the bed and they were able to talk for some time before Professor Slavin entered the room. Jennifer greeted the doctor with her warm personality and he automatically responded with a smile of his own. Along with many others at Hadassah,

Professor Slavin genuinely admired Jennifer's invisible strength that came from somewhere deep within her being.

However, the professor's demeanor became crestfallen as he studied her recent lab results. He looked at the young couple from America and told them that Jennifer was spiking with extremely high levels of bilirubin in her blood stream. Professor Slavin further added that if a miraculous turn-around in her bilirubin was not brought about within the next few days, he must perform a very risky procedure to induce her liver into functioning more effectively. He stayed with them awhile longer so he could answer their emotionally filled questions. Afterwards, he solemnly left the room.

*　　*　　*

The next morning, Keith brought his laptop into Hadassah so Jennifer could contact her friends back home through e-mail. Ever since leaving Plymouth, she kept in constant touch with Mary and Cathy over the telephone, but mostly through e-mail with everyone else. Jennifer spoke with Cathy and Mary yesterday, they were aware of her impending surgery and the serious nature of its outcome.

In the morning sunlight, Keith turned Jennifer's hospital chair to face the window, and then lowered the adjustable food tray to the correct height and turned on her computer. She waited for the familiar musical tone of the operating system and watched her desktop icons come to life.

Jennifer opened her inbox and chose from her distribution list the Jen Possible Team file and this is what she wrote, *'My dearest friends, I am blessed, and God has been good to me. By now, most of you know the doctors will proceed tomorrow with a risky, but unavoidable surgery. I want you to know my faith continues to be strong, and if the operation fails, it does not mean that God no longer heals or performs miracles. No, it will simply mean that it was not His will to save my life. I feel God's presence everyday, and I know His plan for me is perfect and I trust completely in our Sovereign King. I have come to understand that God gave His only begotten Son thirty-three years to complete His work on earth. I am thirty-four years old and who am I to ask God for more time than He gave His own Son? I have much love in my heart for all of you. Being in Jerusalem has meant everything to me. May you be richly rewarded for your selfless acts of kindness in all that you have done for me. Please know that I am not afraid because I know my Redeemer lives and in the end, I will also live with Him. Love, Jen.'*

"Now I want you to know, brothers, that what has happened to me has really served to advance the gospel."
Philippians 1:12

*   *   *

Standing outside the Christian Quarter in Jerusalem, Father Clarke was adjusting the chain lock to his bicycle when Shmuel rushed to his side and after listening to the emotional plea of his Jewish friend, the Franciscan monk wasted no time in responding. Father Clarke left the unsecured bicycle alone and raced with Shmuel to the waiting taxicab. Earlier that morning, with Jennifer's permission, it was Davina who telephoned her brother, asking him to locate Fergus and bring him to Hadassah because Jennifer was in need of prayer.

Moments later, Jennifer closed her eyes and listened to Father Clarke softly pray. She knew God was listening, but as her heart cried out to Him, she found it difficult to concentrate. She was weary, and her thoughts were drifting from the medication administered to her just moments before.

With tears in his eyes, Keith held her hand as the medical staff hurried about with their pre-operation agenda. He knew they would soon ask him to leave the room. He bent over the bedrail and kissed the tip of her nose as his tears fell and moistened her cheek.

Jennifer opened her eyes, but she could barely speak. Her voice was frail and trembling. Her lips moved, but no sound could be heard above the noise in the room. With her left hand she drew her tired fingers inward and holding her thumb in the air she gave a final sign of victory.

At long last, Keith wept.

Davina came alongside him and tenderly removed his hands from the bedrail. She walked him to the doorway where Father Fergus Clarke stood waiting. She returned to Jennifer's side and unlocked the wheels to the hospital bed. Davina stood at the head of the gurney, and like her brother Shmuel, she lovingly served Jennifer. She wheeled Jennifer through the double doors, down the hallway, and into the surgical operating room.

"I have fought the good fight, I have finished the race,
I have kept the faith."
2 Timothy 4:7

~ 46 ~

It was Valentine's Day, 2006, and the morning clouds gave way to an unseasonably warm day with a clear blue Michigan sky. The sun's reflection shone brightly over the blanket of fresh snow and the sunlight sparkled like thousands of tiny diamonds. The parking lot at Schrader-Howell Funeral Home in Plymouth was full, and those who loved her were waiting inside. The fireplace glowed, filling the outer room with warmth and comfort. The colonial decor and dignified atmosphere was exactly what Jennifer wanted.

The visitation room was filled with the fragrance from dozens of Blushing Knockout roses, all of which were the color pink. The Jen Possible Team greeted each other with soft murmurs while silent tears were shed. It wasn't long before the doors were gently closed and everyone was asked to be seated.

Rima held tightly to Bill's hand as they sat on the couch against the wall with Angelina sitting peacefully on her Uncle Bill's lap. Duane stood off to the side while his wife, Janis, sat between their sons, Jacob and Justin, who were all seated in the row behind the Britton family.

Jim placed his arm around Cathy's chair and she inwardly sighed while brushing her bangs away from her watery eyes. Their children, Rebecca, Ryan, and Emily, sat with them in the same row. Al stepped aside, allowing his wife, Sheila, to move in and occupy the seat next to Susan Abraham, who was sitting with her teenage daughter, Michele.

While waiting, Shari read the Prayer of St. Francis on the back of Jennifer's memorial card and her husband, Jeff, placed another damp tissue inside the pocket of his suit coat. Kathy sat two chairs over with several of Jennifer's co-workers from Visteon.

Unstoppable tears streamed down Mary's face as Sue reached into her purse and handed her another fresh tissue. Christopher sat on the other side of his mom and couldn't keep his emotions from showing. Jessica sat next to her brother and her beautiful heart was visibly breaking. In the row behind them, Candice and Walt, sat closely next to one another and wept.

*   *   *

In the first row, Keith sat between Nicholas and Natalie. Today was his wedding anniversary. He listened to the priest talk of a place where there was no pain, no sorrow, and no tears. It was a place where believers in Jesus Christ would spend eternity, a place called heaven.

The priest finished by reading from the book of Revelation 14:13, "Blessed are the dead who die in the Lord . . . they will rest from their labor, for their deeds will follow them." After closing his Bible, the priest invited those who wanted to share their memories of Jennifer to come forward.

Without hesitating Cathy stepped to the podium first. Her eyes seldom left the paper in front of her as she spoke of the great loss she felt for her friend and neighbor. Yet, Cathy rejoiced in knowing one day she would see Jennifer again and they would share eternal laughter and conversation over endless cups of coffee. Cathy spoke of the unwavering faith and trust Jennifer had in God's supremacy and what a remarkable Christian, Jennifer truly was.

Cathy set aside her notes and from inside her pocket she reached for a small card where she had penned her thoughts from earlier that day. Cathy cleared her throat and spoke heartfelt words, all worth remembering. *'Sometimes God sends us to unexpected places. Even as we try to trust, we still can't understand. Rare is the person who listens for His voice, considers His will, and helps God work His plan. But a few will hear and choose to obey. Their lives become blessings for others to see. I want you to know that you were one of the few; you were a gift sent from God to me.'*

*   *   *

Duane's footsteps were barely heard as he walked and stood next to Cathy. He hugged her dearly before he took his place behind the podium. His Christian faith supported him as he looked out on his own family, those he worked with, and those he did not even know.

Duane spoke of fond memories and of happier times, as he recalled the celebrations that Jennifer planned and the unique ways she had of always making others feel special. Jennifer was the *Sunshine* in all their lives. She was a stellar pink star that shined brightly for them to appreciate and love.

Even though their hearts were filled with sorrow, after their time of mourning they would rejoice, knowing Jennifer was made whole again – she was alive and living with her Creator. Duane couldn't stop the tears from clouding his vision as he recalled Jennifer's courage, strength, and hope as well as her smile, charm, and elegance, and how each of them had been richly blessed by knowing her and being a part of her life. He shifted his weight from one foot to the other as he gathered his composure. He was preparing to read a poem he wrote. He loosened his black tie and glanced over at Angelina, then back to Nicholas and Natalie.

Duane's heart was bursting with compassion for Jennifer's three innocent children and it was for them he wrote words that one day he prayed they would understand. *'You may wonder why I left again to travel so far from you. Time and time again it seems it was just what I must do. You may wonder why I couldn't hold you to dry up all your tears, to hug, and laugh, and kiss you, my darling little dears. It's not what I wanted for us to be apart; to really understand this please listen to your heart. I did this because I love you. It was part of God's great plan. In time you will come to see; in time you will understand. I fought, I cried, I prayed for you most each and every day, and as time passed I looked ahead and God showed me the way. Please be strong for me, my children, as you grow in body and mind. Treat others as they would treat you, be courteous, loving, and kind. Love each other, love your father, be each other's friend. Remember me and laugh for me – and I will meet you in heaven again.'*

"Give her the reward she has earned, and let her works bring her praise at the city gate."
Proverbs 31:31

The End

The Jen Possible Team
Autumn of 2006

~ *Epilogue* ~

After their time of mourning had passed, the Jen Possible Team gradually came to terms with Jennifer's passing and everyone rejoiced in the knowledge that one day they would see Jennifer again in heaven. Over a period of time, unique and special stories were shared with each other about Jennifer, and each story told helped to refresh and renew one another's spirit. The stories focused on Jennifer's faith, which she never lost sight of, and it was her faith, which grew from the size of a tiny mustard seed that was securely planted in God's sovereignty.

At the time of her passing Jennifer had not been afraid because she knew God was at her side. She knew He had not forsaken her. It was by faith that she was not afraid to leave her children and travel to Jerusalem in search of a cure for her breast cancer. Jennifer believed in eternity, she believed in His kingdom, and she believed in life after death because her Redeemer lives!

*   *   *

The Jen Possible Team visited the cemetery on what would have been Jennifer's thirty-fifth birthday and now they sat leisurely on the front lawn of her home on Mayflower Drive. Across the street, the leaves on the large white birch tree were clinging to its branches in spite of the fact that winter was soon approaching.

Sheila sat on the porch steps next to Al. She was happy because it was good for him to visit with his team of engineers once again. Duane stretched his long legs out before him and leaned on his elbows, his ball cap, as always, was tipped back over his head. Kathy and Janis sat on the grass next to him.

Mary reached into her coat pocket and handed Cathy a small cloth jewelry pouch. Instantly, tears clouded their vision as Cathy untied the strings and saw neatly wrapped inside, the mustard seed pendant she had given to Jennifer more than two years ago. Cathy hugged and thanked Mary, and then tucked the returned gift into her pocket and walked over to visit with Bill and Rima.

In the driveway Bill held Angelina while Cathy peeked over Rima's shoulder and saw in Rima's hand that she held a shopping bag marked Khan es-Zeit Souk, Israel. Shari leaned against the porch railing watching everyone and smiled when Mary waved her over to come and sit by her side.

Noticeably missing from the group was Susan Abraham. Sadly, during a routine medical exam, a secondary occurrence of cancer was detected. After several more visits with her physician, the unfortunate news was confirmed and Susan's prognosis was heartbreaking. Prayer chains were established and Susan's co-workers began to pray for her daily.

*   *   *

Everyone knew during her stay in Jerusalem, Jennifer had shopped in the Market Place and had purchased keepsakes for them. Several months had passed before Rima felt it was a respectable amount of time to approach Keith and ask him for the mementos. Appropriately today, on Jennifer's birthday, they would receive her gifts of love and visit with her children. Keith was happy to oblige with the arrangements, but unfortunately he would not be able to join them.

Bill, Rima, and Cathy joined the others on the lawn, watching as Angelina entertained everyone by dancing inside the circle of her mother's friends. Rima was nominated to go through the items, and one at a time she gave each their gift. Fresh tears surfaced as they opened their presents and at long last discovered what Jennifer had purchased for them in the Holy Land.

Their small gifts were more precious than silver or gold, and a heavy silence filled the air as they showed their treasures to one another. Gradually, lighthearted conversations surfaced among them and, oddly enough, so many years later, they discovered something short of miraculous, because none of them had known Jennifer longer than two years prior to her cancer diagnosis.

It was a discovery they felt was extraordinary, as everyone had naturally assumed the outpouring of Christian love toward Jennifer was largely based on long term friendships, but that was not the case. They soon realized it was the hand of God that lovingly orchestrated the events that ultimately moved each of them, one at a time, into Jennifer's life – all in His perfect timing. He alone was aware of her future and the help she would need from her brothers and sisters-in-Christ.

*   *   *

Cathy Britton, Bill Hardy, Susan Abraham, and Kathy Walsh first met Jennifer in 1998, but did not become close in their friendship until three years later when in 2001; they were transferred to Al Partington's group of electrical engineers.

Duane Lanyon met Jennifer briefly during cross-section meetings in 1998, but he did not get to know her until he was reassigned to Al's group in May, 2003.

Rima Holland began talking with Jennifer in September, 2002, while caring for Jennifer's grandmother, Mrs. Catherine Toby. Rima met Jennifer for the first time on New Year's Eve that same year.

Mary Richardson clearly remembered Jennifer introducing herself to Mary on her first day assigned to the Powertrain department at Visteon. That day was May 21, 2003, a mere ten months before Jennifer was diagnosed.

Shari Franko casually answered her telephone late one evening in mid-March 2004, which ultimately led her to meet Jennifer for the first time, during her initial visit to Karmanos.

As Christians, sometimes it is easy to recognize God's hand at work, especially when it is something of miraculous proportion, and there can be no other explanation – other than it is simply, Him.

However, it is precious to see God working in the everyday aspects of individual lives, and how sad it would have been for the members of the Jen Possible Team had they not been obedient to the calling of the Holy Spirit. For they would have missed God's hand working through them and they would have missed a great testimony from a remarkable young woman whose name was . . . *Jennifer Ann Hayse.*

*   *   *

Jim walked through his backyard toward Keith's home, and running in front of him were Nicholas and Natalie since they knew a group of special people were waiting to see them. They came around the corner and smiled at the faces they recognized, but shied away from those they had already forgotten.

The children being most comfortable with the Hardys and the Lanyons stayed closest to them, but in the course of time, they soon settled down and, little by little, they joined in on the adult conversation.

Gentle questions of how they were doing in school and who was their favorite teacher were asked, and it was wonderful to see how well adjusted they had become, for time quickly heals all wounds when someone is so young.

Angelina and Natalie unmistakably favored their mother in their young faces while Nicholas was a mirror image of his father, and their mother's inner beauty shone forth in all three of their smiles. The siblings were noticeably, a beautiful blend of their parents.

Once becoming comfortable and perhaps slowly recognizing who the adults surrounding him were, it was Mary who casually asked Nicholas, "What do you want to be when you grow up, young man?" Everyone listened as Nicholas gave a spontaneous child-like answer, "I want to be a Hero – just like my Mom!"

*   *   *

Jennifer Ann Hayse

September 29, 1971
February 10, 2006

About the Author

M ary retired in 2008 from the Michigan automotive industry. She is a first-time author and writing *A Walk with Jennifer* is a promise fulfilled. What you hold in your hands is a labor of love which ultimately led the author into her second career. Since completing this book, Mary has launched *Wicker Chair Publications*, which provides inspirational Christian memoir services.

To learn more about this creative endeavor, please visit her website at www.wickerchairpublications.com, as she would love to hear from you.

"Commit to the Lord whatever you do and
your plans will succeed."
Proverbs 16:3

Sources

᪐᪐

Tetzlaf, Judith. *A Guide to Breast Health Care: How to Examine Your Breasts.* (Henry Ford Medical Center Fairlane, Dearborn, Michigan). Chicago, Illinois: Budlong Press Company (1997-1981).

Hayford, Jack W. *Walk Where Jesus Walked.* Ventura, California: Gospel Light DVD (2005).

Walker, Peter. *In the Steps of Jesus.* Grand Rapids, Michigan: Zondervan (2007).

http//www.mayoclinic.com/health/breast-cancer-staging/ BR00022. Mayo Foundation for Medical Education and Research. Cited November/December 2008

http//www.karmanos.org. Barbara Ann Karmanos Cancer Institute. Wayne State University, Detroit, Michigan. Cited August/September 2009

http//www.cancercenter.com. Cancer Treatment Centers of America. Midwestern Regional Medical Center, Zion, Illinois. Cited August/September 2009 http//www.hadassah.org.il/English. Hadassah Medical Organization. Israel's Leading University Hospital, Jerusalem, Israel. Cited August/September 2009

http//www.bibleplaces.com. Bolen, Todd. *The Sites*. Cited August/September 2009.

LaVergne, TN USA
29 December 2010
210440LV00004B/2/P